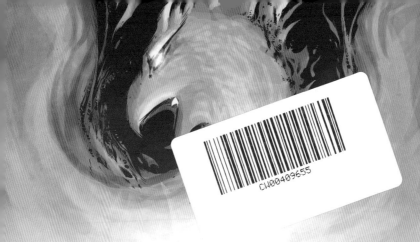

JONATHAN
SKINNER

THE RISE OF
PAGANISM

THE RE-EMERGENCE OF AN OLD IDEOLOGY

The Rise of Paganism

The Rise of Paganism

Jonathan Skinner

EVANGELICAL PRESS

EVANGELICAL PRESS
Faverdale North Industrial Estate, Darlington, DL3 0PH
England

Evangelical Press USA
PO Box 825, Webster, NY 14580

e-mail: sales@evangelicalpress.org

web: http://www.evangelicalpress.org

British Library Cataloguing in Publication Data available

ISBN 10 – 0 85234 624 7
ISBN 13 – 978 0 85234 624 2

All Scripture quotations, unless otherwise indicated, are taken from the New International Version of the Bible.

Printed by Creative Print & Design, Wales

'Rising from the ashes of 5,000 years of oppression and banishment to the religious underground, neo-paganism is now emerging as a viable body of transformative spirituality.'
Anoda Judith, pagan writer.

'the men of Issachar, who understood the times and knew what Israel should do.'
1 Chronicles 12:32

Contents

Part Three – The Biblical Answer to Contemporary Paganism

The biblical arguments against paganism
– we demolish arguments –

Introduction

Cataclysmic changes are occurring in our society and at a rate that is astounding. The religious and spiritual outlook of our generation is undergoing seismic shifts that would have been undreamt of a few decades ago.

People are becoming spiritually hungry, but instead of looking in the direction of Christianity, or indeed even the major religions of the world, they are delving in areas almost unknown for at least one, if not two, thousand years. Citizens of the Western world are revisiting paganism and in phenomenal numbers.

This book examines the come-back of paganism, the rise of the Phoenix. In pagan mythology, the Phoenix was said to rise from the ashes, and it is interesting that one of contemporary paganism's writers refers to its rebirth as, 'Rising from the ashes of 5,000 years of oppression and banishment to the religious underground.'[1] In ancient Chinese pagan mythology the Phoenix was often depicted with the Dragon; it was seen as its subtle and gentler counterpart. Much modern paganism is a gentler and subtler expression of its ancient manifestations. In the Bible, the dragon depicts the devil, or Satan. Today, we are seeing the essential religion of the devil re-establishing itself in the Western world, albeit currently, in a gentle and subtle way. We are witnessing the rise of the Phoenix.

In the following pages we will outline the present resurgence and infiltration of paganism, as well as examine its diversity and roots. Along with this, we will try to answer the haunting question as to why this present rebirth is happening, as well as attempt to get to grips with paganism's essential beliefs and power. The investigation will be critical: we will not only aim at understanding this movement, but will also attempt to give biblical answers to it. In the Bible, paganism is always seen as a main enemy of true religion, and where its ideas have not been obvious outside the church, they have certainly penetrated into it. Satan is attempting to delude the world as well as confuse the church, and so we need to become something like certain heroes mentioned in the Old Testament: 'the men of Issachar, who understood the times and knew what Israel should do.'[2]

Some may feel that this is a subject unworthy of study, that it may be inappropriate, or even unhealthy to explore paganism in this way. After all, we are commanded to be 'innocent about what is evil'.[3] However, although it is clear that we should not immerse ourselves in what may be harmful, or tempting, it is significant that the Bible deals openly and honestly with the sin of individuals and societies. Indeed, the Old Testament is full of what, to many, could be quite shocking material regarding the sin of paganism in those times. The facts of the 'male shrine prostitutes',[4] as well as child sacrifice are clearly mentioned.[5] Paul, while in Athens, made the point that he had observed their objects of worship[6] and when he preached to them it is interesting that he could even quote one of their own pagan poets.[7] Satan is our enemy and we need to be aware of his schemes — whether they are heresies, or false religion. We need to 'be prepared to give an answer to anyone who asks', so that we are ready to 'give a reason for the hope' that we have.[8] If it is right to understand something of the false doctrine that has afflicted the church over the last two thousand years, and if it is right know something of the cults and their dangers, and if it is right to delve into the threat of atheism in order to be able to counter it, then it must logically be right to uncover the rising threat of paganism and provide the much needed answers.

This is a book for all concerned believers — and all believers should be concerned. It is a book for parents, teenagers, youth leaders, Bible study group leaders, evangelists and pastors. It is also a book for those who may feel themselves drawn by the fascination of paganism: it will hopefully reveal that this religion is not only unattractive, but also untrue. The ultimate answer to these things is Jesus, who is 'the way and the truth and the life'.[9]

Chapter 1
The Resurgence of Paganism

'Delusion is the child of ignorance.'
The Bhagavadgita

If the shelves of our bookshops are any reliable thermometer of current interests then we've got problems, serious problems.

Many bookstores have replaced the label over the section called 'Religion' with one called 'Mysticism' — and this is no mere window dressing. Instead of anything like Bibles, commentaries and volumes on Christian living, or even books on the world's religions, these shelves are increasingly weighed down with the most peculiar fare.

If you want the hairs on the back of your neck to stand up, think about this reading material: *Spells for Teenage Witches, White Witching* and *Angel Healing*. Another on the market is, *The Real Witches' Kitchen: Spells, Recipes, Oils and Potions from the Witches' Hearth*. The advertising blurb for this publication boasts that it 'includes around 100 spells and recipes — many revealed for the first time — for eating, drinking and making your life merrier, along with plenty of practical advice on witchy subjects such as potions to improve your looks without ruining your bank balance and brews and teas to heal the body and mind.'[1]

The book, *White Witching: The Good Magic-Maker's Guide to Spell Weaving*, claims to be 'a merry guide to weaving good magic' with 'easy, fun spells and charms for life, love and work'.[2] The introduction states, 'Today, ordinary people from all walks of life are practising witches. From the woman next door to the high-flying business executive.'[3] The list of introductory books on witchcraft goes on and on. *Practical Magic: A Book of Transformations, Spells and Mind Magic* is yet another. This publication claims to offer 'the way towards enlightenment and reconnection, to bring peace, joy and fulfilment.'[4] All this is presented in the most visually attractive manner, bursting with photographs of healthy young adults. The sheer variety and numbers of publications available reveals something about the level popularity of exploring these areas.

Another book is on numerology. The flyleaf tells us that 'Numerology is perhaps the easiest of the occult arts to understand and use.'[5] It claims to give guidance as to 'determine the best time for major moves and activities in life' as well as to 'decide when to invest, when to marry, when to travel, when to change jobs, relocate and much more.' Alongside this — at a level any child could reach — is *Dreams: Hidden Meanings and Secrets*. This book supposes that it can help the reader 'discover the secrets of your sleep' as well as, 'Find out what your dreams are trying to tell you. The answers lie within.'[6]

And it's not just in the media: at the closing ceremony of the Bath International Music Festival finale in 2001, hymns of worship were offered to the sun and moon. But if you think this massive 'spiritual' movement is only for the intellectually superficial, you would be wrong. Bath Spa University College offers a postgraduate degree in Cultural Astronomy and Astrology. The prospectus tells us that this MA course includes studies in Astro-Methodology, Stellar Religion, New Age and Sacred Geography.[7] In the US, this kind of thing is even more developed.[8]

And then there is *The Truth about Neo-Paganism: The Magical World View*. The introduction of this publication makes the following claim: 'Rising from the ashes of 5,000 years of oppression and banishment to the religious underground, neo-paganism is now emerging as a viable body of transformative spirituality. Rather than providing dogmatic answers, neo-paganism focuses on offering powerful techniques, such as ritual and meditation, through which you can search for your own answers.'[9] This book alleges that neo-paganism is the 'world's fastest growing religion'.[10]

The magazine racks are no different: many mainline publications have overtly pagan, neo-pagan or New Age material within them. And there are even specifically pagan magazines: one particularly successful publication is *Know Your Destiny Magazine*, subtitled *Mystic Meg's Magazine*. This is full of extremely alternative spiritual therapies such as palmistry, feng shui, reflexology, tarot cards, psychic counselling, magic spells, astrology, love rites, Zen, crystal balls, mediums and much, much more. For those couples experiencing difficulty in having children the following advice is offered. 'Placing an egg under your bed will increase your chances of conceiving.' And if that doesn't work, how about this — 'On the next Full Moon, hold an egg in your hands, while thinking about why you want a child. Then, draw on it a sun and moon; you may also want to pray to Brigit, the Mother Goddess.'[11] So wrote Silja, whose witch name is White Moon. This is not the stuff of the lunatic fringe — the editor, Elayne Delaurian wrote, 'Welcome to your award-winning magazine. We know how much you love *Know Your Destiny* — your letters keep pouring in, telling us. Well, now you've proved it — by buying so many copies of the magazine that we scooped a silver award for launch of the year at the recent Circulation Press Awards.'[12]

It would be easy to get the wrong impression from all this; people are not becoming 'signed up' pagans in a way that people become Christians or Muslims, but rather, more and more are dabbling in it to find pagan techniques to 'improve their lives'. The following examples all come from one edition of *Mystic Meg's Magazine*, and show the range of techniques people are now attempting. One article is entitled, 'Get Healthy, Wealthy and Famous With Feng Shui'. Here, different businesses are encouraged to change their colour schemes in order to enhance the 'natural energy' and so 'boost business', 'increase health and luck' and 'improve health'. Another article, entitled, 'Two Sides of Love' claims that using astrology and the signs of the zodiac can be the key to finding the perfect partner. And then there is *Happy Ghosts* — 'Not all spirits are mischievous or malicious. Here we meet the people who wouldn't dream of giving up their ghosts.' One of these people is Amy Tan, a best-selling author who 'gets a little ghostly help with her work. In two of her four novels, the main character has the ability to communicate with the dead.' There is also an article on improving lovemaking through the 'Secrets of the Sex Tarot or through Energy Acupressure Massage'. And for those who want to know their future there is palmistry, with an article entitled, 'Your Life in the Palm of Your Hand'. The introductory blurb says, 'Take your hand — and watch your future unfurl before your eyes. It's all there — love-life, weddings, career and children, secret clues to the kind of person you really are.' And if this isn't good enough for a peep into our futures, the article 'Wheel of Destiny' claims that astrology can give deep insights into our lives and our futures. 'In Your Element' tells us that 'According to ancient Chinese wisdom, we each have an element that rules our health and personality. Discover this, and you can reach your ultimate potential in energy and vitality.' And then there is 'Zen Living' — 'the art of creating a haven of peace, away from the stresses of life.' But if this doesn't do the trick then feng shui will apparently help you decorate your house in a way that gets rid of 'negative energy'.

From this brief selection, it is evident that the range of approaches is staggering — and that they are all aimed at tapping into basic human needs and appetites for security, health, wisdom, guidance in life and pleasure. This is why it is all so attractive. More than that, people want another dimension to their lives, something that is 'spiritual' — and this plethora of pagan techniques seems to be filling the gap. In a society where people have given up on biblical Christianity, and are largely secular in outlook, they have grown weary and feel there must be something more 'out there.' Secularism does not satisfy the human soul — which should be of no surprise as our Bibles tell us that God has 'set eternity in the hearts of men.'[13] We are created with a spiritual appetite: we are not meant to be satisfied with creation alone — is it meant to point to the creator. And yet, such is the folly of the human heart, that people tend to look in the wrong places — and Satan is happy to provide alternatives. In a society that has been steeped in agnosticism, atheism and secularism, with a view that God is either not there, or irrelevant, the thirst for something more has now reached epidemic proportions. People are turning back to the old religions of the land in paganism.

What is a pagan?

The word 'pagan' is derived from a Middle English word, which itself comes from the Latin word *paganus* meaning 'country dweller.' This is derived from the Latin word *pagus*, which means 'country' or 'rural area'. Soon a little word that simply described people who lived outside the cities began to have all sorts of connotations. Today, people who live in metropolitan areas usually look down on those who do not with disdain. The same was probably true in the Roman Empire as well. In those days, as now, things always seemed to begin in the cities, and eventually trickle into the country villages. The country villages were always behind in the latest news, fashion and spiritual revolutions. Whatever religion may have been sweeping across the cities was probably not practised out in the country right away. Therefore the *pagani* were probably out of step whenever a new religion came along. So the result was that the *pagani* would continue practising the old religion after the new religion had supplanted it in the cities. The term 'pagan' was adopted by those of a Western Judeo-Christian perspective to mean those who did not embrace their religion or culture.

If the word pagan is looked up in a dictionary, definitions like these would be found:

> *n.* A heathen
> *n.* A non-Christian
> *n.* One who is not a Christian, Muslim or Jew
> *n.* One who has no religion
> *n.* A hedonist
> *n.* One who worships false gods
> *n.* An idolator
> *n.* One who does not acknowledge God

The most practical definition is probably, 'One who adheres to a belief system outside that of established orthodoxy from a Western traditional Judeo-Christian, or a Muslim perspective'. However, this stab at a definition couches the belief in a negative sense: it says what paganism is *not*, but does not say what it *is*. Those who have embraced the label pagan do not see themselves as those who have merely excluded themselves from Judaism, Islam or Christianity, but as those who have embraced certain other beliefs. These beliefs, which we will explore in detail later, include the concept that there is a spiritual reality or domain that we can connect into and even harness, through various techniques and practices. These practices are very diverse, but this diversity is seen as complementary rather than contradictory. Many claim that their approach is that of the original religion of the people of the various geographical regions of the earth, and that these 'old religions' have often been supplanted by what they sometimes call 'the Middle Eastern Religion'. In Britain, and those lands where an Anglo-Saxon heritage influences the culture, Druidism and Wicca (witchcraft) would be examples of the 'old religion', and in the USA many are exploring the native Indian perspectives. The USA is complex in that many of the racial groups that emigrated there have their own pagan pasts, and these are increasingly being explored and added together and given a new spin in a variety of peculiar cocktails.[14] In some areas, like India, the 'old religions' are still the dominant religions. Many in the West are turning to India and other areas of the East, and are drawing on the traditions of those cultures to produce another strain of modern paganism. Modern-day pagans will often feel free to draw from any combination of various traditions, of whatever continent.

Those who are rediscovering the 'old religions' of their own land, or other continents, and are reinventing them with a modern twist are often called neo-pagans, which simply means 'new-pagans'. Many have also taken this a step further and are looking for a future spiritual development of humanity in terms of a higher level of spiritual consciousness. This thought of the evolution of humanity to a new state of spiritual awareness and experience gives the meaning to the label 'The New Age Movement'. This new phase in human history will be the 'Age of Aquarius'. paganism, neo-paganism and New Age are overlapping and sometimes interchangeable terms for a mixed bag of beliefs, techniques and approaches that are flooding various Western societies.

While considering some kind of basic definition of paganism, it is worth outlining its relationship with the word 'occult'. The term 'occult' means 'hidden' and is applied to practices that are below the surface of normal life and involves an investigation of a hidden spiritual dimension. Usually, it is used of phenomena like magic, second-sight, prevision, telepathy, divination, sorcery, omens, witchcraft, spells, mediumship, spiritualism, astrology and consulting the dead. These activities are common in many forms of paganism. Those practices that were once hidden from public view and involvement are now openly available in our high streets; only certain aspects of what was once considered to be of the occult, like Satanism and black magic, are still relatively hidden. In much contemporary literature, the terms pagan and Occult are intertwined and overlapping. Often, 'occult' means gaining access to hidden or mysterious knowledge that can given enlightenment and power. One current dictionary on the subject starts with the phrase, 'knowledge is power'[15] — and this sums up the thrust of the ideology. Interestingly, some of the New Testament letters deal with a developing brand of this in the first century known as Gnosticism.[16] The word Gnosticism comes from the Greek *gnosis*, or knowledge. This shows that there is biblical material dealing with this particular brand of paganism. There is nothing new under the sun, and our Bibles more than adequately equip us to deal with this current manifestation of an old ideology and belief system.

Contemporary occultism has often wrapped itself around various psychological theories: 'Modern occultism, with the aid of Jungian psychology and other developments of the twentieth century, has moved away from obsession with death, blood and the devil that characterised so much esoteric study in the past. Most occultists are seeking to find harmony with the forces that guide the universe.'[17] As we shall later observe, current occult, pagan, neo-pagan and New Age movements often weave psychology and scientific perspectives into their worldview.

The pagan community

All this indicates that there is a growing number of what we might call 'signed up pagans'. These are people who are self-consciously pagan in outlook, belief and practice. There are possibly two million pagan web sites on the Internet, offering a range of services including guidance for pagan parenting, as well as home-schooling and even a selection of pagan libraries. And there are even sites 'serving the needs of the military pagan community'.

There is the Pagan Educational Network, 'dedicated to educating the public about paganism' as well as Pagan Unity Campaign which pushes for a Pagan Bill of Rights, and other political agendas. Other organizations promote a pagan economics programme and even work together forming academic networks. Pagan Solicitors advertise their services like, 'Pagan Osbourne' which claims it is a 'modern law partnership.' And that 'over many years, pagan solicitors have advised several generations of farmers and landowners throughout Scotland.'[18] It is even possible to go on holiday with a pagan holiday company such as 'Skyros — the holistic holiday'. *The [London] Independent* newspaper commented regarding this: 'Let your hair down, take risks, expand your horizons, go on a Skyros holistic holiday.'[19]

The pagan community is served by a whole raft of international journals including *Kindred Spirit: The Leading Guide for Mind, Body and Spirit*, as well as *Resurgence*, which has agents and offices in Australia, Canada, Japan, South Africa, UK and the USA. These publications carry pages and pages of adverts proffering training courses, seminars, conferences, events, retreat centres, holidays, relationships, counselling, therapies, life coaching, accommodation, cassettes, CDs, books and publications, and so on.

Pagan bookshops

All the books referred to at the beginning of this chapter were found on the shelves of main high street bookshops frequented by the general public. But most cities these days also have specialist bookshops that deal with material of pagan, neo-pagan or New Age material.[20] Once the publications within these places are taken into account, the number and range becomes truly astounding. The following is a brief selection:

• *Earth Angels*, by Doreen Virtue Ph.D is 'a pocket guide for incarnated Angels, Elementals, Starpeople, Walk-Ins, and Wizards.'

• *Journey of the Soul: Awakening Ourselves to the Enduring Cycle of Life,* by Dr Brenda Davies apparently 'illuminates the endless nature of the soul as it journeys through birth, life, death and beyond.'

• *Witches' Datebook* — 'Keep track of coven meetings and festivals as well as your more mundane appointments, in the midst of recipes, rituals and pagan artwork.

• *Visions of the Shaman* — 'dynamic art captures the spirit of these healers and initiators who dare to journey beyond the veil of ordinary reality.'

From looking at all these facts it can be seen that the community of self—conscious pagans is of significant size and is growing.

Pagan 'evangelism'

The pagan community is not passive, but is outgoing and even 'evangelistic'. This is clear from a variety of indicators, including the permeation and penetration of the various beliefs and techniques into mainline magazines, bookshops, health establishments and so forth. But what might not be quite so obvious is that there is a plan behind much of it — a plan initiated in the East. In 1966 there was an international Hindu conference where Hindu leaders put together a strategy to convert the world. At this Kumbha Mela Festival, in Allahadbad, India, Gurus were chosen as the first crusaders in this proselytising mission. At the World Congress of Hinduism in 1979 a spokesman declared that 'Our mission in the world has been crowned with fantastic success. Hinduism has been crowned with fantastic success. Hinduism is becoming the dominant world religion and the end of Christianity has come near.'[21] At the 1981 Transcendental Meditation Conference it was stated that 'The entire mission of Transcendental Meditation is to counter the ever spreading demon of Christianity.'[22] Central to Hindu aggressive advancement is the world missionary organization of Hinduism: Vishva Hindu Parishad, whose constitution states that its aim is 'To establish an order of missionaries, both lay and initiate, with the purpose of propagating dynamic Hinduism.'[23]

As many Hindu ideas spread west during the closing decades of the twentieth century, these often also stimulated the rise in interest in the old western forms of paganism, as well as in those from the East. When ancient pagan ideas are repackaged in an acceptable way for our contemporary culture and society, many find them attractive, if not compelling. The ideas are the same, but the language has changed. One New Age activist wrote, 'One of the biggest advantages we have as New Agers is, once the occult, metaphysical and New Age terminology is removed, we have concepts and techniques that are very acceptable to the general public. So we change the names and demonstrate the power. In so doing, we open the door to millions who would not normally be receptive.'[24]

The main spread of paganism, however, is not through 'converts' as such, but through larger and larger numbers of the general public dabbling on the fringes and through its essential concepts infiltrating into mainline thinking concerning business management strategies, martial arts, ecology, health, interior design, counselling and personal advancement programmes. It is in these ways that it is infiltrating our society most effectively. We will look at this in the next few chapters.

Health warning

The fact that something is popular and growing does not mean that it is healthy or true. The Bible clearly states that any form of contact with the spiritual world outside of Jesus is not only dangerous, but is also wrong. A list of prohibited practices are given in Deuteronomy 19:10-11, and in the New Testament Christian converts who had previously practiced magic, burnt their textbooks.[25] The people of Israel were severely punished for their involvement in paganism.[26] The Bible is never neutral about pagan religions or spiritual techniques. 'For there is only one God and one mediator between God and men, the man Jesus Christ, who gave himself as a ransom for all men.'[27]

Questions for Discussion

1. Do you think it is right to understand something of those beliefs that contradict and challenge Christianity? Why? Look up Acts 17:16-34. What evidence is there that Paul had some understanding of the religious views of the Athenians? Notice the word 'carefully' in verse 23.

2. Brainstorm and make a list of some ideologies and religions that actively oppose Christianity.

4. Do you think people with these different beliefs might ask different or similar types of questions to a Christian witness? Turn to 1 Peter 3:16. Note how we are commanded to be prepared to answer people's questions as to why we believe.

5. Make a list of those types of pagan activity that are present in the area you live.

6. What do the following passages tell us about involvement in pagan activities? Deuteronomy 19:10-11; Acts 19:19; 2 Kings 17:7-20; 1 Timothy 2:5.

Chapter 2
Mother Earth

The Spread of Pagan Ideas through Environmentalism

'Behind the cotton wool of daily reality is hidden a pattern. All human beings are connected with this; the whole world is a work of art and we are part of it.'
Virginia Woolf

Even though it is true that there are growing numbers of 'signed up' pagans,[1] only a relatively small proportion of the population would fill in a census form and declare that they are a pagan, neo-pagan or a New Ager. But paganism is still spreading throughout our culture and society: increasing numbers of the general population are not only dabbling on the fringes of the movement, but are adopting facets of the ideology.

The main spread of paganism is not through 'converts' as such, but by larger and larger numbers of the general public imbibing its essential concepts through a whole raft of channels. It is in these ways that it is infiltrating our society most effectively. In this chapter we consider one of the most widespread channels for the infiltration of pagan concepts: care for the environment, reverence for our planet.

Nature is central to modern pagan experience, and Selena Fox, Wiccan high priest and founder of the Circle Sanctuary in the United States, describes this side of paganism:

> I am pagan. I am part of the whole of Nature. The Rocks and Animals, the Plants, the Elements, and the Stars are

my relatives. Other humans are my sisters and brothers, whatever their races, colors, genders, sexual orientations, ages, nationalities, religions, lifestyles. Planet Earth is my home. I am a part of Nature, not the master of it. I have my own special part to play and I seek to discover and play that pat to the best of my ability. I seek to live in harmony with others in the family of Nature, treating others with respect...

I am pagan. Nature Spirituality is my religion and my life's foundation. Nature is my spiritual teacher and holy book. I am part of Nature and Nature is part of me. My understanding of Nature's inner mysteries grows as I journey on this spiritual path.[2]

Over the last few decades there has been an upsurge in concern for our spinning spaceship that we call Earth — and for good reasons. During the previous couple of centuries humanity has ravaged the earth: an incalculable number[3] of species have become extinct; our rainforests have been raped for their resources; pollution has poisoned our oceans and fumes have permeated our atmosphere. The protective ozone layer around our terrestrial globe has shrunk and the Greenhouse effect seems to be warming our environment. Our materialistic and industrial societies are destroying our habit — humanity is behaving like a global bacterial infection. Due to greed to maintain and even improve our standard of living we pump carbon dioxide and other noxious chemicals into the ecosystem.

Many rightly feel we are desecrating our planet and so are reacting against this polluting madness. They correctly feel we should respect the Earth and work to protect it. More than this, they feel that our technological and industrial society has become detached from our natural environment: we rape and do not respect; unlike our ancestors, we have lost a connection with nature. We must return to a respect and veneration for the beauty, harmony, mystery and wonder of our planet.

The living planet

Many feel that there is more to our planet than meets the eye: as well as matter, there is mystery. Something bigger is going on here. The patterns and processes that ripple and flow through the biosphere do not seem to be random, nor the result of blind chance. It is almost as if our planet has some kind of life of its own. In 1979, Jim Lovelock, a scientist who co-operated with NASA and their space programme, and who had been a Fellow of the Royal Society, came up with a novel new theory. Bringing knowledge from astronomy to zoology in support of his radical hypothesis, he explored in his book Gaia[4] the idea that the Earth functions as a single organism. This planetary life-form actually defines and maintains conditions necessary for its survival. In more than one sense, the Earth is alive.

The idea that the Earth is alive had existed since ancient times, but the first scientific expression of the belief was from James Hutton in 1785 in a lecture before the Royal Society of Edinburgh. In the preface to his book, Lovelock writes, 'The concept of Mother earth or, as the Greeks called her long ago, Gaia,[5] has been widely held throughout history...As a result of the accumulation of evidence about the natural environment...there have recently been speculations that the biosphere may have been more than just a complete range of all the living things within their natural habitat of soil, sea, and air. Ancient belief and modern knowledge have fused emotionally in the awe with which astronauts with their own eyes and we by indirect vision have seen the Earth revealed in all its shining beauty against the deep darkness of space.'[6]

Lovelock argues scientifically that the Earth keeps the environment constant and close to a state comfortable for life.[7] In the Gaia theory, he formulates, or perhaps revives, the very ancient pagan concept of the relationship between the Earth and its biosphere.[8] The essence of his hypothesis is 'that the entire range of living matter on Earth, from whales to viruses, and from oaks to algae, could be regarded as constituting a single living entity, capable of manipulating the Earth's atmosphere to suit its overall needs and endowed with faculties and powers far beyond those of its constituent parts.'[9]

A criticism of the theory posed by biologists is that of Ford Doolittle and Richard Dawkins — namely that from their evolutionary perspective, there is no way for natural selection to lead to altruism that is global in scale. Such an event, they said, would require foresight and planning to be included in the genetic structure of living organisms.[10] For Dawkins, it is the individual gene that is selfish and that powers his conception of the evolutionary process.[11] Altruism, the unselfish regard to the welfare of others, as is required for the harmonious interactions of the Gaia model, does not fit well with his perspective. The problem for many scientists has been that Gaia requires some kind of macro-level purpose[12] to come into being, and contemporary biology can only come up with micro-level mechanisms.[13] Interestingly, current evolutionary theory is receiving its greatest challenge at just this micro level — some scientists now feel evolution cannot be explained at the sub-cellular level.[14] The validity of the theory of evolution is being squeezed from the macro and micro level.

Scientists have argued over the Gaia theory, but whatever its merits or shortcomings, it holds no particular challenge to the Christian Faith. Indeed, the Bible reveals that the Earth is the result of intelligent design — God did not just create life, but brought into existence a home for that life to live.[15] Neither came about by chance. If the Gaia concept is in anyway right, what seems absurd in the extreme, is the thought that Earth, our wonderfully balanced and harmonious habitat, which is brilliantly and probably uniquely suitable for life, came about by luck. For those of us who find it impossible to believe that beautifully complex individual species came about by some kind of random chemical lottery, it is equally hard to accept that our environment came about some cosmic quirk. Surely, Genesis 1 is right in showing that our Earth is God-given. It is interesting that Lovelock himself seems to admit this: 'The climate and the chemical properties of the Earth now and throughout its history seem always to have been optimum for life. For this to have happened by chance is as unlikely as to survive unscathed a drive blindfold through rush-hour traffic.'[16] More than this, the Bible shows us that our planetary home was not only created[17] by God, but is also upheld and maintained[18] by him as he provides for our daily needs.[19]

The earth goddess

Lovelocks' Gaia model is fundamentally a scientific theory and not a spiritual one, however, it has certainly been taken up and adapted by those who hold a far more religious perspective regarding our planet, Mother Earth. It is worth quoting more fully one of the contemporary pagan writers, as she explains their perspective regarding our planet.

> Long ago, when humans lived in closer proximity to Nature, we experienced ourselves as enfolded into an intricate and wonderful web. All around us, as far as we could see, were the trees and the grasses, the flowers and the mountains, the Sun and the Moon and the stars. Our effect on the environment around us was minimal. Its effect upon us, however, was not. We were dependent upon the growing season's benevolence to keep us fed and alive through a winter we hoped would not be too harsh or too long... This web around us has power beyond our understanding. It was alive, as we were, yet so much larger and more profound. As women in our tribe swelled in the belly and gave birth, so did the world around us: the animals gave birth in the spring, the trees and plants put forth their fruit. The miracle of human life through the bodies of women was equated with the miracle of the life-giving properties of the earth we lived on, and was seen as divine.

> This intricate environmental web was a deity to be worshipped and honoured. Because it brought forth food in the way that women brought forth life, the divine was worshipped as feminine. Today we think of her as Mother Earth or Mother Nature, for she is the universal mother of us all.[20]

From this quotation it is easy to see why, in some people's minds, there is a link between protecting the environment and pagan belief. Some of those in the environmentalist movement have a veneration for our planet that transcends normal respect for the environment: theirs is a spiritual perspective. New Age and neo-pagan literature is replete with references to ecology and the natural world.[21]

The spiritual perspective of returning to a deeper connection with our planet, which the ancient pagan religions teach, is being positively presented in mainline secular publications. The *National Geographic Magazine*, for example, ran an article by the famous travel writer, Paul Theroux, on Hawaii, where the restoration of ancient religions connected to the land were supported. While commenting on the legitimate concerns Hawaiians have for the destruction of their culture and land, he takes this a step farther, espousing their religion. The young Hawaiians are again becoming *kahu o ka 'aina* — stewards of the land, which sounds fine, until the religion beneath the surface is uncovered: 'The heart of the culture is not music or play but an intense solemnity and an appeal to the pantheon of gods in complex protocols of chants and prayers. In this way Hawaiians proclaim and reinforce their powerful connection to the land.'[22]

The Bible is quite clear: although the Earth is wonderfully made by God and reflects something of his glory, it is not God and should not be worshipped.[23] To worship Gaia is nothing less that idolatry; it is a worship of what is created rather than the creator.[24] Although creation can point to God,[25] because of the perversity of our minds, we lower our gaze and bow to what he has made. Like a stain glass window that was meant to point people to God, it can become a distraction and become itself adored. The Earth may well be far more complex and wonderful than reductionist science can ever comprehend, but that glory should point us to the one who made it rather than to itself. When we see a masterful piece of architecture we praise the architect, not the building. When those who worship Gaia feel they are worshipping the spirit or spirits of this world, ironically and tragically they may well be right.[26]

The healing energies of the earth

A deliberately pagan perspective on the Earth is being promulgated in various books available in secular mainline bookshops in the high street. One book, *The Healing Energies of the Earth*, states on the back cover, that 'The Earth is a living organism. It breathes, it has a circulatory system and a pulse, and its "skin" is sensitive to outside forces. *The Healing Energies of Earth* explores the healing power of the Earth's natural energies. By finding out about its capacity to heal, energise, cleanse and hold memories, we can heal the Earth and at the same time heal ourselves. Heal yourself and the Earth using dowsing, feng shui, and healthy gardening and building practices; explore energetic fields, from electromagnetism and ley lines to geopathic stress; reconnect with the Earth through spiritual journeys, labyrinth walks, organic gardening and simple folk medicine.'[27]

In *The Healing Energies of the Earth*, the author, Liz Simpson, 'integrates ancient and modern ways of looking at Gaia, the Mother Goddess, and discusses each based on a holistic understanding of the Earth's energies...Perhaps it is no coincidence that biologist James Lovelock hypothesized that Earth is a self-regulating, living organism only a few years after humankind first saw the awe-inspiring pictures of this planet seen from space by the 1968 US Apollo 8 mission.'[28]

Pagans see the Earth as an integrated whole — and this is only part of a far larger integrated, interconnected whole — the universe. They have picked up on a development within science in the eighties and nineties that has transformed many people's perception of nature. A perception known as complexity theory started in physics but soon spread to biology and economics. This is best explained by Brian Goodwin, lecturer of Holistic Science at Schumacher College.[29]

> Complex systems are defined as those made up many elements, often of diverse nature, that interact with one another according to well-defined rules. What became evident is that it is possible to understand the behaviour of these elements in isolation and have a perfectly clear understanding of their rules of interaction, but one is unable to predict the coherent behaviour of the whole system.
>
> The patterns that emerged in computers simulating such systems, which include flocks of birds, social insects such

as ants and termites, evolving ecosystems, and the dynamic patterns described in Lovelock's Gaia hypothesis, reveal that the Earth is like a living organism.[30]

This perspective of a totally integrated universe and Earth is sometimes termed the New Cosmology. An advert for a course on this subject at the Schumacher College states that the New Cosmology 'is a way of orientating oneself and one's community in the midst of the overwhelming powers of the universe. At every critical juncture of human history, a new cosmological vision begins to surface. The view that has arisen over the past centuries in the West — that we live in a giant machine — is now giving way to a new understanding that emphasises the centrality of relationships between humans and all beings of the Earth and the universe.[31] This perspective of relating to the connectedness of reality is essentially seen as spiritual, as another advert for the Schumacher College demonstrates. This course, called Shamanism[32] and the spirit of Gaia, is introduced in these words: 'In many ways shamans were the first scientists, and their science was deep ecology. But, living in times and cultures which did not separate the material from the non-material, the shaman's ecology went beyond the limits of the physical earth. This course will be an experiential introduction to the shaman's work, bringing together the physical and world to develop a spiritual ecology. It will involve studying the basic principles of deep ecology and Gaia theory, working outside in nature, and visiting nearby ancient sites.[33]

The view that the Earth should be seen as intimately connected with us in a way that supersedes mere biological and environmental dependency is ancient. Throughout history, many cultures have has a concept of some kind of Mother Earth, who we should venerate and worship. Bertrand Russell in his famous *History of Western Philosophy* states, 'The religions of Egypt and Babylonia, like other ancient religions, were originally fertility cults. The earth was female, the sun male...In Babylon, Ishtar, the earth-goddess, was supreme among female divinities. Throughout western Asia, the Great Mother was worshipped under various names. When Greek colonists in Asia Minor found temples to her, they names her Artemis and took over the existing cult. This is the origin of

'Diana of the Ephesians'. Christianity transformed her into the Virgin Mary, and it was a Council at Ephesus that legitimated the title 'Mother of God'.[34]

The link between veneration for Mother Earth and environmental concern is very strong. pagans believe that not only can the Earth's energies be used to heal us, but also, by connecting in with her forces, we can heal her. Liz Simpson writes, 'By finding out its capacity to heal, energise, cleanse and hold memories, we can heal the Earth and at the same time heal ourselves.'[35] She connects in with many current opinions when she says, 'Our relationship with Earth is becoming increasingly parasitic: we rip out and burn her fossil fuels; decimate her forests and pollute her rivers and oceans; murder animals for sport or vanity; we divest the soil of every ounce of goodness and poison it with chemicals. Only seldom do we take the time to gaze in awe and appreciation at the way Mother Earth continues to create new life from death and destruction.'[36]

So, through a legitimate concern for our environment and a reaction against a dry materialistic perspective that treats the natural world as nothing more than a bundle of randomly generated and innate processes, people are reaching out for mystery and magic. Somehow, the intricacy, complexity and harmony of the balance of nature can't seem to be explained by raw chance. There's more here than meets the eye. The trouble is, that in jumping from materialism to magic, people have missed a far better solution.

The Bible tells that there is indeed more to our planet than the result of some cosmic lottery: the Bible reveals to us that the intricacy, complexity and harmony are hallmarks of design. The biosphere is not a mere chance coming together of obscenely unlikely factors and processes; it is an integrated whole that is magnificently designed and created. There is something about the Gaia hypothesis that fits with a biblical perspective. Our world, and the life that is on it, is the result of a creator, and that creator is God. It is only the biblical view of our world that explains the order that we see around us and that can be explored through scientific exploration. Also, it is only this biblical perspective that reveals that 'something else' which scientific analysis cannot comprehend, and yet to which it points.[37] That 'something' that is beyond the physical, is the creator-God who also upholds his creation. It is not the Earth that we need to 'connect' into, but God himself — and God has given us only one route for doing this: faith in Jesus Christ. Jesus said, 'I am the way and the truth and the life. No-one comes to the Father except through me.'[38]

Christian environmentalists

Of course, Christians should be concerned for the environment. Indeed, with the environment at the centre of so many people's agendas these days, and with many of today's pagans connecting in with this, we need to have a well thought-out response. What is a proper biblical conception of the Earth and all of creation?

The creation account in Genesis includes the refrain 'and God saw that it was good,'[39] which indicates that creation does not exist just for what humanity can get out of it, but has value in God's eyes. The Bible clearly tells us that we have a responsibility to rule over creation in terms of tending and caring for it. Genesis 1: 26 informs us: 'God said, "Let us make man in our image, in our likeness, and let them rule over the fish of the sea and the birds of the air, over livestock, over all the earth, and over all the creatures that move along the ground."' Later, the first humans are explicitly put on earth 'to work it and take care of it'.[40] It is also notable that the move from a state of harmony in creation to the Fall is symbolised by an act of environmental disobedience.[41] Other parts of Scripture build on this foundation. The first covenant in Genesis, is made by God to Noah, his descendants and also to 'every living creature on earth'.[42] Creation is included in the covenant. Creation care is part of the teaching from God in the Torah, where, for example, every seventh year the land was allowed to rest, not only to allow the poor to glean from the fields but also to let the land rest from production.[43] The Psalms add to the picture of a proper relationship between God, humanity and the rest of creation. Psalm 24 opens with the ascription, 'The earth is the Lord's, and everything in it.' Here is a powerful affirmation that the earth belongs to God rather than humankind.

The centrality of Christ in creation is made clear in the New Testament, where John's Gospel, reflecting the opening words of

Genesis, reveals that not only God the Father[44], but also the Word was present at the beginning of creation.[45] Jesus revealed his mastery of creation by calming the storm on Galilee.[46] Indeed, in the face of various claims for lordship, not only for Mother Earth, but also from a whole plethora of pagan gods and spirits, we must contend for the absolute claim of Jesus Christ to be Lord of all, including all creation. The New Testament reveals that, 'He is the image of the invisible God, the firstborn over all creation. For by him all things were created: things in heaven and on earth, visible and invisible, whether thrones or powers or rulers or authorities; all things were created by him and for him. He is before all things, and in him all things hold together.'[47]

More than all this, the biblical perspective on our planet does not conclude with it being destroyed, but after this destruction a new heaven and a new earth being brought into being.[48] It is true that our present creation will be destroyed by fire,[49] but it is also true that a new earth will be established. God will re-establish his physical creation, including the planet earth — we are to be good stewards now, but realistically recognising that the Fall of humanity will work itself out in, first, the ongoing damage of creation and finally, its destruction. In any biblical perspective on our planet, the effect of humanity's rebellion and Fall must be taken seriously. Not only will fallen human beings tend to misuse and abuse God's gift of our environment, but also it needs to by remembered that our environment is under the curse of God.[50] Although this is the effect of the Fall, we are not to lose hope, for the present glories of creation will appear pale in contrast to what will yet be revealed when creation is re-established. The New Testament put this in these words: 'the whole creation has been groaning as in the pains of childbirth right up to the present time. Not only so, but we ourselves, who have the first fruits of the Spirit, groan inwardly as we wait eagerly for our adoption as sons, the redemption of our bodies.'[51] The final future for our recreated planet is glorious: 'The creation awaits in eager expectation for the for the sons of God to be revealed. For the creation was subjected to frustration, not by its own choice, but by the will of the one who subjected it, in hope that the creation will be liberated from its bondage to decay and brought into the glorious freedom of the children of God.'[52]

In contrast to paganism, and in particular the worship of Mother Earth, which is so prevalent today, the Bible has a full, clear and realistic view of our planet. It was created good and reflects something of the glory of God. We are given a mandate to explore and care for this creation. The fall of humanity has damaged and cursed this world, and yet we are still called to respect it and protect it. Nevertheless, when the whole world is judged, it will be destroyed. But this is not the end: God will bring in to being a new heaven and a new earth — it will all be reborn and redeemed. Our planet is to be honoured because it reflects something of our maker and also because we are commanded to be responsible stewards. However, rightly honouring it is very different from worshipping it. To worship the creation but forget the creator is an utter travesty.

Questions for discussion

1. In what ways have you noticed in the media a respect for nature that has become almost veneration, if not worship? How does the Bible anticipate this taking place? (Rom. 1:24-25; Acts 7:42-43)

2. Read Psalm 8 and Psalm 19. How do these Psalms help us to have a correct view of creation?

3. Is the Gaia concept something that is totally alien to the biblical understanding of our world? Explain your answer. Do you feel the biblical comprehension of our planet is closer to the Gaia model or the materialistic model? In what ways does it differ from each of these? In what ways does it agree with each? Do you feel that Genesis 1 helps us to answer these questions? In what ways?

4. In your experience, do you feel that Christians have shown a correct respect and care for our environment? Why? How does Genesis 1:27-31 and Genesis 2:15 instruct us to have a responsible attitude to the world around us.

Chapter 3
Dangerous Doctors

The Spread of Pagan Ideas through Alternative Therapies

The *[London] Times* newspaper runs a Saturday supplement entitled 'Body and Soul', which carries articles on a whole range of topics, including practical advice on things like diet, stress, exercise, human nature, popular psychology and sex. Much of it is good healthy stuff — but the label gives something away.

The title 'Body and Soul', or sometimes 'Body, Mind and Soul', or perhaps even 'Body, Mind and Spirit', is the new lens by which we are invited to look at life in a very holistic way — a way that includes a spiritual dimension. It is certainly not a materialistic perspective, but rather one of a secular culture that has run dry and is now looking for 'that other bit to life' — that which used to be provided by old-fashioned biblical religion.

One series of magazines on our newsagent stands is called, *Enhancing Your Mind, Body and Spirit*. The main sections of this publication are You, Friendship and Love, Foretelling the Future, Spells and Magic, Spirits and Ghosts, as well as Natural Healing.[1] 'Mind, Body and Spirit' is clearly the 21st century label for a perspective on life that includes the physical, but also the supernatural and spiritual.

One has only to walk through a large bookstore to get a feel for what 'Body, Mind and Soul' is all about. In many bookstores the classification 'religion' now only covers a small percentage of publications on spiritual topics, generally the world's biggest religions. Often another label is increasingly being introduced, called 'Body, Mind and Soul',[2] to cover books on every conceivable New

Age, pagan or neo-pagan theme. In essence, the whole thing has a flavour of self-help — ways to make your life better and increasingly fulfilled. The quantity and range is numbing. They span from alternative therapies, through forms of meditation, right the way to encyclopaedias on occult practice.

On the softer end of this range are subjects like yoga, meditation and stress relief. It is important to recognize that many engage in these activities purely from the perspective of simple exercise or relaxation, without any interest in the ideology beneath. However, it is also important to recognize that that underlying perspective is often undeniably pagan. At the initial level, most therapies are explained merely in term of physical and mental health, but with more careful reading and further exploration it can soon be seen that a whole worldview is behind them. Some people undoubtedly practice these therapies without any involvement in or attachment to the underlying philosophy, but others have found them to be a channel into a fascination in pagan beliefs. The full range of alternative therapies is phenomenal — all the way from what appear simple 'healthy living' guides through to blatant things like open witchcraft.

The Health Magazine, is a publication in the UK given out free in many pharmacies, and even at doctors' surgeries. By far, most of it deals with legitimate health issues and includes much worthwhile advice. However, sandwiched within all this are some very alternative perspectives. One article was titled Shantam's Stars — explaining recent changes and interactions between the planets and the stars. This column explains how stresses and strains of life can be reduced by working with the astrological phenomena, apparently occurring out in space around our planet.[3]

In one edition in *The [London] Times* magazine, *Body and Soul*, there was an article entitled the 'Natural way to beat depression.[4] In this double-page spread a leading US psychiatrist and author tells us to say 'no to drugs'. Now, this may be very good counsel, as are many of his other suggestions, like taking time and space to relax, addressing painful memories, maximising omega-3s, contributing to the community we live in and developing a regular schedule. But what is interesting is what is slipped in between all this: 'tap into your meridians' — that is, the spiritual channels for the flow of some mysterious invisible energy. The worrying point is how common sense, or at least plausible advice, surrounds the totally religious and spiritual. Normally hard to swallow pagan beliefs are being sugar-coated in practical healthcare information. Religious propaganda is being camouflaged; Eastern mysticism is being gift-wrapped.

This illustrates that one of the most important things to realise is that in much of the material available, the spiritual bit is part of, and is integrated with, physical aspects. The upshot of this is that much of the advice given in various publications makes good physical sense. Here, the pagan concepts are inserted in a very subtle and mild way. Take for example, the book *Stress Relief Made Simple*, by Sue George. Most of the sections are on straightforward things like considering our workload and lifestyle pressures, personal organization, suitable recreation, diet and exercise. But there are also sections on what the author calls 'mind-body therapies', including Chinese wand workout and t'ai chi. The book tells us that, 'Originating in China and developed as a combative martial art, t'ai chi is mainly practised nowadays as a spiritual and physical fitness regime. It is centred on the Taoist beliefs of balancing yin and yang — dark and light energies — within the body. By circulating energy around the body, stress is reduced and well-being ensured.'[5] After introducing 'hidden energies' in this section, the book then goes on to introduce other natural therapies — some of which also are based on a belief in various sorts of hidden energies, like acupressure: 'In acupressure, body energy is directly manipulated by working on a system of joints and meridians.'[6] Also included under alternative therapies are hypnotherapy, reiki, shiatsu, reflexology and crystal therapy.

Another book that illustrates this popular blending of the common sense with the overtly spiritual is *The Five Minute Healer: A Busy Person's Guide to Vitality and Energy All Day, Every Day*, by Jane Alexander. Again, most of the book concentrates on practical common-sense advice, presented in a very attractive manner. And yet, here and there throughout the book, input is given from a range of alternative therapies including ayurveda, colour therapy, dream therapy, feng shui, meditation, tantric sex and tibetan healing, to name but a few. In one section, the reader is even encouraged to 'talk' to beings that might figure in our dreams: 'Try "talking to your dream." Use two chairs or two cushions. Sit on one and imagine a figure or animal from your dream is on the other. Try speaking to the figure or animal, asking it questions.'[7] Communicating with beings in our dreams is one pagan means of reaching out and contacting spiritual powers. On the next page, visualization is suggested, which is basically a form of witchcraft. The subtle mixing of the normal and the paranormal, the physical and the spiritual, around the theme of health is incredibly common today.

Why is there a revival of pagan medicine?

There are three reasons that can be given for why holistic or alternative medicine is undergoing a phenomenal revival at the moment. The first reason is a recognition that orthodox treatments have unavoidable problems and side affects. Patients do not want to rely on drugs, surgery, or other invasive techniques — and the dangers of side effects of treatments are well established. The second reason for the growth in pagan medicine is because of a renewed and positive emphasis on lifestyle and a personal responsibility for our own health. The third explanation is the expansion pagan beliefs in our society — as people increasingly accept New Age concepts, they of course turn to the health practices that stem from them. In many ways, though, this last point works far more in reverse: alternative medicine is opening many people's minds to pagan ideologies. Through an interest in health and healthy living, many, who would never think of joining any religious group, or visiting a pagan bookshop, are now accepting New Age beliefs and practices. Pagan evangelism is happening through alternative healthcare.

Hidden dangers

New Age medicine is the 'health branch' of the New Age Movement, which involves the application of generally pagan methods of healing, while stressing the treatment of the whole person — body, mind and soul. This approach to healthy living is also sometimes termed 'holistic medicine'. The term 'holistic' comes from the Greek *holos*, meaning 'entire' or 'whole'. Today, the term 'holistic' is applied to many different fields, but usually it has a connection with a cosmic or spiritual perspective. There is a healthy use of the term in reaction to a form of materialistic medicine that assumes that human beings are nothing but biological machines that need to be 'fixed'. There are many dimensions to our being human, including not only the physical, but also the social, emotional, psychological and spiritual. True 'holistic' medicine needs to consider us in our totality, and not just one narrow facet. However, even though this is true, the term 'holistic' is more often than not used as a code word for some form of New Age or pagan perspective. Alternative medicine is another name given for these sorts of neo-pagan treatment.

All these names are rather loose in what they include and some may simply involve techniques or treatments that are simply not proven from a scientific point of view — and have no religious pagan worldview behind them. Furthermore, many use, promote and administer these therapies without believing in the original pagan belief system behind them — feeling that any merit they may have cannot simply be understood by current scientific explanations. Such an approach needs to be carefully questioned. There may indeed be forces that modern science has not explored, but they may also be incredibly dangerous. The trouble with the pagan approaches is that they may have stumbled upon something powerful — but two things need to be born in mind about that something.

With regard to the first, electricity, for example, is an invisible but real force, which may be slightly understood by the average thirteen year old. However, this knowledge could well be fatal. If this teenager started trying to do things with the wires of a house he could well kill himself. Experimenting with the unknown can be fatal. Some alternative therapies are simply medicines that are as yet not accepted or understood. For example, it may well be that some tribal witch-doctor in the Amazon jungle uses a certain plant extract as a potent cure for a particular condition. This may well 'catch on' in the West and finally be offered in a health shop here. Drug researchers here may take that plant and begin to do some research on it to extract and isolate the active ingredient. Having done this, and after much experimentation and years of trials, they may perhaps develop a new and effective drug. There were indeed some therapeutic qualities in the original plant that the tribal medicine had picked up on. However, what was needed was a full series of research procedures including double-blinds and controls — as well as testing thoroughly for any adverse effects. Many of our drugs come this way — an aspirin like drug was found in willow bark and the heart drug digitalis was found in the foxglove. Ancient British pagan medicine made use of both of these. However, research was needed to make drugs not only effective, but also safe.

The second thing to bear in mind with regard to some alternative therapies is not only that they may be dangerous, but they may also be wrong. The Bible clearly teaches that we are to avoid pagan practices. For example, the book of Deuteronomy warns that God's amongst people there must not be anyone who 'practices divination or sorcery, interprets omens, engages in witchcraft, or casts spells, or who is a medium or spiritualist or who consults the dead'.[8] Connecting in with spiritual forces beyond this world and using them for our advantage is utterly banned. Some may come balk at this and question the logic if true healing occasionally occurs. The answer is simply that the Bible recognizes that miracles may sometimes happen, but that the source of the miracle may be opposed to God. Scripture warns that genuine spiritual miracles can occur and yet still be false. For example, God sternly cautioned against a false prophet who would work genuine miracles and then counsel rebellion against him by enticing the people to worship a false god.[9] Indeed, the pagan sorcerers in Egypt performed powerful miracles from their own secret arts,[10] and at the end of time, the lawless one, or Anti-Christ, will have amazing miraculous powers.[11] Scripture clearly states the supernatural powers of the Anti-Christ are the works of Satan and are sent as a delusion.[12] The upshot of all this is that just because something may work, it does not mean that it is good. God has commanded that we avoid any unseen spiritual powers or energies, even *if* their effect seems beneficial in the short term.

Many proponents claim that reliance on allegedly 'natural' and 'spiritual' methods of healing offer medical care superior to that of modern orthodox medicine. Recourse is often made to various concepts about so-called 'life energies' as the reason it 'works'. These 'life energies' are simply a contemporary way of describing spiritual realities that the Bible condemns.

Some pagan alternative therapies may well be based upon something that science has not yet explored, but which may well have a rational explanation. In such a case, the wise course of action may be for the treatment to be avoided until it has been properly investigated. The Bible gives us a mandate to explore God's creation[13] and also to subdue it[14] for our good. But it must be remembered that not all knowledge is good[15] — some parts of God's creation are forbidden territory. Therapies that seem to work must be analysed biblically as to whether they are allowed, and then, even if they are acceptable theologically, they should be tested scientifically. Both God's world, explored through science, and God's Word, explored through careful interpretation, should be used to check any alternative therapy.

Spiritual power

Occasionally, there may be therapeutic results that cannot merely be explained by the placebo effect, nor by natural healing. paganism does have a real power in that it connects into spiritual realities; and these demonic beings can give short-term cures. Their power is very limited, but the Scriptures give clear evidence that it exists.[16] For a variety of reasons this power is constrained, even in the pages of the Bible — but the fact that it is at least sometimes manifest should alert us to the possibility. When this world comes towards its end supernatural powers of darkness may become more evident.[17] Their purpose is always to deceive people; they are a delusion so that people will believe a lie.

Judging carefully

Judging whether a particular therapy is beneficial or not, or is spiritually dangerous, is a difficult business. Some treatments may have a pagan ideology behind them, but they work, not because of the pagan belief system, but rather because the belief system has simply explained something in its own terms, which is actually something natural, that science as not yet investigated. For example, as mentioned earlier, in drug design and development researchers sometimes go off to places like South America to investigate a treatment that witchdoctors used. They looked at the plant substances that they employed and the pharmacological effects produced. These plants are then examined and research programmes set into motion. Often, a substance is isolated that has the medical effect. In the history of medicine various treatments used by witches and shamans have been found to have efficacious effects and then the pharmacological basis has been later understood.[18] The implication of this is that just because a pagan interpretation is given to a treatment, it does not necessarily imply that the treatment itself is false or spiritually dangerous. We must be careful not to see sinister dark shadows where the darkness is simply caused by our ignorance. On the other hand, however, in some cases it could be that although the underlying treatment may have a natural cause, the spiritual ideology is so intertwined with it that it becomes dangerous, at least in the sense that it opens the door to a fascination with the spiritual perspective. And then, of course, there could be nothing actually valid in the treatment itself; it could simply be an outgrowth of a pagan religious perspective. To make judgements with regard to specific treatments is beyond the scope of this chapter. All we are noting here is that the rise of alternative therapies with underlying pagan ideologies fits into the overall picture of New Age perspectives being increasingly imbibed by the general public.

In order to understand and recognize the underlying New Age perspectives it is necessary to examine some common threads that often lie just beneath the surface of this type of therapy.

Common threads in pagan medicine

Even though there is a phenomenally large range of New Age therapies, there are certain ideas that run through most of them:

A belief in a magical worldview

There is the understanding that there are not only scientific laws and principles that govern the way things in the universe behave, but also there are another set of principles and forces to be taken into account. These other laws deal with spiritual forces, energies and beings. By a special range of practices, the belief is that they can be used for the practitioner's own ends. The special practices (or rituals) claim to harness and manipulate these spiritual powers.

Altered states of consciousness

A large number of pagan therapies involve the experience of altered states of consciousness. An altered state of consciousness is the acquiring of unusual conditions of perception, achieved by the deliberate cultivation of abnormal mental states, states not normally experienced apart from certain religious techniques or occult programs. Many New Age practices or techniques and New Age supernatural experiences claim to induce altered states of consciousness by stilling the mind and regulating psychic energy.

Altered states of consciousness are used in approaches like crystal healing, therapeutic touch and visualisation. They are believed to 'orientate' the healer or patient to toward optimum health. The healer claims to receive vital information from a 'higher mind,' spirit guide or 'cosmic wisdom'.

Hidden energy systems

It is claimed that through altered states of consciousness, various psychic anatomies, or hidden energy systems were first discovered. These would include the *chakra* system in Hinduism, or the meridian system in Chinese acupuncture. Various alternative therapists will claim they are manipulating invisible energies, and will attempt to realign or unblock the energy channels. This will thereby permit the hidden force to flow freely through the body and so restore health.

In *The New Guide to Therapies*, sold in many main supermarkets,[19] some examples of this belief are demonstrated. For instance, something as apparently innocuous as performing alternate nostril breathing to relieve stress, gives the following explanation: 'Many Eastern Philosophies believe that as well as containing oxygen, air also contains vital energy. By performing conscious breathing exercises you can accumulate this energy and revitalise both your mind and your body.[20] Likewise, reflexology, a foot and hand massage that has long been used to promote relaxation and improve health,[21] is also based on a hidden energy system of some kind: 'The hands and feet are considered to be a mirror of the body and pressure on specific reflex points is thought to affect corresponding parts. Reflexologists believe that granular deposits accumulate around reflex points, blocking energy flow. The aim is to break down these deposits and improve the blood supply to flush away toxins.'[22]

Behind many of the ideas of there being spiritual energy systems within our bodies, that can be manipulated for our health, is the belief that the whole universe is full of such invisible forces. There is often an acceptance of the existence of a cosmic, mystical, or 'divine' energy supposedly uniting people and the universe. New Age medicine teaches that in order to really understand health and disease, we must switch from thinking in terms of merely matter to that based primarily on energy. This mystical energy has over 90 different names, depending on the culture and period of history. In Hinduism it is known as *prana*; in ancient Chinese medicine and Taoism it is called chi. In Japanese culture it is called *ki*; In Polynesian religion, it is termed *mana*. The developer of modern hypnotism, Franz Anton Mesmer, called it *animal magnitism*. D. D. Palmer, the founder of chiropractic, called it *innate*; the American Indians called it *Orinda*; parapsychologists give it a variety of names, including *psi*. Samuel Hahnemann, the founder of homeopathy, called it *vital force*. In yoga theory it is *prana* or *kundalini* energy. Psychics, spiritists and mediums have referred to it as *paraelectricity, biomagnetism* and *psi plasma*. Occult magicians define it as *elemental energy*.

Some New Age healers believe that either connected with this force, or within this force, are personal spirit beings, or guides, who can assist in the healing process. Not all New Age therapists would be aware of this, but those who have gone further certainly are. Take reflexology, for instance, one therapists writes: 'In channelling for the healing itself, you allow the guides to utilise more of your energy field...Many times the guide will reach in his through the healer's hand and beyond, going right into the body of the patient.'[23] These spirit entities the Bible would identify as beings known as fallen angels, unclean spirits or demons.

Embraces a multitude of diverse approaches

Pagan or New Age medicine is happy to employ a phenomenally wide range of approaches. Clients may end up being treated by methods other than they had initially expected or sought. For example, in reading the literature it is possible to find that someone who seeks help from acupuncture or acupressure may also be offered medical approaches based on astrology, occult meditation, spiritism, psychic diagnosis and healing. Alternative therapists do not see their various approaches in competition with each other, but rather as complementary. The main reason for this is because of New Age medicine's claim to be 'holistic' — they are trying to imply that they treat the whole person — body, mind and spirit. Because of this they feel is appropriate to bring together physical, psychological and spiritual treatments. In many ways, the New Age therapist is claiming to be physician, therapist and minister — all in one.

Potential dangers

In conclusion, it is important to emphasise again that there may be considerable dangers in some alternative therapies. Three concerns can be highlighted, ironically under the titles Body, Mind and Soul.

Dangers to our bodies

Alternative therapists are not usually experts in biological medicine, and so they could miss the diagnosis of a serious condition.

Take, for example, someone who goes to such a practitioner with a continuous sore throat that they have had for a long time. The therapist might suppose that their 'life energy' is blocked and give some kind of acupressure. He may also give an herbal tea. After a while, they feel a little better, but then after a few months they feel feverish, tired and have painful swollen joints, and so go back to the New Age therapist. This time he suggests some other adjustment of their 'life energies' say through reflexology. A month or so later they are feeling so ill that your they experience involuntary jerking movements of the hands, arms and face — as well as their speech becoming slurred. After a visit to a conventional doctor, who arranges bloods tests, they find you have streptococcus-induced rheumatic fever and chorea. They even discover that they now have valvular heart disease — a condition that will remain with them the rest of their life.

This is perhaps an extreme example, but it illustrates the point. Incorrect diagnosis and treatment could lead to missing the development of a serious disease, as well as allowing it to progress.

Another physical danger is that some of the so-called natural remedies may not have been sufficiently tested for adverse effects. Certain plant extracts could well contain potentially perilous substances. Just because it is natural does not necessarily mean it is healthy — after all, death is natural.

Dangers to our minds

False hope is a terrible thing — and the crushing despair caused after we have been let down can cause great distress. Furthermore, an unhealthy psychological dependency could develop, connected with a particular treatment that becomes the alexia of life to us.

More than this, New Age medicine can gradually change our minds, so that we begin to believe that which we earlier thought was unacceptable. Behind much alternative therapy is an ideology, or worldview. This perspective on life is religious, or spiritual. Without realizing it, we can gradually accept the existence of mysterious energy systems that have no more evidence for their reality than the religious views of those who believe that such things have been revealed to them by esoteric supernatural experience. Those who progress in this perspective may then begin to accept the transmigration of souls, spirit guides, visualization, higher levels of consciousness, enlightenment — and so on. The list is endless.

Dangers to our souls

The Bible reveals that there certainly are real spiritual beings like angels and demons, or evil spirits. Those who go deeply into alternative therapies may well make contact with these. The results of such encounters can lead to the most horrendous forms of bondage imaginable.[24] The Bible is clear that such beings are evil and destructive — any contact with them is extremely perilous — which is why Scripture bans it.

Perhaps most dangerous, such activities can develop a fascination in spiritual things that is utterly against that which God has ordained. People's attention is always drawn away from Jesus Christ, the only way to God the Father. It is only by accepting Jesus and following him that we can be made right with God and so be sure of entering heaven after we die. Any distraction from this is the greatest of all dangers we can be exposed to.

Questions for discussion

1. Does engaging in an alternative therapy sit comfortably with Philippians 4:8? Explain your answer.

2. The realities of health, disease aging and death are important things about which to have a biblical framework of thinking. Consider the following passages and reflect how they can be helpful in constructing such a perspective: Genesis 1:31; 3:17-19; Romans 8:18-25; James 5:13-20; Revelation 21:1-5.

3. What preventable things can cause some diseases? Exodus 15:26; Numbers 19:11-16; Deuteronomy 23:12-13; Ephesians 5:17; Proverbs 23:19-21,29-34; 1 Corinthians 3:17; 6:19-20; 10:31.

Chapter 4
Infiltration

The Spread of Pagan Ideas through Various Accepted
Practices

Pagan concepts are gradually being accepted within our society — they are infiltrating our thought processes so that what we would have rejected a generation ago we now tend to believe. As we have observed, our perspective of our planet and the environment have in many ways been used as a channel, as have alternative therapies, to preach pagan ideas. But this is not all; a host of other indirect means have also been adopted. In this chapter we take a glimpse at a variety of these.

Martial Arts

The martial arts are very popular and widespread today, whether through watching films, serious involvement in a club, or simply as an approach to self-defence. Basically, they are methods of physical discipline emphasising the control of body and mind for physical conditioning, health, self-defence and what is called enlightenment. Most of the ideas and practices come from China, but India and Japan have also contributed to their development.

On the surface, to the casual onlooker, they seem spiritually harmless: they appear to simply to assist in acquiring physical fitness and in giving security in a dangerous environment. And indeed, there are nonreligious forms where the stress is strictly put upon physical development. Furthermore, other people are involved in the Eastern forms but take no interest in the underlying religious dimension. Even at this level many Christians may have concerns, as Jesus' teaching would seem to contradict such an emphasis on physical self-protection.[1] However, as soon as we probe a bit deeper, more worrying issues are uncovered. These methods of self-defence claim to work by unifying body, mind and spirit, mainly through physical discipline and meditation. In the religious Eastern forms this allegedly helps to control the flow of mystical energy throughout the body (*chi* in Chinese and *ki* in Japanese) and enable the person to attain a state of mind-body oneness.

Perhaps the easiest way to understand something of the thinking behind many of the martial arts is to look at the Star War's films. In these productions George Lucas clearly portrays an Easter pagan worldview. *The Force* is similar to the spiritual energy or *Chi* that many martial art practitioners try to connect into and use. The Jedi knight initiates are taught in the Great Temple and their reputations are based on their spirits and not their material trappings. In the films, Obi-Wan Kenobi, for example, follows the path on his journey toward Jedi knighthood as the apprentice to the Jedi master Qui-Gon Jinn. These Jedi masters are rather like Eastern Gurus, teaching ideology and philosophy as well as combat skills. The basic pagan concept of connecting into the spiritual realm and harnessing its power for the practitioner's purposes is present throughout. Also, the New Age idea of altered states of consciousness is present as apprentice Jedis are encouraged to 'feel the force' rather than rely on their natural senses. This sort of practice is commonplace in the higher realms of martial art training. So, through the films and through martial arts themselves, many pagan concepts are planted in unsuspecting minds.

In the book, *The Way of the Spiritual Warrior*, the author writes that the martial arts are a kind of 'moving meditation. Meditation is a way of entering a state in which the conscious mind is not active while still remaining awake...When we are attacked, we react immediately: no conscious thought is involved.'[2] This state of mind is meant to help the warrior develop an experience of a duplicate spirit body within them[3] and that ultimately they should feel altered states of consciousness like 'a sensation of weightlessness and expansion beyond the self.[4] Some practitioners are encouraged to be as familiar with their spirit body as their physical body, and should aim to achieve a state where they are able to fly in their spirit as naturally as they can walk with their physical bodies. [5]

Those who practice martial arts simply for physical purposes may still be drawn in to its underlying religious philosophy. As most methods involve pagan teachings and techniques, the martial arts can easily be a doorway into Buddhism, Confucianism, Taoism and so forth. For the unsuspecting, the martial arts can give exposure to beliefs and techniques that are on the threshold of paganism.

Business training seminars

Many businesses have been sending their executives and managers on seminars that are supposed to optimise the participants full potential, making them far more positive and effective in their careers. These 50-60 hour intensive programmes have been run by a whole host of organizations, including names like Impact Seminars, Est, The Forum, Insight Seminars, Actualizations, Silva Mind Control and Life Dynamics. They claim that their training has the ability to radically empower individuals through unleashing the untapped powers of the mind.

These seminars and training programmes are reaching very strategically placed people. For example, one company, called Transformational Technologies claims 'that its clients include 25 of the Fortune 100 companies and that its eight week Executive Excellence programme "has attracted executives from one of the largest corporations in the world."'[6]

The seminars are often an assimilation of a variety of sources, both secular and religious, and have elements of pagan and New Age ideology, along with Eastern mysticism. The leaders and founders of these programmes understand this. Werner Erhard, the founder of Est (Erhard Seminars Training) once said, 'In a seminary I would have been burned as a witch.'[7]

The trainers employ didactic teaching and experientially orientated psychological exercises such as visualization. There is little doubt that a major purpose of these seminars is to transform a person's worldview from a Western to an ancient Eastern or pagan perspective. Participants are indoctrinated, or even brainwashed, to believe that they are part of ultimate reality, or God — and so, in a very real sense, are creators of their worlds and experience.

Astrology and the stock market

In *The [London] Financial Times*[8] there was an article entitled, 'Look to the skies for guidance'. In this article, the author, Peter Temple, reported that, 'Some traders claim that spectacular results have been achieved by studying planetary movements.' He wrote that, 'Some legendary investors have used astrological studies to back their decisions-making. In her book *The Universal Clock*, financial astrologer Jeanne Long says the US trader W. D. Gann (1878-1955) spent much time in the British Museum studying evidence of the theories of astrology unearthed at archaeological sites in Mesopotamia...his trading was spectacularly successful.' Although Gann was a rarity in his day, the practice of using astrology for playing the stock market is growing. *The Financial Times* article went on to say that, 'Devotees use complicated software to plot planetary movements and the relationships between them — and then try and discover whether these planetary "aspects" foretell significant market movements...Financial astrologers have been helped in recent years because the ability to computerise planetary data and share price information has made life much easier. Many financial astrology software packages also combine astrological data with conventional analysis indicators.' In Abu Dhabi, Bill Meridaian, a US fund manager runs money for wealthy Arab investors, using sophisticated financial astrology.

Visualization

Visualization is becoming very popular these days, promoted not only in books sold in any high street, but also in publications offered by many of the nation's biggest supermarkets and mega-stores. It is often seen as a method of meditation. Usually visualization is promoted in material that deals with issues like stress relief, improving concentration, training the mind, increasing self-confidence, positive thinking and problem solving. It uses the imagination and emotions to picture something you want to bring about.

In the book *The New Guide to Therapies*, which has been on the shelves of many supermarkets, visualization is described as 'an extremely powerful technique that uses the imagination to create particular states of mind and being...It can even be used for healing or for helping to achieve spiritual enlightenment.'[9]

At first it is presented as a psychological technique for helping people gain self-confidence. The example is given of a man who has a fear of public speaking: 'He could use visualization to help himself over his fear. He could simply visualise himself in front of his audience, speaking confidently and clearly...he is enjoying himself and feeling very calm and comfortable. At the end of the speech, the audience applauds enthusiastically. He keeps on visualising this situation in the same positive way, eventually the right side of his brain will come to associate the thought of public speaking with pleasure and he will find that his fear disappears.'[10] So the reader is invited to try a technique, which at first glance seems harmless enough. But as soon as one reads on, it becomes clear that there is far more here than merely harnessing the power of the imagination and the emotions. It is also claimed that visualization can be used to bring about physical healing, and other books harness the technique to become prosperous and popular. Indeed, by visualising what you want, it is claimed that you are actually bringing your vision into reality. This technique of visualization is well known among practitioners of pagan magic, and books of witchcraft refer to it as a basic ingredient of casting a spell.[11]

But there is even more to it than this. In *The New Guide to Therapies* we discover that through this technique the participant is encouraged to enter an imaginary visualised world in their mind where they meet a 'guide'. In this state of imagination, or even altered state of consciousness, or perhaps even self-hypnosis, they can ask their 'guide' for help in life's problems. This is thinly disguised witchcraft. In the book *White Witching*, the author encourages new witches to meet their spiritual guide or 'guardian angel.' We are told, 'The guardian angel will guide you to do what is right for you when you listen and follow your "inner voice". To find your guardian angel, you need to work with the powers of creative visualization.'[12] The danger of all this is that it is set out so attractively, that it focuses on some basic human desires for health, wealth and prosperity, and that is so widely available.

Again and again in pagan thought, whatever the technique or particular strand, people are encouraged to contact, embrace and employ 'spiritual' powers. Most of the books in the supermarkets encourage people to contact the spiritual world, or hidden sources of 'energy', for the apparent benefit their health, guidance and peace of mind. The books on witchcraft available in our high streets push this a bit further as a method of obtaining what the participant wants in a given situation. In other words, it is used to bring something about: it is a spell. The person is creating their own reality.

The Bible is absolutely clear that human beings are not allowed to even attempt to contact the spiritual world in these ways; such practices are utterly banned. The Old Testament commands 'Do not practise divination or sorcery,'[13] and indeed, the dangers to a community are so great that 'A man or woman who is a medium or spiritist among you must be put to death.'[14] Although the death penalty was not commanded after the coming of Christ, new believers in Jesus turned away from these practices and burnt their scrolls on sorcery publicly, even though they were of great financial value.[15]

Meditation

Meditation is something that is employed in a whole host of areas from gaining relief from stress to gaining new insight on life. One publication introduces the subject in these words: 'People have used meditation for thousands of years in their quest for inner harmony. All the major religions...use it in their teachings to help attain spiritual enlightenment.'[16] Christianity is included in this description, even though the biblical concept of meditation is radically and profoundly different from that understood by pagans. The Bible employs the term to mean active involvement and concentration of the mind, whereas a New Age perspective is pretty well opposite to this — generally meaning an emptying of our minds.

The pagan claims for meditation are high: 'Meditation improves concentration, increases self-awareness and enables us to combat stress by helping us to relax and cope. It can even help us get on better with others. Many people who meditate improve their physical and mental well-being, and some have been able to conquer depression and the addiction of drugs, caffeine or alcohol.'[17] One publication claims it is a powerful tool for preparing for the day ahead: 'Try to make time for five minutes quite meditation before you leave for work. It stills the mind, combats stress, and mentally prepares you for the day.'[18]

Some may feel that meditation is merely a psychological technique for relaxing. However, this is not the way pagans view it: 'In order to lessen some of the mental stresses you may feel, a spiritual practice such as meditation can be very beneficial...turn to your spiritual side.'[19] Eileen Cady wrote, 'All you need is deep within you waiting to unfold and reveal itself. All you have to do is be still and take time to seek for what is within, and you will surely find it.'[20] The Buddha claimed to reach enlightenment through meditation and then devoted the rest of his life to teaching others what he had learned. The Buddha used a mantra to help achieve this, and this is something that many books today encourage. These are statements that someone repeats to himself or herself until they are said to resonate through the body and bring about a transformation of consciousness. Gaining an altered state of consciousness is a thread that runs through almost every variety and style of traditional and contemporary paganism. In this state of mind one is said to be in contact with the spiritual world. This altered state of consciousness leads to an alleged self-realization or spiritual enlightenment, which has as its final goal union with the ultimate reality and resulting in dissolution of the individual personality.

New Age meditation is derived from Eastern or occult methods and uses the mind in an abnormal manner to radically restructure an individual's perceptions of the self, the world and the universe in order to support pagan philosophy and goals. Almost all forms of pagan meditation can lead to the eventual development of psychic powers and the possibility of spirit possession.

Yoga

The introduction to the section on yoga in the book on therapies available in most supermarkets begins with these words: 'If this section of the book inspires you to explore the system of yoga, it could become your first step towards the liberating journey of self-realization. Many people find that they choose yoga as a fitness tool to increase their flexibility and improve their muscle tone, *but also gain a great deal from the philosophy behind it.*'[21] This very clearly reveals the aim of many behind the pushing of yoga: to accept the philosophy behind it. That philosophy is undeniably pagan. The spread of yoga in the West has been encouraged and supported by Hindu missionary organizations that believe it is an effective way of capturing hearts and minds for Eastern pagan philosophy.[22]

This is not hidden beneath the surface, *The New Guide to Therapies* is typical when it states, 'It is important to learn to let go of the negative conditioning of the past in order to become more conscious of how the emotional content of the thoughts you have today will determine your future reality. So what begins as a simple quest for a fitness programme can lead to a greater understanding of "where I am coming from" and a much healthier lifestyle. The true meaning of self-realization may take years to achieve, but yoga will shape your present and create a positive future along the way — it's a fascinating journey. As we spiral off into the 'New Age of Aquarius' the energy around us is beginning to vibrate at a higher frequency.'[23] Note how yoga is seen as a spiritual activity and one linked with the New Age, as well as involving mysterious energy forces.

The thinking behind yoga is intensely religious. Let me quote *The New Guide to Therapies* again, this popular book available in supermarkets throughout the UK (I am quoting from this basic book to make the point that the religious side of yoga is hardly hidden):

The Universal Mind choreographs everything that is happening with ultimate intelligence. It permeates every fibre of existence, and everything is alive as an expression of this intelligence. Our bodies and all we perceive is the transformation of this consciousness from the unknown and invisible into the known and visible. The process of creation is how Divinity expresses itself. The physical universe is pure consciousness (energy) in motion. When we see that our true nature is universal intelligence expressing itself, we begin to realise the unlimited potential of who and what we are.[24] Prana is the subtle force that animates all manifestations of creation. We extract this 'life current' from the oxygen we breathe and it then circulates throughout our bodies. By practising yoga, more prana is obtained and stored and one feels greater connection to the 'oneness of all things'.[25]

The origins of yoga are now lost in the mists of time, but believers in it understand that the so called ancient wisdom known as 'the supreme science of life' was revealed to the ancient sages of India three to four thousand years ago. From this is it should be noted that several of the factors usually present in pagan belief are evident. For example, the belief in hidden, or mysterious energy forms, which have been mystically revealed to some guru. Furthermore, there is the basic understanding, present behind many forms of paganism, of some kind of cosmic spirit, which we need to connect into — 'The Oneness of all Things'. This spiritual connection between the participant and the 'Oneness of all Things' is at the heart of yoga. The word yoga means 'union' — union of mind, body and spirit, and union with the 'Oneness of all things' — the cosmic spirit of the cosmos. This psychic connection is seen a state of enlightenment and involves an altered state of consciousness — another concept and desire in many pagan, neo-pagan and New Age practices.

It is difficult to separate yoga practice from yoga theory. Without being fully conscious of the fact, an innocent practitioner may be exposed and subjected to pagan practices and belief systems.

To the law and to the testimony

In response to all this it needs to be asserted that Christians need to listen to the cry of Isaiah the prophet: 'To the law and to the testimony.'[26] These words were uttered when the king of the day ran after pagan beliefs and practices,[27] and the people sought supernatural inspiration and guidance.[28] The law and the testimony are to us the Word of God, the Bible. This supreme and final revelation from God tells us that the thinking behind these practices is wrong — and more than that they are dangerous.[29] What may appear innocent and even healthy may in reality sinister and deadly.

Questions for discussion

1. Why do you think these sorts of activities have become so widespread over recent years? In what way does Romans 1:18-25 throw light on this?

2. Some Christians feel that some of these practices are not harmful if the ideology behind them is avoided. For example, some feel that yoga is fine if it is used merely as a means of exercise or relaxation. In 1 Corinthians 10:14-11:1, the apostle Paul deals with the issue of whether it is right or not for Christians to eat food that has been offered to pagan idols. Do you think that the principles revealed in that passage are in any way relevant to the practices outlined in this chapter? Give your reasons for feeling that such an application is appropriate, or inappropriate.

3. Read 2 Kings 16 and Isaiah 8:11-22. List the ways in which the people of Judah were turning from the true God. Beside each item in the list, write a modern-day equivalent current in our society today. In particular, look again at Isaiah 8:21-22. What do these verses teach us about what will happen to those who seek pagan enlightenment, guidance and health? In what ways is this being fulfilled in our contemporary society?

Chapter 5
Magic on the March
The Current Rise of Pagan Religions

It has been the basic thrust of this book that pagan ideas and beliefs are permeating our society at the moment. The really startling
thing is that it is the 'normal' person on the street who is absorbing
all these ideas. Whereas a decade or two ago, there were always a
few people who were linked to some 'way-off' religious group or
cult, in general they were the exception rather than the rule. The
difference today is that, although most people still aren't becoming
signed-up members of particular pagan religions, they are adopting a worldview, or outlook, that is definitely pagan.

There are various reasons as to why people aren't joining cults
and groups. In particular, we live in a very individualistic culture
and we don't want to commit ourselves to anything, or come under
any sort of badge or label. Today, we are far happier with a 'pick
and mix' approach, where we take this practice from over there,
and this perspective from here, and then make up our own distinc-
tive combination. Of course, this fits totally and happily within our
pluralistic society and it also gels nicely with the pagan religions
themselves. Generally, pagans see all the different styles, not as
contradictory, but as complementary — what we have to do is find
the particular approach, or combination of approaches, that works
for us. Like in ancient Rome, pagans are happy for us to follow
any approach or religion we want, as long as we don't say ours is
the only way — if we do that, we incur their wrath. And this is exactly what happened in the first century with the early Christians.
Political correctness is being used today as a hammer to suppress

religious freedom so that the only acceptable view is that everyone is right. You are not allowed to say that anyone is wrong — this is pluralistic fundamentalism or, totalitolerance. Today, the acceptable path is that every path is acceptable.

What all this means for the average citizen is that they can bolt-on the spiritual activity they are interested in onto their life, without being seen as peculiar or bizarre. Basically, they behave as a normal secular citizen, but have added a particular spiritual dimension to their lives that inspires and helps them. They don't force it on anyone else; their only claim is that they find it helpful. Truth claims are left out of the religious arena — and it is totally non-PC to get anyway near them bringing them back in. For a society that is post-modern and does not believe in the concept of truth, that is pluralistic in practice, and is yet spiritually hungry, such an approach fits the bill wonderfully. Religion is for my benefit, to do in the way I choose. Furthermore, it does not dictate any morality to me – this is an added and beautifully attractive bonus. In effect, I become god of my own little world — and ironically, that is what the New Age teaches we are: Everything is One, God is in us — and so, we are God.

So, rather than Westerners suddenly all signing up to some religious cult, we are ever so gradually accepting the belief systems of paganism. If all our neighbours suddenly became Hindus, Buddhists or Wiccans, we would find this too much, but if we come to the position of essentially believing the same as much of these religions without actually joining them, then everything is wonderfully acceptable.

The gradual nature of this being immersed in pagan thought and practice is very significant. There is the old story that tells us that if you want to boil frogs alive, don't throw them in boiling water — they will jump straight out. However, if you add them to cold water and gradually heat the pot, they will stay where they are and be cooked alive. This describes exactly where we are with regard to the present onslaught of pagan concepts and activities.

Having said all this, our analysis of the rise of contemporary paganism would be incomplete without at least taking a peek at the 'finished article' of the pagan religion as adhered to by practitioners. Although most people will not sign up to a pagan cult or religion, it is necessary to discover what some people link up with. In the light of this, we will now take a brief look at neo-paganism as a religious movement and then consider a particularly successful form of that movement in more detail.

Paganism as a movement and a religion

Neo-paganism is coming out of the closet in force — as a self-conscious religious movement it is beginning to find its political teeth. In one of Britain's most reputable intellectual journals, *British Archaeology*, the case was made for Druid priests to be consulted regarding the new road proposals at Stonehenge: 'The project team, including the Highways Agency, construction contractors, landscape architects and archaeologists, have acknowledged Stonehenge to be a working temple for modern pagans and sacred for many others. Should the work go ahead, all site personnel will be briefed about the sanctity of landscape and monuments. Archaeologists will talk to pagan priests who will feed information back into their faith communities worldwide. Rituals to ease environmental and ancestral spirits will be made.'[1] Contemporary paganism is not hiding away in an obscure corner; it is making its voice heard in the public arena.

For an overview of modern pagansm it would be best to hear from a pagan themselves. The pagan writer Anodea Judith, in her book *The Truth about Neo-Paganism*, writes:

> The term neo-paganism describes a modern social and religious movement based on the reconstruction and adaptation of our ancestral polytheistic nature religions. The prefix 'neo' is used to distinguish modern pagan practice from those of the ancestors, because many of the rites have changed and evolved along with our culture. Believing that there is no real separation between self and the environment, between races or sexes, neo-pagans see their world as an incredibly rich and complex interconnected web of which all things are a part. This view of interconnectedness empowers the individual as an agent of change. As part of the web, we are able to effect subtle changes within

it — changes that help to bring it back into balance once again, from its precarious state of environmental threat, social oppression, and spiritual bankruptcy.

Neo-paganism is a religion connecting the worlds of myth and reality, heaven and earth, life and death, person and planet. It is a religion that is inclusive rather than exclusive, life-affirming rather than self-denying, cyclical rather than linear. Predating Christianity by more than 30,000 years, it is the common ancestral religion of our people and our planet, once brutally repressed, and now returning at a time of great crisis and need.[2]

Emma Restal, author of *Living Druidry* and the current head of the Druid Network writes, 'The root of my spirituality is reverence for nature. Its practice is the forging of sacred relationships within humanity and the environment.'[3]

As to the variety and range of this modern pagan movement, Anodea Judith writes that today's pagans,

Include practitioners from many different traditions, including Native Americans, ceremonial magicians, Witches, Druids, feminist theologians who honour the Goddess, Hindus, some Buddhists, and those who follow shamanic paths. Still others would call themselves pagan if they had had informed knowledge of what the term really means. Many people who receive an explanation of pagan belief say, 'That's what I've always believed, but I never knew what to call it!' They do not change their believes to join the movement, but instead find a movement that is in harmony with the values they already hold.[4]

She later continues:

Like Christianity, with its subdivisions of Catholic and Protestant, and the many widely differing Protestant denominations, neo-paganism comes in many flavours and styles.

The following is an attempt to describe the major influences and contemporary styles that make up the larger body
of the neo-pagan community. it is by no means exhaustive,
for neo-pagans pride themselves on the diversity of their
ways, and many groups are eclectic blends of the traditions listed below.[5]

Anodea Judith, in summarising the contemporary pagan scene,
then lists the following under the heading of Wicca, or Witchcraft:
Gardnerian Witchcraft, Alexandrian Wicca, Seax Wicca, Fam
Trads, Dianic Witchcraft, Faerie and Radical Faeries. The pagan
traditions outside of Witchcraft are then also listed as Feraferia and
Norse paganism. After this are itemized groups that may choose to
focus on a particular culture or pantheon, such as Celtic, Middle
Eastern, Egyptian, Greek, Oceanic, Oriental, Hindu, or Tibetan
Buddhist. Although originally distinct, many contemporary prac-
tioners emphasise diversity and borrow heavily from each other, as
well as combine the traditions in any way they wish. These cultural
traditions include, Druidism (Celtic), Huna (Hawaiian), Santeria
(Africa), Umbanda (Brazilian), Voudoun (Haita), Hinduism (India), Tantra (India), Tibetan Buddhism, Ceremonial Magick and
Native American Shamanism.[6]

Before looking at one of these in detail, it is worth quoting
Anodea Judith again to appreciate the fervour and missionary en-
thusiasm within the movement:

> Neo-paganism is a religion that is alive and thriving. Its
> rituals are meaningful, passionate, colourful, and fun. Its
> philosophies are relevant to today's world as well as being
> deeply embedded in the past. It works with both the con-
> scious and the unconscious, with rich symbolism, ecstatic
> music and drumming, colourful costumes, and potent ar-
> chetypal images. It is a religion that honours the individual
> and as a carrier of the divine, and honours the world we
> live in as equally divine. It is a religion that answers the
> needs of our time — the environmental crisis, the loss of
> faith and purpose, and the emptiness and despair within so

many individuals and society. It is a religion with a strong sense of community, forged perhaps by centuries of persecution, but supported by common purpose, mutual respect, and the sharing of joy.[7]

Paganism is advancing; magic is on the march.

Neo-paganism has a strong presence in the USA. One of the great American forefathers of the pagan revival there was Gerald Gardner, who was born in 1884. His book *Witchcraft Today* is one of the foundation stones of modern witchcraft, or Wicca. Gardner constructed a neo-pagan religion, which drew upon such authors as Margaret Murray (*Witchcraft in Western Europe*, 1921) and Robert Graves (*The White Goddess*, 1948).

The Pagan Federation was founded in 1971 'to provide information on paganism and to counter misconceptions about the religion'. The Federations Information Pack defines modern paganism as 'a religion of joy and self-realization ... Pagans follow a nature-based spirituality and worship the old gods — the deities of pre-Christian times'. The Pagan Federation is a coordinating body based in London, and its principle role is to provide a network of pagans and to facilitate communication between various pagan groups operating in Britain. It organises conferences and day meetings, and it publishes a quarterly magazine, *Pagan Dawn* (formerly called *The Wiccan*), which deals not only with Wicca but also with other neo-pagan movements such as Druidry, Odinism and Shamanism. The British Pagan Federation has it its counterpart organizations in America: the Midwest Pagan Council and the Pagan Front are just two of many such coordinating groups. The movement is truly international in flavour.

Susan Greenwood is a lecturer that has taught an anthropological and historical approach to magic and witchcraft at various universities in the UK, including Goldsmiths College, University of London, Sussex University and King Alfred's College, Winchester. She believes her subject 'has been widely misunderstood and misrepresented.'[8] In her book, *The Encyclopedia of Magic and Witchcraft: An Illustrated Historical Reference to Spiritual Worlds*, she brings together material covered on these courses. In the introduction to the section entitled, Modern Magic, she writes:

Magic today has had a bad press — it is either associated with the work of the Devil, or it is reduced to conjuring tricks and sleight of hand. Magic is seen to be separate from religion, but the way we view magic in the West has been shaped by Christianity, which has branded it evil. Magic is neither good nor evil in iself and can be used in a variety of ways depending on who is practising it. During he seventeenth century magic was increasingly seen as irrational when compared to science. At this time, those who practised the occult arts went underground, and many secret societies — such as the Rosicrucians and Feemasons — were formed. Magical practices today reflect this history.[9]

This explains why the movement has historically been on the fringes of society, but now, with the relative weakening of Christianity and the philosophical undermining of science as the arbiter of truth,[10] pagan beliefs and public organizations are becoming far more acceptable to the general public. This is demonstrated by the fact that in 2004 a Satanist had his religious practices recognised by the British Royal Navy and is now allowed to perform Satanic rituals on board his ship. Leading Hand Cranmer from Edinburgh became the first registered Satanist in the British Armed Forces after the captain of *HMS Cumberland* agreed to recognise his beliefs. A spokesman for the Royal Navy said: 'We are an equal opportunities employer and we don't stop anyone from having their own religious values. Our policy is that, wherever practical, reasonable requests for time and facilities that do not impact on operational effectiveness or the welfare of other personnel are met.'[11]

Perhaps the most well known public face of contemporary neo-paganism is the New Age Movement.[12] This originated in 1971 when it emerged in America as a self-conscious form of spirituality. Through bookshops, conferences, magazines, journals and retreat centres like the Findhorn community in northern Scotland, this movement has made its mark on contemporary society.

When all this is put together it is evident that that it is not just that increasing numbers of the general public are quietly imbibing pagan beliefs, but also that more organised and official forms of neo-paganism are growing as well.

As part of our glimpse at this powerful religious movement, it is worth considering one particular aspect in detail: Wicca.

Wicca

Essentially, Wicca is based on one of the original ancient faiths of the British Isle and of many who emigrated to countries such as America, Australia, Canada and South Africa. It was also prevalent in different forms in much of Europe.[13] This religion was driven underground by the advance of Christianity, which generally referred to it as witchcraft. Again, so as to be careful not to misinterpret them, I will quote the pagans' own words on their faith. Christine Seville, a practising Wiccan, writes the following in a popular introduction to her faith:

> Most of us have grown up with an image in our minds of what a witch looks like, normally an ugly, wicked old crone, dressed in black robes and a pointed hat, armed with a book of evil spells and a broomstick and always accompanied by her ever-faithful black cat.

> This misconception was born out of the anti-witch propaganda of the Christian Church as it tried to suppress the practices and religions of the past. Even until relatively recently, witches were portrayed as evil villains in such films and fairy stories as The Wizard of Oz and Sleeping Beauty.

> Thankfully, the perceived role of the witch has now started to change from that of villain to a wise and honourable hero or heroine, as seen in television series like Sabrina, the Teenage Witch, Bewitched, and Buffy the Vampire Slayer.[14]

She continues her explanation of this faith that is undergoing resurgence in the following words:

The Wiccan faith can trace its practices back for many thousands of years and most likely derives its early roots from the animal cults and shamanistic beliefs of Stone Age Europe. These animal cults formed the core of many of the faiths of early human society and helped our ancestors begin to understand the patterns of the natural world, leading them to a basic psychological understanding of themselves and the world in which they lived.

The tribal shaman would explain complex ideas through the symbolism of the natural world, including animals, seasons, changing weather patterns and stars. In time, these cults developed some very sophisticated beliefs about magic and religion, and although their names and interpretations varied throughout the world, the symbolic meanings behind them were virtually the same in every civilization and culture. This is one of the main reasons why the Wiccan faith has seen such a revival in the last century; its symbolic meanings are familiar and relatively easy for everyone to understand.[15]

Having outlined its background and development, she then draws attention to this particular contemporary pagan religion's essential beliefs:

Although Wiccans worship and honour many deities, or lesser gods, and elemental lords, their focus of worship is on the 'divine creative force' (resembling the 'great spirit' in Native American tradition), which is subdivided into the male and female principles of the God and Goddess (similar to the Chinese concept of yin and yang). As well as making up the divine creative force, these two opposing forces, or aspects of nature, can be subdivided into further deities, many of whom were proclaimed saints by the early Celtic Christian Church.

> The God is the masculine force, the master of life and death. In pagan belief, the image of the Horned God (or god of the hunt) is a very powerful symbol, which, despite having been used by the Christian Church to represent the devil, is, in fact, far from evil, representing as it does the darker side of nature...
>
> The Goddess is the female, or light side of nature, equivalent to the Native American Mother Earth.[16]

In her book, *White Witching*, Mariano Kalfors tells us that witches, or Wiccans, believe that we are all part of 'the Wyrd' or 'web of life'. The word 'weird' comes from this 'Anglo-Saxon word "Wyrd", which people thought of as an all-powerful sense of destiny that shapes the world. It can be thought of as a magical web in which all life is interconnected'.[17] She goes on to explain that as part of this web of life we are 'intimately connected to all things and one another via invisible forces and energies. These energies radiate from everything in the universe — from the moon and stars in the heavens to rocks and stones on earth, sending out subtle vibrations along invisible energy pathways. The art of white magic is about tuning into these "vibes" and working with the natural and elemental ingredients of the universe to bring about positive change'.[18]

Morally destitute

One of the things that becomes obvious when reading pagan literature in general, and Wiccan material in particular, is how devoid of moral teaching it is. Professor Miranda J. Green, head of The Centre for the Study of Culture, Archaeology, Religions and Biography, at the University of Wales College, summarises the pagan ethic as 'Do what thou wilt but harm none.'[19] And practising witch Christine Seville tells us that any spell will always come back on the initiator 'in three ways and at three levels.'[20] Anodea Judith confirms this ethical position when she writes 'it is believed that it only harms oneself to harm another...Pagans do not believe in a concept of "sin and forgiveness," but instead see things in terms of cause and effect, sometimes called karma'.[21] Another Wiccan, Marion Green, writes, 'so long as you cause no harm to any person, animal or thing, you may follow your True Will. True Will is not personal choice or want, but the purpose of your existence on Earth...If you cause harm to anyone, that harm will be reflected back on you, if not in this life then in another incarnation, there is no escape'.[22]

All this is very weak in constructing an ethic for living — there is no real practical morality here. As Mario Green admits, the witches maxim, '"If you harm none, do what you will," on the face of it looks like a licence to do anything.'[23] And it certainly does. Indeed, in practice it is a form of situation ethics that allows you to reason out what you feel is the best course of action. A specific illustration of this is given by Anodea Judith in *The Truth about Neo-Paganism*: 'Pagans believe in allowing people privacy and freedom for their own actions. Within this framework, small acts must be weighed against larger effects, such as a woman's decision to end a pregnancy, where the decision to terminate is weighed against the effects of the potential harm in raising a child without proper emotional and physical support, and contributing in this way to over population, poverty, and potential child abuse.'[24] In the end you can really do what you want.

We will consider this whole topic in more detail later, but here it is worth comparing with the ethics of the Bible. From the first page in Genesis to the last page in Revelation, the Bible reveals a consistent and detailed ethic for practical healthy living. Moreover, it deals with the whole issue of forgiveness, something that Wiccans reject.

Old verses new

Wiccans often make the point that they are a far older religion than Christianity — and are therefore a more authentic faith of our planet. They also feel that theirs is the original religion of the British Isle, rather like Native Indian shamanism is the authentic regional faith of North America. Wicca is also popular in the US, and it is suggested that this was the original faith of some of the racial groups that settled there. Wiccans, and other pagans, often refer to Christianity as 'the Middle Eastern religion'. In response to this, at a superficial level it should be noted that just because something is older does not mean it is correct. And furthermore, neither is something necessarily true for a given group of people, just because it is associated with their geographical location or race. Behind this initial response is the biblical perspective that truth exists — and absolute truth at that. The Bible claims to reveal God's truth — a truth that is true independent of time, place and race — a truth that is always true.

To more specifically answer the charge of Christianity merely being a 'young' faith, we have to understand the Bible's concept of truth being progressively revealed by God.[25] The Bible shows us that it has been God's will and purpose to gradually reveal his truth to us. Although some knowledge of God is available through creation around us,[26] and from our consciences within,[27] God built on this in successive stages. Most particularly, he revealed his righteousness and his righteous expectations through Moses, as well as his mercy and the potential for forgiveness.[28] Through Moses the Law and the sacrificial system of the Tabernacle was instituted. Various signs, wonders and miracles validated this revelation.[29] The people who received this revelation were meant to be a light to the other nations. Miracles were given again as this light-bearing nation was rooted into the land of Israel under Joshua, and then later when they rebelled and were called back to God's ways by the special prophets Elijah and Elisha. Significantly, what he was calling them back from was paganism. God then supremely and miraculously validated his final revelation of truth when Jesus Christ came[30]. Jesus brings God's good news to the whole world. This answers the two objection to Christianity that Wiccans sometimes raise: that theirs is the oldest faith and the faith of our geographical locality or race. Biblical Christianity is based on God revealing himself step by step in history and it is a message for all nations.

Ignition point
- when East meets West - and old meets new -

Christine Seville, in her book on Wicca, attempts to give a positive spin on her faith, as well as change our perception of witchcraft, when she writes:

Belief in Wicca has long been misunderstood, and even in more recent history, those called witches have been feared and hated. Yet in today's world of fast-living and high-technology, with more and more people seeking spiritual or natural guidance, peace and enlightenment, Wicca is enjoying a resurgence of popularity. With one of its central tenets of balance and harmony, it shares similarities with many other belief systems, particularly those of eastern origin.[31]

It is worth noting how she focuses on the increasing appetite folk have today for spiritual exploration and satisfaction. Two centuries of secular atheistic propaganda, along, in many instances with exposure to a liberal, dry and watered-down Churchianity, have left an aching void in our society, which paganism is now filling. It is also significant that in the above paragraph she links her paganism with eastern religion. In many senses, the return to paganism in the neo-pagan and New Age movement dovetails completely with people's experimenting with eastern spirituality. Eastern religions and western paganism share many basic beliefs. This is emphasised by Anodea Judith when she writes regarding Hinduism:

Practitioners of Hinduism are beginning to join forces with the neo-pagan community because they have discovered so many neo-pagans worshipping their gods and goddesses. There are many commonalities of beliefs, as well as a multiplicity of deities, most of whom come in pairs of divine couples, such as Brahma and Saraswati, creators; Vishnu and Laksmi, preservers; and Shiva and Kali, destroyers. Hindu gods are frequently invoked in neo-pagan circles, and in India these gods have living traditions, temples, and unbroken lines of worship through history. [32]

She then continues to reinforce the link between the rebirth of western paganism and fascination with eastern religions in her comments on Tibetan Buddhism:

There are enough neo-pagans simultaneously involved with Eastern religions to have coined the term, Buddheo-Pagan. While some forms of Buddhism may imply rigorous self-denial and withdrawal from the world, other aspects are extremely polytheistic, honouring Goddesses as well as Gods. Buddheo-pagans contribute the threads of deep meditation; philosophical constructs, such as the Bodhisattva, who work for the enlightenment of all sentient beings; and the power of compassion and prayer. Tibetan deities also have a time-honoured tradition of uninterrupted worship.[33]

Eastern and Western forms of paganism have many basic ideas in common and generally do not see themselves in competition, but as complimentary. Generally, both believe in some great creative force that permeates the universe; this is often subdivided into two opposing forces or aspects; and from this emanates many deities. Human beings can, through many mystical means, 'connect into' this spiritual domain and so 'tap into' its power. The ultimate aim is enlightenment, which is an altered state of consciousness where we perceive we are one with the universe and its creative force; we grasp that this divine power of the cosmos dwells within us — we are divine; we are God.

This basic package of ideas permeates much Eastern paganism, ancient Western paganism, neo-paganism and the New Age. Here, East meets West and ancient meets modern; here are the central tenets that could lead to the merging of all these forms of anti-biblical belief into a One-World faith. Here is the basic belief system that has always set itself against the revealed religion of the Bible — and is almost as old as humanity.

Satan's lie, that started in the Garden and fought against true faith in God, continued through the Bible period, was suppressed and sometimes assimilated by Christianity, but is now poised for a massive come-back of demonic proportions.

Questions for discussion

1. Does it surprise you that people can find paganism so attractive today? What do you think that 2 Corinthians 11:14 can teach us about this? In what ways does this make neo-paganism so dangerous?

2. In this chapter we have seen that pagans often see all their different varieties, not as in competition with each other but complementing each other. Indeed, many would accept Christians until they make exclusive claims for Jesus Christ. How does John 14:6, 1 Timothy 2:5, Philippians 2:5-11, Colossians 1:15-20 and Exodus 20:1-7 interact with this? Why do you think Christians are justified in making exclusive claims for Jesus Christ? Give specific reasons.

3. Do you think that the present rise of paganism is more of a threat or opportunity for biblical Christianity? See Acts 19:23-41; Acts 13:4-12; Acts 19:13-20.

Introduction to Section 2

In Part One of this book we looked at the phenomenal rise of paganism in our contemporary society, observing that it is fast becoming a religious force to be reckoned with. We noted that, far from people having to join a pagan group or sect, the majority of our population are becoming increasingly exposed to a pagan worldview through their everyday lives. Particularly through environmental concerns and alternative therapies, the average citizen is increasingly accepting New Age perspectives. On top of this, various pagan practices are becoming widely practiced by a significant percentage of the population; through martial arts, business training seminars, astrology, meditation and yoga, neo-pagan concepts are being effectively disseminated within our society. And then there are the self-confessed 'signed-up' pagans, be they Druids, Wiccans, Hindus, or whatever — and their growth is unprecedented.

When all this is put together, along with the fact that books with a pagan mind-set are available in most of our large supermarkets, the majority of bookstores, almost every natural health food shop, various gift shops as well as dedicated New Age outlets, it becomes apparent that they have the market cornered. Almost all newspapers carry subtle and not-so-subtle neo-pagan perspectives, and its presence in one form or another is present in the rest of the media.[1] By stark contrast, Christians appear holed up in our buildings, preaching to the converted, having lost our grip on the main mechanisms of communication within our society. To the casual observer, Christianity appears to be at war with itself, confused, inarticulate and irrelevant. Most churches have given up on the basis of their beliefs: they have rejected the Bible. Moreover, most evangelicals are incurably naïve as to the key question of why they believe what they believe. In the battle for hearts and minds, paganism is gaining the upper hand.

In order to understand this further it is necessary to have a deeper look at contemporary paganism. In this section we will analyse the history and roots of the movement, along with some of the reasons for its phenomenal growth. After this, we will untangle what appears on the surface to be a disordered collection of contradictory beliefs and practices, showing that behind them is a coherent, but nevertheless false, set of ideas. We will then examine neo-pagan attempts to justify their beliefs with 'science'. And then, we will uncover how paganism has penetrated the church, before finishing by taking a look at the movement's perspective of its own future: the New Age.

Chapter 6
The Mists of Time

The Early History of Paganism

'The Academy, where Plato had taught, survived all other schools, and persisted as an island of paganism, for two centuries after the conversion of the Roman Empire to Christianity. At last, in A.D. 529, it was closed by Justinian because of his religious bigotry, and the dark ages descended upon Europe.'
Bertrand Russell[1]

In order to understand any movement or religion, we need to comprehend their view of themselves and perhaps the most significant thing to understand is where they think they have come from. Because of this we will now take a brief look at the history of paganism from their own perspective. Of course, different forms of paganism would have varying views of their history, and it needs to be appreciated that what is stated here is only one of these — but it is probably the most widely held outlook in the West.

Essentially, most modern forms of paganism growing within our society see themselves at Nature religions; they feel that through the industrial revolution we have become disengaged from the forces of the Earth. Indeed, we are now often found to be antagonistic to our planet and the environment.

Long ago, when people lived in closer proximity to Nature, we found ourselves enfolded in a wonderful and intricate web. All around us, as far as we could see, were grasses, mountains, flowers, trees, the Moon, the Sun and the stars. Our effect on this web of interactive forces[2] was minimal; its effect on us was matter of life and death. Humans were dependent on this dynamic interactive web of natural relations for good seasons to grow crops and an abundance of game to eat. Our very lives depended on our environment and what it provided for us. Fair weather could give us life; ferocious storms could destroy us. The natural web around us had immense power, power beyond comprehension.

In the light of people's understanding of Nature giving birth to life in the spring, as plants bore their flowers and fruits and animals their young, it was seen as miraculous. And their women mirrored this as they became pregnant and then gave birth. Because of the parallel with what they saw happening in their women's bodies, this divine being or force was thought of as feminine. Here was the concept of Mother Nature, Mother Earth — the universal mother of us all. Here is the Earth Mother — the Goddess. Figurines of women with symbolically large bellies and breasts have been found throughout Stone Age Europe.

Many of these early societies were also hunting communities, and the men, it is supposed, would often dress in the skins and horns of animal and dance in order to better results in their pursuits after wildlife. Behind this was the concept of the great animal God, sometimes called Pan by the Greeks and Cernunnos by the Celts. There is a belief in many pagan groups of this masculine side of the deity, the master of life and death. Sometimes he is seen as the consort of the Goddess in neo-pagan beliefs.

This male God is often called The Horned God (or the god of the hunt). As one writer puts it, this Horned God was 'used by the Christian Church to represent the devil.' And then goes on to comment that he is 'in fact far from evil, representing as it does only the darker side of nature. Cave paintings dating back to about 30,000 B.C. have been found in France showing depictions of the Horned God.'[3] Another contemporary pagan source notes regarding the classical image of the devil that 'it is derived from early patristic writings of the fourth century, which merged pagan elements (such as the half-bestial Pan) with a semi-human form, so in Medieval times was sometimes pictured as almost a carton figure of fun became a sort of hierarchical great god Pan, with cloven hooves, goat head and a curiously anthropomorphised form'.[4] What is particularly fascinating is that this image of the 'Horned God' is very linked to the hunter and his virility and success. In the Bible, Nimrod, the man who built Babylon, often representative of all that is against God, was 'a mighty hunter'.[5] He was probably also the builder of Babel, the centre of human pride, false religion and possibly even pagan magic.[6]

It is thought that the Horned God and the Mother Earth, male and female sides of Nature,[7] spawned other lesser deities. These became the gods of wind and rain, Sun and Moon, reaping and sowing, heaven and Earth — and other aspects of the natural world. Although specific cultural pantheons varied, with their own rituals and rites — the 'Godhead' was often split into different aspects of life and its natural cycles.

A golden era

Some writers look back to some golden period in the distant past. Feminist pagans envision a time when the Goddess was supreme and there was an absence of war: 'Warriors, weapons, scenes of battle, military fortifications, lavish burials of chieftains, evidence of slavery, or other hierarchical structures were simply not depicted in the art of these ancient peoples.'[8] It is claimed that the art of the cave paintings of this period abound with nature symbols — those of butterflies, birds, plants, Sun and Earth — as well as various images of the Goddess herself. This is seen as a period before the patriarchal gods of war.

Other pagans look back to an ancient civilization that had far greater connection with pagan spirituality than is seen today. They gaze back to a culture that was destroyed by water and is passed down to us in the legend of Atlantis.[9] The first account of Atlantis was given by Plato in various dialogues around 350 B.C. Plato recounts the story of the Egyptian priests who 200 years earlier had reportedly described Atlantis as a powerful island empire seeking to dominate the Mediterranean world.

In the nineteenth and twentieth centuries various neo-pagan theories emerged regarding this lost race that was obliterated by water. Madame Helena P. Blavatsky, cofounder of theosophy, claimed the information came from the Book of Dyzan, an alleged Atlantean work that had survived and was now in Tibet. The occultist and philosopher Rudolf Steiner then claimed to have access to what are known as the Akashic Records, sometimes called the Akashic Chronicles. These esoteric records are claimed to be indelibly imprinted upon what is know as the Akasha and may under normal circumstances be read only by initiates or adepts. The Akasha are, in Hinduism and Buddhism, the all-pervasive life principle of the universe. According to theosophy these are the supernatural historical records of all world events and personal experiences of all thoughts and deeds that have taken place on the earth. Through reading the Akasha with mystical enlightenment it has been revealed that this ancient Atlantis was some kind of pre-flood world that was alive with demonic contact and psycho-spiritual power. Many neo-pagans look back to this 'glorious' period as they yearn forward to the coming of something similar, if not 'better' — the Age of Aquarius. One significant person who may have been influenced by the example of Atlantis was Adolf Hitler.[10]

It is interesting that all this is possibly a reference to the world that existed prior to Noah's Ark and the flood that covered the earth because of God's judgement. Jesus remarks are salutary when he comments: 'As it was in the days of Noah, so it shall be in the days of the coming of the Son of Man.'[11] When we examine our Bibles it becomes clear that one of the things that God judges and punishes most severely is idolatry and pagan religion. This was the primary reason why Israel was put into exile. With this in mind, it could possibly be conceived that one of the main reasons for the judgement and punishment of the flood at the time of Noah was such occult pagan practice.

The middle eastern religion

In various forms, organised and public institutional paganism existed throughout much of the world until the growth of the Christian church. Pagan writer Anodea Judith writes of this period in these words: 'With the advent of Christianity, demanding loyalty to the church and to the "One True God," the remains of pagan peoples and their practices were systematically suppressed by the ruling priesthood. As early as 430 C.E. (Common Era), heresy was punishable by death.'[12]

Pagans write with considerable antagonism against this period, often referring to Christianity by the title, the Middle Eastern Religion. Furthermore, they oppose Christianity's stamp on history in the dating system B.C. and A.D. by supporting the alternative labels B.C.E. (Before Common Era) and C.E. (Common Era).

Yet even in the ascendance of the Roman Catholic Church, many of the rural population of Europe still held basic pagan beliefs and clung to the cyclical seasonal rites of sowing and harvest, celebrating the dance of the Moon and Sun openly or in secret, passing their traditions down through families and communities. Those out in the country, the heath dwellers, or heathens, as they were called, continued their craft. Their witches, a term that comes from the Saxon word for 'wise', and the wiccans, which comes from the Saxon word 'to know', were driven underground. With the coming of Christianity, these terms became derogatory and witches were persecuted. However, just because kings and those in authority claimed some kind of Christian allegiance did not mean that those in rural areas turned from their old beliefs.

Indeed, in many ways the formal and political church took on pagan festivals and practices, trying to Christianise them. Christmas being near the winter solstice is a case in point, taking over the pagan Yuletide. Easter covered up the older festival of Ostara, or Spring Equinox. The famous Easter Egg hunts are actually an old pagan rite of Ostara Eggs. Many of the old gods became 'saints' and churches were often built on pagan sacred land. Indeed, the Goddess did not die either, but resumed her presence in society as the 'Mother of God', the Virgin Mary. As we shall see in a later chapter, pagan beliefs die hard and always tend to grow up again within the church's beliefs, structures, rituals and festivals. Like the chameleon, paganism so easily re-colours its public image within an apparently Christian gloss. Paganism continually reinvents itself.

The burning times

In 1227 a period of history began that has been called the bitterest phase in pagan history — the burning times. It is absolutely essential for any Christian who wishes to witness to pagans, or argue against the present upsurge in paganism, to understand something of this phase of history. For neo-pagans and many others, this makes Christianity seem abhorrent as an unjust and evil tyranny of torture and murder. For others of a feminist perspective, this phase of persecution fits in with their concept of the oppression of women. Indeed, for many, one of the main reasons for rejecting Christianity is the church's brutality — even against those who would profess to be Christian themselves. Lord Byron once wrote, 'Christians have burnt each other, quite persuaded that all the Apostles would have done as they did.'[13] This charge of bloody brutality needs to be met by Bible believing Christians.

And it is not only contemporary Pagans who make Christianity responsible for what many would call genocide. Dr A. C. Grayling, Reader in Philosophy at Birkbeck College, University of London, writes in his popular book, *The Meaning of Things* writes:

> Apologists might say that without the accident of Christianity's becoming the official religion of the Roman Empire, we would be without the glorious Annunciations and crucifixions of Renaissance art. But in balance with the sanguinity of Christian history — its crusades, Inquisitions, religions wars, drowned witches, oppressive morals and hostility to sex — this seems a minor loss.[14]

For many today, including atheists, Jews, Muslims, all the way to pagans, Christianity is conceived as a cruel, violent and bloody religion. The Inquisition is a byword for injustice, torture and murder. A main part of this charge against Christianity is the burning of witches.

The distinguished writer and broadcaster, Ludovic Kennedy, in his attack on Christianity in his book *All In The Mind: A Farewell To God*, has a whole chapter entitled, 'The Christian Killing Fields'. This section catalogues what Kennedy feels are historical facts that undermine the case for Christianity. A significant part of this chapter is called, 'The Burning of Witches'. Here he writes:

> The newly formed society of Jesuits were fanatical witch-hunters but even the great reformers were not far behind. Luther, for instance, arranged the burning of four witches at Wittenburg and Calvin quoted Exodus the authorise that witches should be killed: and they were in their hundreds of thousands.'[15]

1227 is seen by neo-pagans as the start of 500 years of brutal thievery, torture and murder. This was 'the persecution of the Witches, whose name comes from the old English *wicce*, or wise ones. They were the teachers and healers, the herbalists and midwives, as well as the stubborn women and men who supported them, by refusing to give up their personal power and freedom to the power-hungry Christian priesthood.'[16] The numbers of witches executed is usually placed in the millions, and sometimes over ten million.

In 1484, two years after the first Papal Bull of Pope Innocent VII, two German monks wrote a scathing manual, called the *Malleus Maleficarum*, for the identification and persecution of witches. It was then presented to the Theological Faculty at Cologne, who promptly rejected it. The monks forged the signatures and passed it through Europe, its forgery remaining undiscovered until 1898. It is claimed that through this forged endorsement to burn and torture witches as many as 200,000 people were tortured for confessions and then burnt at the stake.

In Britain, James VI of Scotland and later James I of England not only sponsored the publication of the so-called King James Bible, but also published a book called *The Discouverie of Witchcraft* — another kind of 'how to find a witch' manual. This led to possibly hundreds, if not thousands, being put to death. Pagans claim that King James influenced the Bible he authorised, so that it contained pieces of anti-witch propaganda:

> In this version of the Bible's book of Deuteronomy, for instance, it is stated that 'Thou shalt not consult astrologers

or soothsayers', the text later going on to say, 'Thou shalt not suffer a witch to live'. In this instance, the word 'witch' is a mistranslation of the Greek text. The correct translation is 'poisoner', but as a result of the witch's knowledge of herbs, the word 'witch' and 'poisoner' became synonymous.'[17]

Ludovic Kennedy comments on the use of torture to bring about confessions in Scotland: 'For proof of the efficacy of torture, [to produce confessions of witchcraft] one need look no further than England where torture was forbidden and where fewer than 1,000 witches were hanged in a hundred-year period, and compare it with the much smaller population of Calvinistic Scotland where torture was permitted and in roughly the same period some 4,500 witches were hanged, strangled or burned.'[18]

Many writers refer to the specific case of persecution in East Anglia. Here, Matthew Hopkins, a Puritan who held the infamous and self-appointed title of 'witch-finder general', oversaw the trials of many hundreds of alleged witches, hanging sixty in Essex in one year alone. Hopkins was eventually challenged and subjected to one of his own witch-finding tests. The test was simple: if a suspect was thrown into a river and drowned, he or she was innocent, if the suspect floated, then he or she was deemed a witch. Hopkins failed the test and was put to death.

In America the famous Protestant Salem witch-trials were held in 1692, where 150 were accused and 31 condemned. Witch burnings took place in France until 1745, and in Bavaria a witch was beheaded as late as 1775. The last witch-burning took place in Ireland in 1902, the sentence of death being passed not by a court, but by an angry mob. The last trial for witchcraft in Britain was in1944. One Helen Duncan was accused after receiving a vision of the sinking of the Royal Navy cruiser Burnham, which was classified information. She was found guilty and imprisoned.

Answering the charges of bloody brutality

It is vital that these charges against Christianity are challenged; the accusations are serious, and if true give adequate reason to undermine faith and put off seekers after truth.

The first response must be to challenge the historical accuracy of the accusations. Philip J. Sampson, in his book *Six Modern Myths Challenging the Christian Faith* has a whole chapter entitled, *Witches: A Story of Persecution*. He writes:

> In recent years...various explanations of the 'witchcraze' have appeared increasingly doubtful as scholars have studied witchcraft more carefully. The picture which emerges is not one we have been led to expect. As long ago as 1928, Montague Summers called the belief that witches went to the stake in England 'a popular and fast-grounded, if erroneous, opinion' of the 'ignorant', better suited to the 'romanticist and story book' than the scholar and historian.'[19]

It has become apparent that the witch-hunts of history, are not so much a phenomena of the church as such, but of society in general. Most societies tend to have their scapegoats, whether they be witches, Jews, Blacks, Whites, Communists, or whatever. There seems to by something in human society that picks out some minority to blame for all the ills it is facing. As Sampson comments:

> Contrary to the orthodox story, witchcraft was not principally a 'church' matter, nor was the Inquisition the prime mover in its persecution of witches. In fact, the majority of prosecutions concerned not abstruse heretical opinions about the devil, but the run-of-the-mill suspicions and tensions of village life when property was lost or stolen, the beer failed to ferment or the bread rise. People commonly appealed to magic and witchcraft to explain tragedies and misfortunes, or more generally to gain power over their neighbours.[20]

In other words, in many cases, the church was merely the functionary in witch-hunting because of the confusion over relationships between church and state meant that it was often the representative of social authority and cohesion. The church sometimes became the instrument of popular frenzy. All this took place in societies that prosecuted folk and executed them for a whole variety of crimes. Having said that, it is also worth noting that, 'recent research has shown that, far from "stimulating the persecutions," the church, whether Catholic or Protestant, often had a moderating effect.'[21] And regarding the Puritans in New England in the Salem cases, the historian Chadwick Hanson has concluded that 'the clergy were, from the beginning, the chief opponents to the events at Salem.'[22]

Another challenge that needs to be made to the evidence offered against the church is that the numbers have almost certainly been exaggerated: 'Most recent estimates put the number of executions at about 150 to 300 people per year throughout all Europe and North America, three quarters of whom were women. Over a period of about three hundred years this amounts to between 40,000 and 100,000 people. This is an appalling enough catalogue of human suffering, but to refer to it as 'genocide' or a 'holocaust' is both misleading and offensive to those groups who have suffered actual genocidal assaults in recent generations.'[23] Indeed, when thinking of this 300 per year, it should be remembered that one of the worst persecutions of the twentieth century was by Adolf Hitler, who as we shall see in the next chapter, was himself almost certainly 'paganised' in his thinking. In that period of history, 6 million Jews were butchered – and on top of that, all the millions of casualties of the World War II can also be laid at his door. Furthermore, pagan writers who wish to push the point should also consider that Columbian Aztecs sacrificed about 15,000 people each year from a far smaller population base than that of Europe.[24] And it is certain that the older pagan religions of Britain also engaged in human sacrifice, although numbers are hard to estimate.[25]

To conclude the discussion on numbers of people hunted down and killed as witches, it has recently been estimated that, 'somewhere between 90% and 99% of the cruel deaths reported by the story of witch-hunting are fictional.'[26]

And just in case 'enlightened' atheists feel superior in this regard, they should read the butchery of Stalin and his minions — again, millions were destroyed. Fifteen to twenty million people died in Soviet forced labour camps. On top of this, if we include the fatalities of war since 1945, at least eighty million have been killed, with a high proportion of women and children. All this puts the witch-hunt figures into their proper context.

The devil's schemes

One of the most potent of Satan's schemes is not so much the spread of witchcraft, but heresy within the church. It is significant to note when the apostle Paul was followed by a girl involved in fortune telling and possessed by an evil spirit crying out against him, he ignored her for a long time before he acted to cast out the demon.[27] Yet, in his Epistles, his deep concern is for a church that either dilutes the truth given to it in Christ, or compromises with regard to ethics. And history teaches us that the greatest problem for true Christianity is false doctrine and lax morality within the external church. If Satan can put wolves in sheep's clothing within the church, then he can destroy it more easily than by persecution or other religions, including paganism.

In this light it is significant to look at the challenge made with regard to John Calvin in particular. Like Paul, it actually seems that he was not especially interested in witch hunts at all — indeed, he regarded witchcraft as a delusion for which the only cure was the gospel, not execution.[28] Many of those fanatics within the outward formal church, whether Catholic or Protestant, were doing Satan's business, causing a distraction and blemishing the reputation of Christianity in the process. Jesus said the wheat and tares grow up together — and even in the most biblically sound community this will be true.[29] Believing the right doctrines does not necessarily mean we have become true believers.[30] It may well be to Satan's advantage to both encourage witchcraft and witch-hunts, both can distract people from Jesus Christ and the gospel and well as malign the reputation of the church. The important thing to realise is that this in no way diminishes the fact that true biblical Christianity is true.

Confused believers

Another point to remember is that true believers make mistakes. We are all men and women of our times and we should be careful in judging folk of a different culture when all the influences around them were so different from ours. In the days of the witch-hunts, superstition was ingrained in the population, and more than that, executions were commonplace. This was bound to affect the way Christians responded to what they saw as wrong. On top of this, there was a lot of confusion over the relationship between church and state, as well as Old Testament social regulation and New Testament expectation. In essence, since the Roman Empire has become 'Christian' in the fourth century, the concept of Christendom had become deeply engrained. This meant that people saw a geographical area and political entity as 'under the rule of Christ.' The results were unfortunate in that this allowed the development of the crusades, where 'Christ's kingdom' could be advanced through the sword. Power struggles inside this empire were rife. Holy Roman Emperors, Papal Princes, Prince Bishops and Kings all contended for authority and claimed Christ's support. And those within 'Christendom' who did not tow the party line could be persecuted.

Even after the Reformation, church leaders found it difficult to disentangle theology from politics and in many cases tried to establish 'Christian' countries by force and rule of law. They looked to the OT nation of Israel to set up some kind of theocracy. This meant that officers of the state used their authority to contend for their brand of Christianity. As a result of this mind-set and political context, persecution of those who disagreed with the state still occurred. Many would argue that the reformation had not gone far enough — church and state should be separated. The gospel of Christ and true doctrine should be spread through the sword of the Spirit, the Word of God, and not the secular sword. Jesus told Peter to put away his sword. Witchcraft is to be dealt with through the power of the cross and the proclaiming of the gospel, not persecution.

The challenge of pagan history

The pagan's perspective on history up until the eighteenth century is a great challenge for Bible believing Christians today. Much is misunderstood concerning early paganism and the coming of Christianity — and in particular the persecution of witches. The record desperately needs to be put straight; the honour and reputation of true Christianity is at stake here.

Questions for discussion

Read Romans chapter 1:18-32.

1. One of the key differences between a biblical religion and paganism is that pagans tend to worship creation rather than the Creator. What do you feel Paul is communicating as to the place of deifying creation in the decline and judgement of a society? Is this trend happening in other ways outside of the directly religious? List some specific examples.

2. In this chapter in Romans, Paul on one hand points out that creation points to the existence of the creator, and then outlines how people tend to slip from this and forget the creator and worship creation. Why do people tend to do this?

3. Read Genesis 6:1-8; 8:20-22; 2 Peter 2:12; Romans 1:18-32. It was suggested that some pagans look back to a golden age in the past, whether that be Goddess worship, or a higher level of 'spiritual' consciousness. Why do you think God judged the world prior to the flood? Do you think false religion had anything to do with it? And what about the tower of Babel? Compare Genesis 6 with Romans 1 to note the intellectual, religious and ethical decline of a society under judgement.

4. Why was Israel commanded to deal so harshly with the Canaanites when they entered the land? What 'leftovers' from this culture so plagued Israel through the centuries?

5. What do you think is the correct biblical response to doctrinal error and developing paganism today? Should force ever be used? Read Matthew 26:47-56; Acts 8:9-25; Acts 16:16-18; Acts 14:8-18; Acts 19:13-20.

6. In what ways do the roles of state and church differ with regard to the use of force? Romans 13:1-7.

Chapter 7
The Fall of Christianity and the Rise of Contemporary Paganism

'Many strokes overthrow the tallest oaks.'
John Lyly

Although often corrupted, the West did have some kind of allegiance to Christianity and Christian values. Biblical thought patterns permeated many of our laws; obedience to the Ten Commandments was at least a theoretical expectation. In northern Europe and those new nations that stemmed from its peoples, biblical ideas shaped the thinking of many. In the USA, Australia, New Zealand, South Africa, and Canada, to name but a few, biblical Christianity was incredibly influential. But what caused this Christian perspective on life to begin to fall in the West and now to be replaced by a rising paganism?

In order to have some understanding of this it is necessary to grasp something of the flow of ideas over the last three hundred years, where step by step a Christian perspective on the universe was dismantled in the popular market place of ideas. It is important to note that as materialism, the belief that only matter exists[1] directly challenged Christianity, it led to a perspective that left a spiritual void in people's hearts and minds. This led to various attempts at filling the gap, all of which failed. The resultant vacuum became the ideal context within which a new restored paganism could develop.

A bird's eye view

From the early Middle Ages until around 1700 very few challenged the existence of God. Christianity had so penetrated the Western world that, whether people personally believed it or not, they lived in a context influenced by the Christian Faith. Then there was a radical shift in emphasis from God's special revelation to us in the Bible to reason as the way of knowing about God and spirituality. As people began to study and discover the mechanisms of the universe by reason, they didn't see why they should not think towards God in the same way. It was claimed that reason now became the route to God instead of God's revelation in Scripture.

For many, the concept of God began to change drastically, instead of being personal, he was increasingly seen as an impersonal force. This God created the universe with all its mechanisms, like a clockmaker might make a clock, but was not seen as involved in its running, or with the people in it. To these people, often called deists, God is distant, an architect, but nor a lover. In reality, deism is more of a link between theism and naturalism, which followed it, rather than a school of thought itself.

Christians saw God as the infinite personal creator and sustainer of the universe; deists reduced him to Creator, but lost his personality. Naturalists reduced him still further — for them he ceased to exist. Natural history began with some self-activating process in the cosmos whereby the universe came into being, and humanity was given its origin in the theory of evolution.

Most people who hold this view do not bother to think thoroughly about its assumptions, nor where it leads. In reality, Materialism is built on a whole load of baseless assumptions. After all, if all I am is a machine, how do I know I can really think accurately and logically at all — my hardware might have faults and my software might be corrupt. As Charles Darwin put it, 'The horrid doubt always arises whether the convictions of a man's mind, which has developed from the mind of the lower animals, are of any value or at all trustworthy.'[2] Also, as I am merely composed of a bundle of cause and effect equations, I am totally determined. Even my thinking is simply the result of the falling of biochemical dominoes. If this is the case, I can't really know anything and my life is utterly pointless — and more than that, my extinction at death undermines any point of living. Those who thought this through to its disturbing end were called nihilists — this is a denial of everything, of knowledge, and even existence. Nothing has meaning; there is no knowledge, no morality, no beauty; everything is one great zero.

Ruth Rendell, in her detective thriller, *Murder Being Once Done*, describes Chief Inspector Wexford investigating the scene of a murder in a graveyard. He comes upon the old Victorian Montfort vault, the size of a small cottage. On this was a copperplate inscription, which powerfully portrays nihilism in all its despair.

> He who asks questions is a fool.
> He who answers them is a greater fool.
> What is truth?
> What man decides it shall be.
> What is beauty?
> Beauty is in the eye of man.
> What are right and wrong?
> Today one thing, another tomorrow.
> Death is only real.
> The last of the Montforts bids you read
> and pass on without comment.[3]

When naturalism, or materialism, is taken to its logical conclusion the results are very disturbing indeed.

By the end of the First World War, nihilism finally began to affect the attitudes of ordinary men and women.[4] The nightmare of the World War I, the depression, the eventual rise of Nazism and its horrors all pointed to the absurdity of life. Human life really did seem meaningless. A nihilistic perspective was becoming increasingly common; more and more were seeing it as the logical conclusion of naturalism. Into this dark void another perspective was heralded as the answer to all this despair: existentialism. The main strand of this thinking at this time was atheistic existentialism,[5] which developed as the answer to the problem of naturalism that inevitably led to nihilism. Basically, atheistic existentialism sees the cosmos in a similar way to the materialist — history is a linear stream of events with no overall purpose. Existentialists try to answer the question, how can I be significant in a meaningless world? They say that within our mental subjective world, where we are aware of own existence and are free to choose and act. By our actions, based on our choices we define ourselves — while we are alive and conscious we can create value. The atheistic existentialist makes a decision to create his own meaning in the face of absurdity.

The trouble with this is the all-too-apparent problem that it is a form of self-delusion. In essence, the existentialist is trying to convince himself that he can make his life have meaning. Western thought has turned down a cul-de-sac. Naturalism has led to nihilism and the answer to that in existentialism is a farce.

By the time we got to the 1960s, many were so disillusioned by dead religion,[6] sterile and pointless materialism and farcical existentialism that they began to look to other places to find some meaning and purpose in the universe and for their own lives. As western thought had reached its cul-de-sac, some began to glance to the East. Along with the Beatles, many began to explore Eastern ways of looking at the cosmos. To the new generation in the sixties, the materialistic reasoning seemed to only lead to sophisticated weaponry and economic oppression. Western religion appeared, largely, to support those who controlled the system. Whereas the West was a maze of despair, violence and farce, the East by comparison appeared a world of quietness, simplicity and spirituality.

Some of the spiritual perspectives proffered at that time taught that what was needed in the individual was an altered state of consciousness where the individual could connect into the universe at large and make contact with spiritual beings. One of the ways it was claimed that this could occur was by the use of drugs. Drugs had been used from antiquity for this end in all kinds of esoteric religions, particularly shamanism. As the 1960's drug culture expanded and the hippy movement came into being, some began to experiment with pharmacological substances for this purpose. Experimenting with drugs was seen as a psychedelic route into bizarre spiritual encounters and experiences. The Beatles with their Strawberry Field perceptions began to disseminate these ideas to the younger generation. Alongside this, they also assisted in importing religious ideas from the East.

Eastern views began to creep into the West, and over the ensuing decades have become more and more common. The core Eastern perception that became popular in the West included the idea that the essence of any person is the essence of the cosmos. At the very core of each of us is the essence of the universe. In Eastern thought, the essence of each person is called Atman and the essence of the universe is called Brahman. Their relationship is best expressed by the phrase Atman is Brahman, that is, the soul of each of us is the soul of the cosmos. In pantheistic terms, this ultimate God[7] is the One, infinite impersonal reality — God is everything; nothing else exists. Each of us is God. The distinctions between us, and the distinctions between anything in the universe are all an illusion — we are all One.

Alongside this, people began to explore the ancient beliefs of their own geographical regions before the time of Christianity. As part of this trend, people have explored native American, Aborigine traditions, Wicca and Norse beliefs, among many others. In many ways they found that these world-views fitted in with Eastern perspectives of connecting in with some ultimate reality of the cosmos that expresses itself through various gods and spiritual entities that are supposed to be one with and behind Nature. The emphasis on Nature lines up well with contemporary thought. The aim is to 'connect into' the ultimate reality behind the universe. Through a kaleidoscope of paths or techniques, practitioners try to achieve some alternative form of consciousness, where they feel one with the universe and gain contact with spiritual beings. The hunger left by the voids of deism, atheism, naturalism, nihilism and existentialism is being filled by a spirituality that is both very old and very new.

In parallel with this and even within it, the New Age movement developed. This movement originated in 1971 when it emerged in America as a self-conscious form of spirituality. Susan Greenwood tells us in her *Encyclopaedia of Magic and Witchcraft* that within this perspective, 'The Earth was seen as entering a new cycle of evolution[8] marked by a new human consciousness, which would give birth to a new civilization — the "Age of Aquarius" which would overcome the present corrupt culture by cataclysm and disaster. The idea of a New Age was an amalgamation of various predictions: those of Nostradamus; the American psychic Edgar Cayce; the Theosophical Society; and the Lucis Trust, as well as Rudolph Steiner's anthroposophy. These prophecies were founded in the spiritual traditions of the Maya, Aztecs and Hopi people, and also the Judaeo-Christian belief in the Second Coming of Christ. When the anticipated apocalypse did not arrive there was a "turn inward" and nature became a source of revelation rather than something that obscured real spirit.'[9]

By the time we get to the early 21st century, eastern ideas and ancient pagan western concepts are commonplace. Running through our society are parallel and far from contradictory threads of belief and experience from East and West, past and present. Christianity has been effectively and efficiently removed from its former position as the predominant accepted belief within society.

A closer look behind the scenes

'The nineteenth century was an age of independent spiritual teachers in a time of declining established religion, when many people were looking to find a single key to solve the mysteries of the universe.'[10] Susan Greenwood

The theosophists and the new age

In order to understand something of the current spiritual and mystical views that are prevalent today, we need to say something more about the development of the New Age movement. The New Age Movement received its modern start in 1875 with the founding of the Theosophical Society by Helena Petrovna Blavatsky (1831-91). A basic teaching of this organization was that all world religions had "common truths" that transcended potential differences. The term derives from the Greek *theos* ('god') and *sophia* ('wisdom') and so claims to be wisdom about God.

Theosophy refers to a broad spectrum of mystical or occult philosophies, often pantheistic in nature. Pantheism (from *pan*, 'all' and *theos*, 'god'.) can be summarised by the expression 'God is All, All is God.' It is a way of seeing that identifies everything with God and God with everything.[11] This belief system is characterised by an emphasis on the hidden tradition passed down in a succession from the ancients. This tradition is thought to provide a key to nature and to humanity's place in the universe. Strongly propounding the theory of evolution, Theosophists also believed in the existence of 'masters' who were either spirit beings or fortunate men more highly 'evolved' than the common herd. Some claim that this was a belief system, which was to have a substantial impact on the development of Hitler's Nazism several decades later.[12]

Madam Blavatsky worked in 'telepathic communication', serving as a 'fulcrum' for the masters[13] starting in 1867 and continuing until her death in 1891. Achieving 'illumination' or enlightenment was one of the Theosophists' goals. And that meant more than mere light bulbs to at least one of their more famous initiates — Thomas Alva Edison, who joined the organization and signed its pledge of secrecy in 1878. Blavatsky elaborated an amalgamation of previous theories that were claimed to have derived from ancient India. The Theosophical Society grew rapidly in Europe and the United States, its two most influential adherents being Annie Besant and Rudolph Steiner.

Through the Theosophical Society, the budding movement demonstrated hostility to Christianity from its beginning.

In 1875 Helen Blavatsky wrote in her scrapbook:

> The Christians and scientists must be made to respect their Indian betters.
>   The Wisdom of India, her philosophy and achievement must be made know in
>   Europe and America and the English made to respect the natives of India and
>   Tibet more than they do.[14]

From Buddhist High Priest Mohottiwatte Gunanana, to Prince Emil of Wittgenstein, from General Abner Doubleday (founder of baseball) to Swami Saraswati, the famous of East and West met in a concerted effort to eliminate orthodox Christianity. In fact, many theosophists intended to eliminate all Christianity. Two theosophists attempted to institute a branch of Theosophy — known as Esoteric Christianity — that would be a revival of Gnostic Christian teachings along the line of the Kabala[15] — a form of Christianity that is Christian in name only.

A Theosophical Society brochure made clear the anti-Christian aims of that movement:

> ...To oppose the materialism of science and every form of dogmatic theology, especially the Christian, which the Chiefs of the Society regard as a particularly pernicious; to make know among Western nations the long-suppressed facts about the Oriental religious philosophies, their ethics, chronology, esoterism (sic), symbolism; to delude the so-called 'heathen' and 'pagans' as to the real origin and dogmas of Christianity and the practical effects of the latter upon the public and private character in so-called Christian countries.[16]

Proudly drawing their inspiration from 'masters', 'spirits', or 'elementals', the leaders of the Theosophical Society believed they were under the direct supervision of 'adepts' and 'initiates' belonging to a branch of 'The Great White Brotherhood'. Following written orders from these spirit beings, the New York-based leadership moved to India in 1875. Another order from these messengers told them to keep the society and teachings secret — at least for the time being. This was a dictum that was to prevail for 100 years — until 1975 — the year initiates were at last permitted to make the initiatory teaching public. It was claimed that psychic phenomena and seemingly miraculous signs also characterised the early days of the Society. These apparently included precipitating of letters, materializations of objects and production of strange sounds.

Alice Bailey did more that anyone, except perhaps Helena Petrovna Blavatsky, to build the foundation for the 'New Age'. Alice wrote nearly two-dozen books laying out the specific instructions for disciples of the 'masters' in the latter part of the 20th century. Her work was immense. She organized the Arcane School, the New Group of World Servers, Triangles, World Goodwill, and assisted with a host of other foundational activities to help build the 'New Age'. The Lucifer Publishing Company was established in 1922 to help disseminate her works. The name was changed the next year to Lucis Publishing Company for reasons unknown.

The year 1962 was another landmark year, for that was when the Scottish community of Findhorn was founded. Findhorn is run according to messages and guidance received by Eileen Caddy, one of its founders. It has become a horticultural Mecca for communication with so-called nature spirits, devic presences, fairies and other such postulated beings.

At the same time Findhorn was blossoming, esoteric groups around the world commenced their networking operations. Serving as a focal point, Findhorn itself attracted visitors and residents from a worldwide base. Its residents meticulously studied and mastered the works of Alice Bailey, Helena, Petrovna Blavatsky, Agni Yoga and a host of other esoteric "saints" and societies. David Spangler wrote a book that purported to be a transmission from unearthly sources — or 'his higher self'. *Revelation: The Birth of a New Age* quickly became mandatory reading for Findhorn residents.

This New Age became 'concerned with a transformation of nature, both internally as healing and a form of development of a higher consciousness, and externally as a relationship with the wider environment. The interconnectedness between all beings, within a network symbolised as Gaia, is very important to its thinking. Healing is an important aspect of the movement, and contemporary or alternative therapies such as shiatsu, acupuncture, reflexology, reiki and various visualization techniques are very much part of the whole picture.'[17]

To avoid misrepresentation and misunderstanding, the New Age movement can best be understood by considering how a dictionary that is positive towards its beliefs defines it.

The term New Age became popular in the 1980s and is used to describe a nebulous, quasi-religious set of beliefs encompassing a wide array of notions, such as spiritualism, astrology, mysticism, the occult, reincarnation, parapsychology, ecology and planetary awareness, as well a commitment to complimentary medicine and pseudo-scientific applications of the 'healing powers' of crystals and pyramids. New Age beliefs and practices are largely confined to the industrialised West, and the origins of the movement can be traced to the social and political unrest in the 1960s, dissatisfaction with obsessive materialism, the influence of Eastern religions, experimentation with psychedelic drugs, the development of human psychology and increased eco-consciousness. Despite hostility from the popular media and the establishment, New Age ideas now permeate many areas of mainstream culture, notably areas of behavioural medicine, physics, psychology and even business.[18]

The hippies have had hair cuts

The last sentence of the above quote is of paramount importance and significance: New Age ideas now permeate many areas of mainstream culture, notably areas of behavioural medicine, physics, psychology and even business. This radical movement has sent out tendrils of ideas and belief that have captured the hearts and minds of many average citizens. Most would not now call themselves occultists, shamans, wiccans, witches, neo-pagans, pagans, New-agers, or whatever, but they would share more than they realise with these alien and fringe groups. The beliefs of these groups are all now settling in and bedding down into normal contemporary thought. We will now try to distil out what these essential shared beliefs are.

Questions for discussion

1. Mysticism and occult practices are often claimed to be a search for 'wisdom'. Where can true wisdom be found? How can we become truly wise? Consider Solomon's words in Proverbs 1:1-7; 2:1-22.

2. Read Ecclesiastes 12:9-14. What warning does Solomon give with regard maintaining wisdom? (12) What does Revelation 22:18-19 and 2 Timothy 3:14-17 tell us in this regard?

3. Solomon was one of the wisest men that ever lived (1 Kings 4:29-34), but he became a fool. Why was this? List the mistakes that he made. What can we learn from this personally? (1 Kings 11:13)

Chapter 8
Pulling the Threads Together

The Essentials of a Pagan Worldview

'Delusion is a vivid false belief, often felt by its victim to be threatening or exciting, often associated with psychotic states.'
A. C. Grayling[1]

'Delusion is the child of ignorance.'
THE BHAGAVADGITA[2]

We must now to pull the threads together. Having looked at how eastern and older western paganism are reasserting their values and beliefs on our society, and how these are being redefined and 'modernized' in neo-paganism and the New Age movement, we now need to distil out the essential beliefs that hold them all together.

This is vital because many who follow these sorts of teachings do so in a dialectic way. They pick something up from the East and combine it with a pinch from the ancient West, and then they add a dash of the occult, with no problem or sense of contradiction. The reason for this is that all these approaches have far more in common than we would initially think. There are a set of basic beliefs that most of these geographically and historically diverse religions share.

This is not to say that there are not contradictions, disagreements and differences between all these belief systems. More than that, it is not being claimed that the essential shared beliefs are not in tension with each other, or that everyone believes every-thing. This is not a rationalistic philosophy, nor the construction of a 'logical' worldview. However, having said this, most of the belief systems from the East, ancient West, neo-pagan, New Age and the occult, as well as the average citizen who has constructed his own unique mind-set, share some combination of the following.

The majority today would not label themselves with any of the above; they see themselves as people who have bolted on to their secular lives a belief in a spiritual dimension. And increasingly, this belief in some spiritual dimension is growing.[3]

Today's paganism appears to be a piecemeal assortment of allegiance to diverse deities, apparently contradictory techniques and different dogmas. From ancient to modern societies, and from the different continents of the globe, it seems to be an unconnected collection of beliefs to the casual observer. Nothing could be further from the truth: these manifestations of paganism are connected and often have certain controlling ideas in common.

So, what are these controlling 'big' ideas? What are the common denominators of belief that are now increasingly permeating our society?

All is One, One is All

The wise realise everywhere that
which is invisible, ungraspable,
without source, without senses,
without body,
That which is infinite,
Multiformed, all pervasive,
Extremely subtle and undiminishing,
And the source of all.

Mundaka Upanishad 1.i.6[4]

This is the perception that everything is the same essence. The whole universe is One basic stuff, or energy, or 'something'. Exactly what this uniting thing is we don't know, but we are all made of it. Whatever it is, we are all seen as expressions of the way it shapes itself.

Einstein tried to condense everything into the formula $E=mc^2$, where E equals energy and M designates mass, and so show that they are actually interchangeable forms of each other. That is, everything consists of this energy, which can express itself as mass and therefore 'stuff' — everything is one basic reality[5] and has an elegant harmony of being.[6] Many today reduce all reality into a similar, but more fundamental equation. They take this idea far further than mere physics; they would say everything, absolutely everything, is simply an expression of one basic essence.[7] This includes dimensions beyond our everyday experience, dimensions that include the spiritual, whether, gods, or demons, or spirit guides, or angels, or whatever.[8] Everything is One. We are all connected. We are all part of this One ultimate reality. This is sometimes even extended into the area of morals; right and wrong do not exist.

The upshot of this is that we are all One, we are all connected. The human problem, from this way of thinking is that we just don't see it that way; we perceive things wrongly. 'Salvation' from this perspective means attaining an enlightened state of consciousness where we come discover and appreciate our 'oneness' with all things.[9]

There are several varieties of this belief, 'All is One, One is All', but together they are generally termed slants of what is called monism, from *mono*, meaning 'one'.

'God is All, All is God'

This is a perspective that identifies everything with 'God' and 'God' with everything, although what is meant by 'God' here is not the view presented in the Bible. By 'God' may be meant the One great reality — everything — the temporal, the infinite, the seen, the unseen, the animate, the inanimate. It may be designated as Nature, the Cosmos, the Self, to include but a few names. Everything is seen as part of 'God', or 'God' itself, and so absolutely nothing is separate or distinct from 'God'. From this perspective we can all say 'we are "God"'. Echoes of the serpent's lie in Eden are more than apparent here.[10]

This perspective is sometimes termed pantheism (from *pan*, 'all,' and *theos*, 'God') and has been held from antiquity in Hinduism and Brahmanism in particular. In Brahmanism the one great reality is called Brahma (n), who dreams the universe and our world. This dream is called *maya* (illusion), and people are supposed to find 'salvation' by understanding that they are merely part of Brahman's dream and have been deceived by *maya* into thinking that the world is real.

A view called panentheism (where 'en' means 'in') has a slightly different slant. This view holds that the universe is included in 'God', but that 'God' is more than the universe.

Increasingly, all these view are being merged into what is sometimes called pantheistic monism. This can be summarized as 'All is One, One is All, All is God.'

Monism, pantheism and panentheism are all in contradiction with a biblical view of reality. God is seen as within ourselves and encourages people to participate in the divine life without the necessity of a mediator between them and God. In the Bible, not only is God distinct from this universe,[11] but also God is separate from us because of his just reaction to our sin.[12] We can only have access to him through Jesus Christ and his work on the cross.[13]

Energy — connecting into spiritual power

Many pagans see within the universe some kind of creative energy, which is part of the total Oneness of the cosmos. This creative force is meant to account for the existence of all things. Using this idea, many in the New Age movement make their beliefs sound very contemporary, after all, we know that we are surrounded by invisible forces like radio waves, magnetism and electricity. They imply that this creative force is a type of energy not yet discovered and analysed. The ultimate implication of this for many is that the ultimate cause of the universe is impersonal.

This spiritual energy is given many names including, The Force, vital force, life force, chi (yin/yang) universal life energy, vital energy, prana, animal magnetism, the innate, orgone, cosmic energy and mana. Many mishaps or diseases are thought to occur if this life force gets out of balance or blocked in some way. Holistic healthcare often uses this understanding and some of the therapists see themselves as those who know the 'spiritual technology' to make the appropriate correction.

This idea of cosmic energy, or force, is seen to fit well with monism, that is the belief that everything is essentially One. From this angle, matter, including us humans, is merely a highly concentrated form of this impersonal energy. And pantheism, where 'God' is one with the universe, fits with this as well. When New Age folk speak of themselves as 'God' they are sometimes seeing themselves as inseparable from the Oneness of the universe, or this universal life energy. From this perspective we can see why they think we are all 'God' or gods. The secret of life for many of them is getting in harmony with one's life energy - this is how we are supposed to achieve peace, life, health and the well-being of oneness. Using crystals or some other technique, believers in this view of the universe tap into 'cosmic healing energies'.

All this leads to one fundamental idea that permeates many forms of paganism: human beings can 'connected into' spiritual power. Through a whole host of techniques, rituals, altered states of consciousness, chanting mantras, or whatever, spiritual power and knowledge can be grasped and manipulated. This is the basis of the magical worldview.

Many supernatural beings

In many forms of paganism, this great Oneness or Cosmic energy of the universe is utterly impersonal, in others it may be conceived of as a personal reality of some kind, but totally beyond our comprehension. It is believed that this ultimate reality that permeates everything sometimes concentrates, or 'congeals', producing inanimate objects; in a special way it can also focus and form various life forms. These range from the simplest protozoa, through the plant and animal kingdoms, human life and beyond, to more 'advanced' life forms than our imaginations could possibly conceive. These 'higher' forms of life are given a whole range of labels and descriptions: ascended masters, angels, gods, aliens, fairies, demons, elemental spirits and so on.[14] Here, science fiction, beliefs in UFOs,[15] ancient religions, the New Age movement, animism, polytheism, spiritualism and many more all manage to coalesce and synthesise into one world view.

One generally shared, 'big idea' is that around us and above us — or alongside us — exists another dimension or 'plane'. This parallel universe is controlled by cosmic forces and inhabited by supernatural beings, which have been given a variety of labels and names throughout human history, and across different cultures. Whether you consider ancient Egypt, Greece, South America, Britain — or wherever, these forces and beings were seen to exist. The aim of paganism is to 'connect into' this dimension in some way and harness the powers for the individual practitioners' own purposes. It does not matter what particular technique is used, only that it works for the individual. Hence paganism does not see all these different approaches, whether they be crystals, mediums, idols, meditation - or whatever, as contradictory, but as complementary alternatives.

These spiritual beings are thought of in varying ways. As mentioned earlier, depending on the exact form of paganism, they may be seen as, or called, gods, angels, demons, spirits, ascended masters, UFOs, aliens and a host of other designations. As the whole of reality is often seen in evolutionary terms, these beings are sometimes conceived as more highly evolved forms of life than us. The merging, or synthesis, of religious, philosophical, scientific, pseudoscientific and science fiction ideas is often apparent here. These beings are also seen as part of the 'Oneness' of the universe; they also are part of the 'All is one, One is All, All is God'. In other words, everything is made of this great 'Oneness' and within him, or it, is every reality, including every being from a one-celled organism up through humans, to a whole range of spiritual beings.

A belief and interaction with the lesser of this supposed myriad of spiritual beings is often called animism (from *animae*, 'spirits'). Many societies around the world have been animistic, believing in a myriad of spiritual beings that are concerned with human affairs and are thought to be capable of harming or helping people's interests. Even in the West this is reemerging with a rediscovery of personal connection with fairies, pixies and the spirits of the countryside. In the West, the animism of this sort has historically been subsumed into cultural fairy tales, but the religious root is the undisguised belief in supernatural spirits of the woods and glades. Animism usually includes the belief that stones, plants, rivers, trees and animals all have their own animating force, or spirit. There are many contemporary forms of animism, including shamanism, wicca and Native American beliefs. People contact these spiritual beings, not so much to find answers to the big questions of life but to help with more immediate concerns like averting danger, getting food, finding wisdom and curing illnesses.

In many cultures and civilizations some of these spiritual beings are seen as far more powerful and are conceived as gods, or divine beings. When a society believes in many gods it is seen as polytheistic; belief and interaction with greater spiritual beings is often called polytheism. Throughout the world there has often been a worship of such beings, from the old Norse Gods, though those of ancient Greece and Rome, Egypt, Babylon, South America, Africa, India and so on. These beings are seen as malevolent or benevolent and have varying levels of dominance or authority. People claim to interact with these gods and enter into relationships with them, often through the worship of idols.

From a biblical point of view there is only one God, but there are many beings that seem to claim the title 'god.' The Bible does reveal to us that there are spiritual beings, which it calls angels and demons. Demons are spiritual beings that are opposed to God and his good purposes for humanity; they are utterly evil and are totally opposed to Jesus Christ and his gospel. In Ephesians, the apostle Paul tells us, 'Our struggle is not against flesh and blood, but against the rulers, against the authorities, against the powers of this dark world and against the spiritual forces of evil in the heavenly realms.'[16] More than this, specifically, when someone is engaged in pagan practice they may well be encountering such beings. The apostle Paul writes that 'We know that an idol is nothing at all in the world and that there is no God but one. For even if there are so-called gods, whether in heaven or on earth (as indeed there are many 'gods' and many 'lords'), yet for us there is but one God, the Father, from whom all things came and for whom we live; and there is but one Lord, Jesus Christ, through whom all things came and through whom we live.'[17] More than this, he goes on to indicate that many of these 'gods' are actually demons, and that people do really engage with them in pagan worship: 'The sacrifices of pagans are offered to demons, not to God, and I do not want you to be participants with demons.'[18] Jesus always clearly demonstrated a belief in demons.[19] These are the beings, acting as angels of light,[20] that are more than happy to oblige pagan worshippers and are part and parcel of their belief system. Paganism does have real supernatural powers. Remember, our Bibles inform us that the woman in Philippi really could predict something about the future,[21] physically overpower men,[22] and Pharaoh's wise men really could turn their staffs into snakes and even imitate a few of the plagues.[23] On top of this, the Bible appears to predict a rising in evil and real supernatural phenomena towards the end of the world.[24] These beings are seen as awesome.[25]

Fitting it together — isn't there a contradiction here?

How can people believe in some divine being that is everywhere and in everything ('All is one, One is All, All is God') on one hand, and yet also hold to a belief separate spiritual beings, or gods, on the other. For a start, paganism does not claim to be a thought out system with no contradictions; some of them would say that there are too many unknowns and each view is a different, but limited perspective on the divine reality. Furthermore, some would merge the views by saying that 'God', the divine entity, or Oneness, whatever term is given, actually sits comfortable with pantheism or panentheism, because this is seen in countless expressions of gods, spiritual beings, animals plants and humans, indeed everything. In fact, the whole universe is often conceived as evolutionary with gradations of being from mere molecules, through men and 'gods' of various levels, all of which are expressions of this ultimate Oneness, or God. All are understood as part of an intricate web of being.[26] As we shall see later, this is in total opposition to the biblical perspective and breaks down at various points. God is robbed of his true divinity, Jesus is reduced to 'a lord' rather than the Lord of all, and the Holy Spirit becomes impersonalised to the spirit that transcends everything.

Perhaps the best antidote to all this is when the apostle Paul writes in his letter to the Colossians,

He is the image of the invisible God, the firstborn over all creation. For by him all things were created: things in heaven and on earth, visible and invisible, whether thrones or powers or rulers or authorities; all things were created by him and for him. He is before all things, and in him all things hold together. And he is the head of the body, the church; he is the beginning and the firstborn from among the dead, so that in everything he might have supremacy. For God was pleased to have all his fullness dwell in him, and through him to reconcile to himself all things, whether things on earth or things in heaven, by making peace through his blood, shed on the cross.[27]

Reincarnation and karma

Common to many who follow some variation of the New Age mindset is often a belief in what are called Karma and reincarnation. Karma is an old Sanskrit word meaning 'works, actions, deeds'. Reincarnation means to 'come again in the flesh'. These two ideas work together.

The basic viewpoint is that people have lived many lives before, possibly hundreds or even thousands. People's karma ('works, actions, deeds') in previous existences determines the circumstances of the present and future lives. The physical, spiritual and practical circumstances of each lifetime are dependent upon their good or bad karma from previous lives. Good deeds lead to progress and eventual liberation from the continual round of rebirths, whereas people can go backwards through bad karma, possibly regressing to the animal kingdom, or even lower forms of life.

When all the bad karma is paid off by good deeds, a point is supposed to be reached where the individual has evolved spiritually (a recurring New Age theme) to a point where they no longer need to reincarnate. They then understood to have become pure spirit and reached nirvana, a state of absolute blessedness. In Buddhism this implies the extinction of the self, but this is not so common an understanding in more western variations.

When this is put together it can be seen in essence to be a belief in self-salvation — we pay for our own wrongdoing in future lives. There is no need in this belief for the substitutionary death of Jesus as our substitute to pay the price for our sins. Of course this is in direct contradiction with the Bible which states, 'Man is destined to die once and after that face judgement.'[28]

The idea of spiritual or psychological evolution runs through all of this. Many New Agers hold that their so-called spirit guides are former humans who have evolved to a point that they no longer need to reincarnate. Becoming one of them is the promise held out to many New Age seekers.

Mystical knowledge

The key question that all this raises is why do all these people think they know all this? Where do they claim their knowledge comes from? What authority do they use to back up their claims? The key question, then, is all about knowing. How do they claim to know all these ideas?

In essence, it is often believed that the spiritual dimension cannot only be connected into in order to get power, but also to get knowledge. Secret, hidden, or supernatural knowledge is claimed to be available to those who have mastered the right techniques. One neo-pagan book says,

> Knowledge is power. 'I know something you don't know' is a well-known childish chant, but is mirrored in the adult world by the respect and sometimes fear, claimed by and given to those who have special knowledge. The dictionary definition of occult is 'kept secret; beyond the range of ordinary knowledge; involving the supernatural, mystical or magical.'[29]

One example, who claim to obtain such knowledge would be the Shamans, a role and activity that is present in most forms of paganism in one form or another. The word shaman comes from Siberia, and its origins lie in the words meaning 'to become excited'. Shamans are claimed to perhaps be the 'first people to seek to penetrate and interpret the secret currents of life. The essence of shamanism was to be able to enter a state of trance in which this communion with natural powers could be experienced … In trance, the Shaman's spirit left his body and traveled … to meet godlike beings from whom he would receive knowledge … it has become of great interest in recent times, partly through syncretism and partly through the feeling that its simplicity of approach, its closeness to nature, has much to teach the modern mind.'[30] Shamans are claimed to 'mediate between the human and the spirit worlds.'[31]

Shamanism is only an example of people claiming to connect into some spiritual dimension to obtain supernatural knowledge. Paganism is full of other techniques including among many others, various methods of divination, astrology and spiritualism. Contacting the 'other world' for knowledge is a central theme.

One particular type of this emphasis on esoteric knowledge is called *Gnosticism* (from *gnosis*, 'knowledge'). Some groups of Gnostics in the time of the early church believed that salvation came through knowledge (*gnosis*) rather than through faith (*pistis*). The Scriptures are quite clear that not all knowledge is good, indeed, certain types of spiritual and moral knowledge have produced damage of cosmic dimensions.[32] Some things are revealed to us, but other things are kept from us, as Deuteronomy 29:29 states: 'The secret things belong to the Lord our God, but the things revealed belong to us and to our children forever, that we may follow all the words of this law.'

Against alternative forms of spiritual 'enlightenment,' the words of the prophet Isaiah ring very clear:

When men tell you to consult mediums and spiritists, who whisper and mutter, should not a people enquire of their God? Why consult the dead on behalf of the living? To the law and to the testimony! If they do not speak according to this word, they have no light of dawn. Distressed and hungry, they will roam through the land; when they are famished, they will become enraged and, looking upward, will curse their king and their God. Then they will look towards the earth and see only distress and darkness and fearful gloom, and they will be thrust into utter darkness.[33]

One world religion

Paganism seems to be a religious approach that is a sort of lowest common denominator for cultures as far apart as the Pacific islands, eastern Asia, native Americans, tribal Africans, aborigines and the older western beliefs. The basic pagan tenets seem almost universal, from the ancient primal beliefs all the way through to the current New Age Movement. Indeed, paganism is literally everywhere — it is the linking spirituality that human beings seem to be prone to.[34] Under the surface of the various guises in different cultures, the shared threads indicate what could be conceived of as a One World Religion. Biblically, the suggestion is being made here that it is the common lie Satan is foisting on us.

Throughout the Scriptures, paganism and idolatry are seen as one of the main enemies of God's people. We have only to survey the history of Israel to get an appreciation of this. Consider, for example, tower of Babel, the battle with Pharaoh's magicians, the judgement on the Canaanites, the failings of the people of Israel in worshipping on the high places and around Ashera poles, along with child sacrifice to Molech, the leadership of the witch-queen Jezabel, the crisis on Mount Carmel and the underlying reasons for the exile. Even in the New Testament, which although particularly in the gospels, addresses dead hypocritical religiosity, paganism is still seen as a primal enemy. Outside of Israel, which by that time had largely learnt her lesson regarding paganism, the New Testament often describes believers meeting the challenge of paganism. Consider for instance the believer's interaction with Simon the Sorcerer, the citizens of Lystra, Derbe, Athens, Ephesus and Rome. In his letter to the Romans, where Paul unpacks the process of God's wrath against mankind, he starts the diagnosis of the continuing ongoing fall of societies with what is essentially paganism. This facing into paganism continues elsewhere as well.[35]

What we are seeing in our generation, that is perhaps unique in the history of the world, is the synthesising of East, West, North, South, ancient and modern pagan beliefs. They are coming together, accepting each other, converging and merging into a unified whole that is becoming one integrated perspective. There may be many varied expressions, but underneath a ruling paradigm is emerging. A current handbook on the occult put it this way:

Syncretism, 'the process by which systems of belief, which once were separate and which arise from different sources, begin to blend and to take elements from one another. This is particularly marked in modern occultism, although it has always been a feature, since practitioners have always been interested in what they could discern about other teachings. The development of mass global travel and of electronic media has accentuated this trend to the point where many occult processes are combined. The same person may use tarot and the American Indian medicine wheel or combine Kabalistic[36] and Tibetan means of divination. This potentially confusing procedure is justified by the underlying resemblances of all occult studies. They share the same intention, which of seeking harmony with the invisible and not fully understood forces of the cosmos.'[37]

The occult tradition has evolved with other fields of knowledge, and New Age thinking has given it a new dimension. The urge towards the practicable and the provable, which has characterised the rise of modern technology and science, has inevitably led to a counter-reaction towards the mystical, the Earth-related and the natural. Ironically, it is the achievements of modern technology that have made possible the fusion of different — although often similar — traditions and teachings from all over the world ... Will the combination of all these millennia-old ways of thought, ways of seeing the universe, lead to a new and definitive synthesis? Time will tell.[38]

Religious expressions throughout the world and history now seem to becoming together to form one shared understanding, or religion.[39] This is made easier by the attitudes within our society to various religions. The politically correct view now seems to be that in a pluralistic society the only acceptable position is that no view is right and no opinion is wrong. This rising dominant view in the West is what may be called pluralistic fundamentalism, or totalitolerance. By these terms I mean that are only allowed to hold that all views are correct. Ironically, this in itself is a form of intolerance, for it only accepts one perspective. The danger is that religious freedom will be reduced on the grounds that others will be offended.[40] What this does is that it provides the sociological and ideological context within which all the pagan religions can come together in a way that is acceptable to the general population.

The underlying similarities of many pagan, neo-pagan, New Age and occult perspectives are increasingly being recognised. A fusion, or synthesis, of religious perspectives is now happening on a scale that may possibly be unprecedented in the history of humanity. Whereas in a previous generation, the ecumenical movement, powered by liberalism, attempted to merge Christian denominations, a syncretism of a different order of magnitude is now fusing faiths. The final outcome is probably beyond our imagination.

Questions for discussion

1. Read Genesis 1. How does this passage relate to pantheism? Does it support such a view, or contradict it?

2. Read Colossians 1:15-23. How does this passage relate to a belief in an impersonal cosmic life force?

3. Read Philippians 2:5-11, Revelation 21:1-7 and Hebrews 9:27. In what ways do these passages support or contradict the belief that some pagans have of continual cycles of reincarnation, until we reach nirvana, where our personal identity is obliterated and we are absorbed into the supposed ultimate Oneness of the universe?

4. In what specific ways do Revelation chapters 4 and 5 give a different perspective of the cosmos than that outlined in this chapter?

Chapter 9
Pagans in White Lab Coats

*'Buddhism has the characteristics of what would be expected
in a cosmic religion for the future: it transcends a personal
God, avoids dogmas and theology; it covers both the natural
and the spiritual, and it is based on a religious sense aspiring
from the experience of all things, natural and spiritual, as a
meaningful unity.'*
Albert Einstein[1]

Increasingly, many following the rising contemporary spirituality
are turning to science to give some kind of credulity to their perspectives.[2] The New Age Movement has often dressed up classic
occult concepts in more modern pseudoscientific language to make
its ideas more generally acceptable, but now it is going beyond a
makeover in linguistics — it is claiming scientific justification for its
views.

We are all attracted by the possibility of guidance for our daily
lives, and desire to gain insight into our futures — this seems to
be a human trait. Throughout history people have sought inspiration for the present and have longed to have a glimpse into their
destiny. Almost all manifestations of paganism have this idea of
seeking spiritual counsel to make the most of life. Whether consulting the tea leaves, astrology, the tarot, spiritism, numerology, or
interpreting dreams, people seek advice on living their lives in the
light of their predicted future. Perhaps they can discover whether
the time is right to take risks in business, or to take initiative in ro-
mance. More and more, folk are experimenting with these things

today, all the way from columns in our newspapers, through dabbling with many self-help aids available, all the way to fully validated Master of Arts courses in our universities. As we saw earlier, Bath Spa University College offers a postgraduate degree in Cultural Astronomy and Astrology. The prospectus tells us that this MA course includes studies in Astro-Methodology, Stellar Religion, New Age and Sacred Geography.[3] More than all this, people are also increasingly employing techniques such as ritual, spells and visualisation to achieve specific purposes. The use of magic is gaining acceptance.[4]

Many feel that all this is almost laughable. How can the movement of stars and planet out in space possibly affect human lives here on Earth? How can events dictated by some view of fate possibly be revealed in tea leaves or set of tarot cards? How can some incantation or spell influence people and events thousands of miles away? It all sounds utterly absurd. However, some pagans are now justifying their beliefs in scientific terms.

The big idea: everything is connected

The work of British former NASA scientist James Lovelock is significant here. We saw earlier, that in 1969, he proposed the principle known as the Gaia hypothesis — that life shapes and controls the environment rather than the other way around. As neo-pagan writer Susan Greenwood puts it: 'Every individual life form, from microbe to human, is involved by its own life processes. Earth's atmosphere is actively maintained and regulated by life on the surface for all the species of living beings. Lovelock's work has helped promote a new scientific understanding of life at all levels, from organisms to social systems and ecosystems. It involves a distinct shift in perception from the mechanistic worldview to an encompassing ecological view.'[5] Everything on our planet is seen as interconnected whole, an interactive web, or network.[6] This holistic perspective, seeing everything as interconnected, is basic to a pagan, or magical, worldview.[7]

It is not only in the biological sciences that this holistic perception is gaining ground; a reinterpreting of physics is also involved. Erwin Schrodinger, the physicist who perfected quantum mechanics, believed in the eastern idea that our innermost self (Atman) is identical with the entire universe (Brahman). He once said, 'I consider science an integrating part of our endeavour to answer to answer the one great philosophical question which embraces all others — who are we? And more than that: I consider this not only one of the tasks, but the task, of science, the one that really counts.'[8]

The case for an alternative interpretation of physics is most popularly put by the physicist Fritjof Capra. He critiques normal mechanistic science in *The Turning Point (1983)* and explores the parallels between post-Einsteinian physics and eastern religions in *The Tao of Physics* (1976). Capra claims that in twentieth-century science there is a shift to a holistic perspective, involving a change in focus on the parts to the whole. Again, this holistic paradigm is sometimes used to explain magic or the prediction of the future. The great web of existence, which is seen as totally interconnected and is as part of the One essence of the universe, is given as an explanation. Events right over here in this part of the cosmos are connected with and influence parts right over there. Furthermore, the One, or Force, is understood to be controlling, or the cause of 'fate'. In the weaving of a spell the magician claims to manipulate the web of existence.

Mystery explains magic

The universe is more complex and weird than we can possibly imagine

Pagans claim that today, increasingly, people believe that their lives are networked with a far bigger reality. A pagan view of the universe, or reality as a whole, is that it has it be viewed 'holistically'.[9] Everything is a united whole, or Oneness. It is all part of the one integrated cosmic reality — it is all One. This is part of the perception, or paradigm, of holistic science, which is growing so much at the moment. What this means is that everything is linked, or networked.

They believe that conventional science only looks at the relationship of cause and effect in a very blinkered and limited way.

So, normal science may study the relationship between say heating a vessel of water and temperature changes in the water, but it conceives of no possible relationship between the movement of the planet Saturn and my speculating on the stock market. They postulate, in other words, that conventional science studies the universe in a particulate way, but not a cosmic way.

Professor Paul Davies, an internationally acclaimed physicist, writes, 'there is a growing appreciation of the structural hierarchy in nature: that holistic concepts like life, organization and mind are indeed meaningful, and they cannot be explained away as 'nothing but' atoms or quarks or unified forces or whatever.[10] In other words, it may be that our universe cannot be explained by a multitude simple cause and effect laws — that may not be the whole story. The complexity of the whole may be just as important. Davies also comments, 'One of the unsolved problems for modern physics is whether the holistic features of a physical system require additional holistic laws that cannot be reduced to the fundamental laws of elementary forces and particles.'[11]

Many pagans feel that mentally we need to have a paradigm shift, or radical change of perception, and to view the universe as a whole, like a multidimensional web. In this view, something that happens right over there could well influence something right over here. Just because we can't understand the mechanism does not mean that it doesn't happen. Furthermore, there could well be mysterious laws governing the relationship between what happens right over there and how it effects what happens right over here. So, somehow, it is argued, embedded in the universe are principles that might well control these influences. For example, if I am born on a certain day, and the planets do certain things years later, then they will tend to influence me in these particular ways. An illustration of the human body might be helpful here. If I stub my toe it causes my voice box to cry out in pain. This is because my body is an integrated whole, and something at the extremity of my body can cause an effect in my lungs and throat. Some believe that this is the way the cosmos operates, we just have not understood how, as yet. These hidden, or mysterious, principles are claimed to have been revealed to certain seers over the centuries and passed down to initiates.

With regard to these claims that holism might offer a mechanism for astrology, magic and so on, Professor Paul Davies comments, 'So far we have no evidence for truly holistic laws.'[12]

Mathematics explains magic

To bolster and justify their position, pagans will also look to other contemporary scientific ideas, like chaos theory. Chaos theory is a 'mathematical theory that describes chaotic behaviour in a complex system'.[13] The name 'chaos theory' comes from the fact that the systems that the theory describes are apparently disordered, but chaos theory is really about finding the underlying order in apparently random data. Perhaps, underlying what many view as our apparently chaotic universe is an order of some kind – an order that the astrologers and mystics of past civilizations had uncovered. Basically, they are saying that the universe is a lot more complicated than we can possibly conceive and is linked and networked to itself in ways beyond human comprehension. This appeals to many as the popular view today, most eloquently expressed by Bill Bryson, is that 'we live in a universe whose age we can't quite compute, surrounded by stars whose distances from us and each other we don't altogether know, filled with matter we can't identify, operating in conformance with physical laws whose properties we don't truly understand'.[14] Bryson also tells us in his survey of contemporary science, that physicists have encountered, as James Trefil puts it, 'an area of the universe that our brains just aren't wired to understand'.[15]

Trying to apply chaos theory to pagan belief is really grasping at straws.

The miniscule explains magic

He then expresses a contemporary scientific concept that many pagans have tried to cease upon to explain how things out in space can affect things on earth.[16] It is worth remembering that this is quoted in a popular level book that won various awards and spent many months high up in the best sellers list. The point is this: weirdly erudite and complex physics has been made widely available to the population at large. Bryson is only a current example of this popularising of scientific ideas; there are many other examples, but his is possibly the most readable. What this all means is that complex ideas that are simplified can be misconstrued and misapplied by readers — something that pagans have been guilty. The concept they have ceased upon, then, is this:

> Perhaps the most arresting of quantum improbabilities is the idea, arising from Wolfgang Pauli's Exclusion Principle of 1925, that certain pairs of subatomic particles, even when separated by the most considerable distances, can each instantly 'know' what the other is doing. Particles have a quality known as spin and, according to quantum theory, the moment you determine the spin of one particle, its sister particle, no matter how distant away, will immediately begin spinning in the opposite direction at the same rate.

> It is as if, in the words of the science writer Lawrence Joseph, you had two identical pool balls, one in Ohio and the other in Fiji, and that the instant that you sent one spinning in one spinning the other would spin in a contrary direction at precisely the same speed. Remarkably, the phenomenon was proved in 1997 when physicists at the University of Geneva sent photons seven miles in opposite directions and demonstrated that interfering with one provoked an instantaneous response in the other.[17]

So, from chaos theory pagans feel that there is the theoretical possibility that there is an underlying order in apparently random data. We can't see the connection between, say, Saturn and a car crash, but that doesn't mean there isn't one. From quantum physics they feel they have proof that objects far apart are in some way causally connected. This could apparently explain both astrology and the casting of spells.

The evidence claimed from physics is out of place. It may be that subatomic particles can affect each other at great distances, but, as we are continually discovering, subatomic particles behave in totally different ways from those at our level of existence. Just as Newtonian physics does not apply at the subatomic level, so, quantum mechanics does not apply at the macro level. The rules seem to be utterly different for the different domains and therefore applying the behaviour of things at one level to the other is totally inappropriate.

Debunking 'scientific' mechanisms for magic

The trouble with all this is that it is pure conjecture. There is no point looking for a model or mechanism to explain causal links between events millions of miles apart, if those causal links have never actually been demonstrated as happening. Nothing here has ever been shown to be fact. If things like astrology really do work, then it would not be too difficult to conceive of a series of experiments to demonstrate their veracity. But no one has ever proven any causal links. The 'knowledge' is being dresses up as scientific, when in reality it is merely blind and hopeful belief, based on the occult revelations of various seers, gurus and mystics of history.

A striking example of a holistic law of physics having practical application would be psychokinesis or telepathy. Proponents of what are called paranormal phenomena claim that the human mind can act to exert forces on distant matter; spells in essence claim a similar thing. Any conceivable mechanism is unknown at a reductionist level: they are not, for instance, electromagnetic, nuclear or gravitational. The most direct illustration of these psychic forces is in the spectacular cases of remote metal bending, where, without physical contact, the subject appears to deform a metallic object by mind-power alone. Professor Paul Davies once 'devised an extremely stringent test of this phenomenon using metal rods sealed inside glass containers from which the air has been replaced by a secret combination of rare gases to preclude tampering. In a recent trial of arch-metal benders not one was able to produce any measurable deformation.'[18]

Our brains are hardwired for spirituality

Experiments on the brain have led scientists to suggest that the capacity for religion may somehow be built into us.[19] A report in *New Scientist* magazine asked: 'Are our religious feelings just a product of how the brain works? Einstein felt it. Chances are you've felt something like it too — in the mountains, by the sea, or perhaps listening to a piece of music that's especially close to your heart.'[20]

'More than half of people report having had some sort of mystical or religious experience. For some, the experience is so intense it changes their life forever. But what is it? The presence of God? A glimpse of a higher plane of being? Or just the mystical equivalent of déjà vu, a trick the brain sometimes plays on your conscious self?'[21]

Andrew Newberg, a neuroscientist at the University of Pennsylvania has been fascinated by the neurobiology of religion for more than a decade. He admits it's an awkward role for a scientist. 'I always get concerned that people will say I'm a religious person who is trying to prove that God exits, or I'm a cynic who's trying to prove that God doesn't exist.'[22]

Neuroscientists generally agree that religious experiences originate in a region of the brain called the limbic system. Researchers have found that this part of the brain becomes unusually active during intense religious experience.

Plenty of evidence supports the idea that this limbic system is important in religious experiences. Most famously, people who suffer epileptic seizures restricted to the limbic system sometimes report having profound experiences during seizures. As a result, epileptics have historically tended to be people with great mystical experiences.

Neurosurgeons who stimulate the limbic system during open-brain surgery say their patients occasionally report experiencing religious sensations. And Alzheimer's disease, which is often marked by a loss of religious interest, tends to cripple the limbic system early on.

Newberg has worked with Budddhist, Michael Baime, to study the brain during meditation. 'By injecting radioactive tracers into Baiime's bloodstream as he reached the height of a meditative trance, Newberg could use a brain scanner to image the brain at a religious climax. The bloodflow patterns showed that the tempio-ral lobes were certainly involved but also the brain's parietal lobes almost completely shut down. The parietal lobes give our sense of time and space. Without them we may lose our sense of self.'[23]

Anyone who doubts the brain's ability to generate religious experiences could visit neuroscientist Michael Persinger at Laurentian University — he claims 'anyone can meet God, just by wearing his special helmet.[24]

For several years, Persinger has been using a technique called transcranial magnetic stimulation to induce all sorts of surreal experiences in normal people. Through trial and error and a bit of educated guesswork, he's found that a weak magnetic field rotating anticlockwise in a complex pattern about the temporal lobes will cause four out of five people to feel a spectral presence in the room with them. What people make of this presence depends on their own biases and beliefs. Pagan's, atheists and Christians can all attempt to interpret the data their own way.

So where does all this leave us? For whatever reason — natural or supernatural — our brains clearly allow a novel sort of experience, which we call religious. But it is difficult to say more than that. Sceptics of religion are quick to claim that the brain's hardwiring proves that God has no real existence; that it's all in the brain. 'The real common denominator here is brain activity, not anything else,' says Ron Barrier, a spokesman for *American Atheists*. 'There is nothing to indicate that you are somehow tapping into a divine entity.'[25]

Newberg isn't so sure. 'If you're a religious person, it makes sense that the brain can do this, because if there is a God, it makes sense to design the brain so that we can have some sort of interaction.'[26] Perhaps this research simply reveals that God has made our brains capable of religious experience.

Out of their bodies, or out of their minds?

Is death the end? Does the soul exist? Has science finally proved that there is life after we die? Britain's leading medical journal, *The Lancet*, published a study which shows that large numbers of people believe that they have experienced their souls leaving their bodies while they were proclaimed clinically dead.[27] The evidence is from 'dead' people whose hearts stop beating and then claim to experience a form of afterlife before they are finally resuscitated.

Doctors who studied 344 heart attack survivors found more than one in 10 had experienced emotions, visions or lucid thoughts while they were 'clinically dead' — unconscious with no signs of pulse, breathing or brain activity. This two-year study in 10 Dutch hospitals is the largest study into the phenomenon. It found that 12 per cent of cardiac arrest survivors reported having various 'near-death experiences' (NDEs) before being resuscitated.[28]

Some reported having 'out-of-body' experiences. This included one man who remembered, a week after his heart attack, that one nurse treating him removed his dentures while he was unconscious. He believed he had seen this while floating above his body and watching the doctors working on him.

The research, by a Dutch team, will be seized on by academics who support the theory that the mind can continue to work after the brain has stopped. It is being held up by some as proving that the mind — or soul, can survive death. This study also showed that patients felt better about death and more spiritual for as long as eight years after their NDE.

Over the last few years various research teams from different universities and hospitals have been trying to make sense of NDEs. It was reported that doctors at the University of Southampton had spent a year studying patients who were resuscitated in the city's general hospital after suffering a heart attack.[29] The people brought back to life were all, for varying lengths of time, clinically dead with no respiration, no pulse and fixed dilated pupils. EEG studies have confirmed that the brain's electrical activity, and hence brain function, ceases during this time. Out of 63 patients who survived their cardiac arrest, seven recalled emotions and visions while they were 'dead'.

In this study, the heart attack survivors were interviewed within a week of their cardiac arrest and asked if they remembered anything during their period of 'death'. Some recalled feelings of joy and peace, lost awareness of body, heightened senses, time speeded up, seeing a bright light, entering another world, encountering a mystical being or deceased relative and coming to a point of no return.

Not all NDEs are alike — and some are not positive experiences at all. Typically they involve feelings of deep peace, followed by sensations of floating up through a tunnel towards a bright light and into a beautiful kingdom. However, it has become clear that other NDEs involve terrifying accounts of being pulled downwards – towards a pit inhabited by demons. An article in *The Telegraph* called, 'Patients near death see visions of hell', focused on the research of Tony Lawrence, lecturer in psychology at Coventry University who has probed the nature of negative NDEs.[30] There was a startling account of a woman who fought for life after a miscarriage: 'It was an awful feeling — like I was going down a big hole and I couldn't get up. I was going into this big pit. I was going further and further down, and trying to claw my way back up and kept slipping.'

But what do the results of all these studies show? The cardiologist who led the Dutch research team, Dr Pim van Lommel says it, 'pushes at the limits of medical ideas about the range of human consciousness and the relationship between mind and brain.'[31]

The question is: Are these people out of their bodies, or out of their minds? Perhaps the drugs given to the patients can explain their experiences. However, researchers at the Southampton hospital were able to rule out claims that unusual combinations of medications were to blame, because the resuscitation procedure was the same in every case. Other critics have suggested that these experiences were the result of a collapse of brain functions caused by a lack of oxygen. Yet an examination of the medical records of the Southampton cases reveals that none of those who had these experiences had low levels of oxygen. *The Lancet* report also mentions that epilepsy and electrical stimulation of the brain may possibly be the cause.

The problem with near-death experiences is that they are exactly that — *near-death* experiences and not *death* experiences. The difficulty is in assessing when the brain, an organ we hardly understand, actually dies. Does the cessation of electrical activity, of necessity mean that the person is dead, or are they actually in the *process* of dying? Body tissues are sensitive, and real death very quickly brings irreparable damage. The fact that these patients were resuscitated means that that damage had not occurred and therefore begs the question as to whether they actually did die. All that may have happened is that one of our measurements of life could no longer be detected.

As to the question of the emotions and visions, which the patients experienced, the difficulty is in understanding what happens to the brain when it is nearly dead. When some cells die, others become damaged and brain chemicals are no longer controlled, what sort of hallucinations are possible?

The fact that many people who testify to having NDEs have similar experiences needs to be taken seriously, but this might simply be a common psychological phenomenon, which occurs as the mental software begins to crash.

The essential point is that, even if we give credit where the evidence is at best dubious, such experiences can provide no reliable information about an after-life. An after-life is by definition in another dimension, and we can have no confidence that the tools and methodology of our science applies — the laws of that universe might be totally different from ours. When trying to explore that other dimension, which many call the spiritual dimension, we have to use a totally different approach.

The Bible's claim is that it is a source-book, provided by God to reveal certain aspects of that different dimension to us. God uses it as a dimension-crossing-communication-device to show us spiritual realities. It is interesting to note that the Bible records a story, told by Jesus, which touches on the whole area of people bringing back revelation from the grave. The story goes like this: There was an evil rich man and a good poor man who both died. The rich man was in torment an cried out to Abraham for the poor man to rise from the dead and warn his five brothers, 'so that they will not come to this place of torment.'

'Abraham replied, "They have Moses and the Prophets; let them listen to them."

"No father Abraham," he said, "but if someone from the dead goes to them, they will repent."'

Abraham's response is shocking: 'If they do not listen to Moses and the Prophets, they will not be convinced even if someone rises from the dead.'

In telling this story Jesus was saying that, if people don't accept Moses and the Prophets (that is, the Scriptures), they will certainly not be convinced by someone coming back from the dead. There was a bitter irony in that statement, for Jesus knew that he would soon die, and then on the first Easter morning, rise from the dead himself. And the ironic point is this: most people didn't — and don't — believe him.

Near-death-experiences are certainly interesting, but probably do not prove much about an after-life. But even if they did, I doubt if it would make any difference to most people.

The challenge

What we are seeing today is that not only are these pagan activities are becoming increasingly popular, but also that the 'secrets' are being more widely publicized. Furthermore, through holistic science, chaos theory and other means, these practices are being intellectually defended and promoted. Paganism is developing its own brand of apologetics — and Christians need to be ready to respond.

Questions for discussion

1. Read Genesis 1:27-31 and Genesis 2:19-20. What can these passages teach us about a biblical view of scientific endeavour? Do we have a mandate to explore, classify and use God's creation? Does that mandate have any constraints?

2. Read Daniel chapters 1-2. Daniel was studying at a pagan university and coming to grasp a pagan view of the universe. What challenges did he face? What series of stands did he have to make, and why? In what ways was his worldview different from the Babylonians?

3. Read Luke 16:19-31. How does this passage relate to the claims of NDEs giving data from beyond the grave?

Chapter 10
The Seduction of Christianity

'I thought Constantine was a Christian,' Sophie said.

'Hardly,' Teabing scoffed. 'He was a lifelong pagan who was baptized on his deathbed, too weak to protest. In Constantine's day, Rome's official religion was sun worship — the cult of *Sol Invictus*, or the Invincible Sun — and Constantine was its head priest. Unfortunately for him, a growing religious turmoil was gripping Rome. Three centuries after the crucifixion of Jesus Christ, Christ's followers had multiplied exponentially. Christians and pagans began warring, and the conflict grew to such proportions that it threatened to rend Rome in two. Constantine decided something had to be done. In 325 A.D., he decided to unify Rome under a single religion. Christianity.'

Sophie was surprised. 'Why would a pagan emperor choose *Christianity* as the official religion?'

Teabing chuckled. 'Constantine was a very good businessman. He could see that Christianity was on the rise, and he simply backed the winning horse. Historians still marvel at the brilliance with which Constantine converted the sun-worshipping pagans to Christianity. By fusing pagan symbols, dates and rituals into the growing Christian tradition, he created a kind of hybrid religion that was acceptable to both parties.'

'Transmogrification,' Langdon said. 'The vestiges of pagan religion in Christian symbology are undeniable. Egyptian sun disks became the halos of Catholic saints. Pictograms of Isis nursing her miraculously conceived son Horus became the blueprint for our modern images of the Virgin Mary nursing Baby Jesus. And virtually all the elements of the Catholic ritual

— the mitre, the altar, the doxology and communion, the act of "God-eating" — were taken directly from earlier pagan mystery religions.'

Teabing groaned. 'Don't get a symbologist started on Christian icons. Nothing in Christianity is original. The pre-Christian God Mithras — called *the Son of God* and *the Light of the World* — was born on December 25, died, was buried in a rock tomb, and then resurrected in three days. By the way, December 25 is also the birthday of Osiris, Adonis and Dionysus. The newborn Krishna was presented with gold, frankincense, and myrrh. Even Christianity's weekly holy day was stolen from the pagans.'

'What do you mean?'

'Originally,' Langdon said, 'Christianity honoured the Jewish Sabbath of Saturday, but Constantine shifted it to coincide with the pagan's veneration day of the sun.' He paused, grinning. 'To this day, most churchgoers attend services on Sunday morning with no idea that they are there on account of the pagan sun god's weekly tribute — Sunday.'

The Da Vinci Code, Dan Brown[1]

'See to it that no one takes you captive through philosophy and empty deception, according to the tradition of men, according to the elementary principles of the world rather than according to Christ.'

Colossians 2:8

There are a core set of spiritual beliefs that homo sapiens tend to gravitate towards — and these beliefs, like the tendrils of some subterranean beast, find their way into almost every society. They are always the enemy of biblical religion.

In essence, we are drawn towards believing in some creative force that is one with Nature and the cosmos. This force brings life into existence, from the extremely simple, through plant, animal and human, to a whole host of advanced spiritual beings. Gradually, we are seen to evolve from one level to another. In order to help us in our lives here, we can connect into the levels above ours and solicit the aid of beings more powerful than ourselves. Through various techniques and rituals, we are tempted not only to receive supernatural aid, but also mystical wisdom. This is the basic worldview of paganism, neo-paganism and the New Age. It is the essential perspective of many of the religions of the East and the old religions of the West. This is the fundamental belief system the Israelites of the Old Testament had to contend with, and it is religious psyche that made up the world within which Christianity spread. It is the enemy of the faith; it is the doctrine of demons; it is the heart of Satan's spiritual delusion. It is *The Lie*. We all desire power and supernatural wisdom; we all want to progress to a higher level of existence. We all want to be like God.

With this in mind, it is not difficult to appreciate that it was hardly likely that *The Lie* would curl up and die with the coming of Christianity. No, after an initial struggle in the West, it simply played dead. If it couldn't defeat the church from outside it would infiltrate from inside. trojan horses are just as effective as warhorses. Paganism would reinvent itself in Christian disguise. After all, Satan had plenty of practice; the Old Testament is full of examples of the Israelites compromising their religion and taking up what was essentially paganism as a way of worshipping Jehovah.[2] This was part of a slippery slope that quickly led to unadulterated paganism.[3] Likewise, the history of the church is littered with instances of where pagan practices and beliefs have wormed their way into the most surprising of places. Quite how correct this is in regard Dan Brown's *Da Vinci Code* is a matter of debate, but what is certain is that there is more truth here than is comfortable.[4]

Throughout church history Christianity has often struggled with how much to absorb and adapt from the culture within which it was trying to grow, and how much to suppress. As one contemporary pagan writer puts it concerning Christianity's adaptation and absorption of the festival of Easter: 'Many of the symbols associated with Easter reflect an older past ... The Easter bunny was originally a hare, a sacred animal that is seldom eaten because of its associations in Britain with the Goddess of Spring ... Eggs, which are one of the man indicators of returning life at Easter, are fertility symbols in many lands.'[5] A different current pagan writer states, 'The

Christian festival of Easter, which is traditionally held on the first Sunday after the first full moon following the spring equinox, is another example of a Christian festival that is based on a much older, pagan tradition. The Easter bunny was once the hare of the Saxon goddess Eostre, who gave her name to this Christian festival.'[6] And regarding Christmas, present day pagans write: 'December brings a collection of festivals celebrated by different people. There is the Winter Solstice on or around 21st December ... some call this by its Saxon name of Yule ... a bundle of sticks ... burns in the hearth for the 12 nights of the festival ... The pagan Yule is the time of the birth of the Star Child, the Mabon, the sacred Son of the Mother, Modron. He is the Child of Promise, whose coming brings hope into the wintry world. Christmas has its own traditions in the giving and receiving of presents, eating a special meal, and visiting relatives. Carols, which are now sung, were originally dances. The story of the birth of Jesus and all its symbolism has far older sources. The tradition of a lit and decorated Christmas tree spread from Germany, but dressing up a tree with candles and ribbons in midwinter is a very old tradition.'[7] Quite how dangerous, or harmless, all this is has often been disputed among Christian believers, but the underlying serious point is that if the church found it so easy to absorb pagan festivals and images, it may well have found it just as easy to absorb pagan beliefs and practices.

The trojan horse

The Lie has entered the church. Over the centuries, Satan has continually infiltrated the ranks of believing people with his confused teachers who preach pagan ideas dressed up in Christian disguises. Today, such ideas have massive influence.[8]

A reliance on ritual

One of the keynotes of pagan worship is a reliance on ritual. It is believed that through certain activities, words and chants, spiritual power can be unleashed. The New Testament, by contrast, reveals a non-ritualistic religion, which is simple and straightforward. Throughout the ages this has often been forgotten, and we end up with priests wearing ornate clothing, performing intricate rituals. Rather than people hearing God directly by studying his revelation in the Bible and approaching him directly in prayer, the whole thing becomes buried in mystery and symbolism. The magic of the ceremony replaces the centrality of the Bible and prayer. This has even happened to the Lord's Supper when it became the Mass in the Roman Catholic Church, so that a memorial of Jesus' death turned into a re-enactment of his sacrifice and a kind of magical rite. It is the spiritual elite who are alone allowed to administer the ceremony, keeping the power in the hands of the privileged.

Certain places are seen as having special spiritual significance. Many churches throughout history were built on ancient pagan sites that were meant to be endowed with power. The building becomes the place where we can connect with spiritual reality. Even in conformist churches, buildings are sometimes given undue respect, termed as sanctuaries where we can meet God. The building becomes God's house. At best this is an unjustifiable harping back to the days of the Old Testament temple, at worst it is tiptoeing towards a paganized worldview. As the special places of spiritual encounter are held by the religious institution, these hold the keys to power. At its heart, paganism is concerned with the wielding of power, power over nature, power over spiritual realities and power over people. At its core, biblical Christianity is concerned with free access to God, the priesthood of all believers. Jesus is our only mediator, the Bible our only authority.

The sorcerer's apprentice — connecting into power

Essential to paganism is the idea that spiritual forces can be connected into and used for our advantage. What the secular world calls 'mind power' many Christian believers confuse for 'faith'. The ability to exert 'mind over matter' is no longer considered as something weird or occult, but is now often seen as part of the normal human potential that can be used by anyone who uses the right techniques. Many sincere Christians have been influenced by the sorcerer's gospel to imagine that faith has some power in itself. To them, faith is not placed in God, but is a power directed at God, which forces him to do what we want. Prayer becomes a spiritual technique for forcing our will on the world. Prayer ceases to be God centred, focusing on his revealed will and submissive to his hidden will.

This is taken to extreme proportions in what is often called the prosperity gospel. Here our Christianity is seen as a means of achieving personal success and wealth. By our faith we are told we can become rich; Jesus will give us whatever we ask. Success becomes the name of the game.

In their teaching on praying some Christians even promote visualizations. Paul Yonggi Cho who pastors one of the largest churches in the world in South Korea once said, 'I discovered that the reality of that dynamic dimension in prayer that comes through visualization.'[9] Teachers like Yonggi Cho push the perspective that through imagining and visualising what you want in prayer you can bring it about. This is a totally pagan and occult practice.[10]

Blocking out God — intermediaries

One of the recurrent themes of ancient mysticism and paganism is the belief in a cosmology that comprises of multitudes of supernatural beings. Above us are spiritual entities of increasing levels and power, called variously ancestral spirits, spirits of the land, angels, demons and gods. If the specific form of paganism has some ultimate personal 'God', or impersonal Spirit of the Universe, then he or it is obscured by all these levels of being. The believer has to get those above him to plead his case, or give him aid or information. From a biblical perspective, supernatural spiritual entities do indeed exist: they are angels and demons. Angels do the work of God, but demons, or fallen angels, take on a whole host of guises in order to confuse and pervert the human race. These later inject the doctrines of demons into human thinking. One of these delusions is this belief in intermediaries to act on our behalf in the spiritual world; and in doing so they often achieve our worship. Human beings, in seeking, bowing, obeying and worshipping these intermediaries are prostrating themselves before evil spirits. Whether it is the ancient Greek pantheon, the *gnostic* aeons, or the New Age ascended masters, the essential system of belief is the very similar.

With the rise of the church after the time of Christ, Satan did not seem to find it necessary to change his strategy. As the church grew and often moved away from the anchor of the Scriptures, he introduced exactly the same confusing lie. Instead of the 'one mediator between God and man, the man Jesus Christ', he subtly introduced the idea of praying to the saints, and in particular to the Virgin Mary, the so-called Mother of God. The delusion was powerful and effective and built on the emphasis on ritual and priesthood. God was blocked out of view: ritual replaced reality; priests replaced personal access; saints mediated prayers and Mary replaced Jesus. Paganism was reinvented within the church; the church became pagan in belief and practice.

This delusion did Satan's kingdom good service until other lies and delusions came to pre-eminence in western culture. The devil's opposite and equally effective strategy came with the Enlightenment in the eighteenth century: agnosticism and atheism. There is no God, no gods and no spiritual dimension at all. And if there is, it is unknowable anyway. The nineteenth and twentieth centuries have been dominated by these perspectives and their logical out workings. The deadness and spiritual void they produced created the void into which Satan could reintroduce his first lie: God obscured by a myriad of spiritual beings. Neo-paganism and the New Age is filling the gap. 'Angels', demons, gods, ascended masters, UFOs, alien and so on are increasing common parlance. The basic conception is evolutionary: we are all evolving into higher spiritual beings as we climb up through the heavens.

Some sections of the church today are absorbing this emphasis on spiritual entities. Guardian angels, personal angels, spirit guides. In their excellent *Encyclopaedia of New Age Beliefs*, John Ankerberg and John Weldon write,

> There are ... ways in which deceiving spirits have infiltrated the church. The dramatic increase in the number of books advocating angel contact began many years ago with the late Rev Roland Buck's Angel's on Assignment. The book, however, has little to do with the holy angels. The content of the book involves spiritistic deception ... One issue of The Christian Parapsycholgist, a magazine devoted to merging

Christianity and the occult, was devoted entirely to angels ...In Some Thoughts about Angels, J. Dover Wellman, vicar of Emmanuel Church ...includes virtually all spirits into the category of deceased humans and encourages various occult methods to contact them ... Brian Kingslake is a minister of the New Church ... In his article A Heaven of Angels from the Human Race, he accepts the common mediumistic ... teaching that "all the millions of spirits inhabiting the spiritual world – angels and devils alike – are human beings who once inhabited the earth ... The popular late Christian preacher William Branham claimed to speak for God, but throughout his life he was at times guided by lying spirits (his "angels") who would whisper to him and, apparently, occultly "heal" many people each year ...The Rev. Edward W. Oldring, author of I Work with Angels and I Walk and Talk with Angels, supposedly had "angels" appear to him and assist him in "preparing many [Christian] people to work with God's angels."[11]

In his book, *The Other Side of Silence: A Guide to Christian Meditation*, Morton Kelsey wrote, 'If one does not shut the door by disbelief, dream images can bring contact with other entities of psychic power beyond oneself.'[12]

It is chilling to observe again and again in the literature examples of people who claim to be Christian, but who advocate some kind of contact with spiritual beings. History is repeating itself: Jesus Christ is being supplanted as the one mediator between God and man; he is being subtly removed from his supreme position as the only way to the Father.

Sorting out your soul — psychology unleashed

Barely disguised pagan beliefs and practices have been worming their way into the church through a variety of counselling techniques, masquerading under the label 'Christian'.

Christian counselling has increased radically over the last half a century, and although many have tried to develop a biblical approach to this area, others have been far more open to non-

Christian input. Indeed, some workers in the field have borrowed ideas almost indiscriminately from people whose approach contains anti-biblical material. This lack of biblical discernment becomes particularly apparent when thinking about the subconscious. The roots of some schools of psychotherapy run deep into the fertile soil of the occult.

One of the first researchers to delve below the level of the conscious was the idiosyncratic Franz Anton Mesmer (1734-1815). The enduring importance of Mesmer's influence can be seen in the following statement from a prominent psychiatrist writing in the prestigious *Journal of the Royal Society of Medicine*:

> What is important is the impact and influence [Mesmer] had on the subsequent development of psychiatry. It would be no exaggeration to say that he was one of the world's first psychotherapists.[13]

It is not often realized that Mesmer believed the planets influenced the human body, and that his work was highly influenced by 'the occult work of a Jesuit priest, Maximillian Hehl, one of Maria Theresa's court astrologers who had used magnets to cure people.'[14] Mesmer believed in a form of mystical pantheism, where what he termed a 'Magnetic Fluid' that permeated the universe was equivalent to the Japanese Buddhist *Ki* or *Chi*, the transcendental magician's Grand Elixir, the spiritualist's *Elan Vital*, the occultist's *Philosopher's Stone*, or the Hindu's *Prana*. This thinker's work was used as a foundation stone for hypnotism[15] and the word *mesmerize* comes from his name.

This idea was later picked up by one Sigmund Freud (1856-1939) who for some four and a half months studied at the Salpetriere in Paris, where Jean-Martin Charcot (1825-1893) was reviving interest in hypnosis, but from a materialistic perspective. In his autobiography Freud wrote, 'I received the most profound impression of the possibility that there could be powerful mental processes which nevertheless remained hidden from the consciousness of men.'[16] He was also far more interested in the occult than is generally realized, declaring, 'Behind all so-called occult phenomena lies something new and important: the fact of thought transference, i.e., the transferring of psychological processes through space to other people.'[17] Freud, one of the fathers of modern psychology and psychotherapy, had two favourite students who carried on and developed his work: Wilhelm Reich (1897-1957) and Carl Gustav Jung (1875-1961).

Welhelm Reich was responsible for the concept of 'bioenergy' which he believed permeates all matter.[18] His basic theory was that psychological problems are fundamentally caused by sexual repression. He believed that the Lord Jesus Christ was murdered because the sexually maladjusted world could not cope with his dynamically healthy sexual energy.[19] From his work developed Orgone Therapy and Bioenergetics. Bioenergetics is very similar to Tantric Yoga, where specialized sexual experience is meant to lead to Cosmic Consciousness, *ananda*. In other words, sexuality is seen as a spiritual ritual to connect into the spiritual world.[20]

The other key student of Freud, Carl Gustav Jung, developed theories that have been taken by many churches to provide the impetus to what is commonly called 'Inner Healing' and 'Healing of the Memories', with their visualized images of Jesus.[21] Jung attempted to produce an apparent synthesis between psychological investigations and 'spirituality.' He developed a very complex view of human personality, delving into the apparent depth of the unconscious. He postulated that far down within man's inner life there was something he called the *collective unconscious*, which contains the memories of a whole race of people. He argued that within the collective unconscious there are hidden primordial images, or *archetypes*. These often take human form, could be contacted and could counsel their human hosts as inner guides. Jung himself developed a relationship with a spirit guide, a disincarnate entity called 'Philemon'.

Jung was plagued with dreams and visions which caused a continuous nightmare for his family. It is reported that on one occasion the doorbell of his house started ringing by itself and continued without stopping. One biographer writes: 'The whole family looked uneasily at one another and Jung knew that "something had to happen". It was, he wrote, as if "a crowd were present", and the whole house "crammed full of spirits."'[22] Jung interpreted this event later as being part of a collective mental breakdown, or an encounter with the archaic materials of the collective unconsciousness. Christians may well come to a different conclusion.

With this background to much of modern psychotherapy and various schools of counselling, it is perhaps surprising that many who claim to be Christians have adopted and adapted it. But this is certainly the case.[23] Morton Kelsey, is a case in point here. In his book *Encounter with God* he 'evaluates the work of Carl Jung in some detail, demonstrating a great deal of compatibility between the thinking of the Swiss professor and some aspects of traditional Christianity.'[24] A whole raft of popular books and so-called Christian counselling strategies have been overly influenced by the works of Mesmer, Freud, Reich and Jung.

The point is not that non-Christians should not be listened to. Although the Bible is completely true, it does not contain all truth.[25] In a whole range of academic disciplines, through the work of common grace and an intelligent look at general revelation in creation, people have discovered the most amazing things about our universe and ourselves. However, for the Christian, the Bible contains controlling truth. The point is that we should always filter ideas biblically in order to ascertain whether they should be accepted, rejected or modified. The Bible should act like a firewall, protecting us from dangerous ideas and practices. What has happened with some areas of 'Christian' counselling is that the spiritual and intellectual firewall of the Bible has turned off. It is not therefore surprising that demonic hacking is infiltrating the church.

Diminishing the Bible — mystical knowledge

One contemporary introduction to the occult opens with the words, 'Knowledge is power.'[26] From the very beginning Satan attempted to reveal information to people that they should not hear.[27] The heart of the Satanic lie to humanity is the offer of knowledge that is illicit. Much of pagan religion is concerned with the revelation of secret, hidden spiritual knowledge. Through and ecstatic state of mind, ritual, trance, drugs or some other means, practitioners claim to disclose esoteric knowledge. Classically this was the work of shamans, sorcerers, seers, spiritists and mediums; today it is sometimes the work of so-called Christian pastors and teachers. In some churches, members of the congregation are encouraged to exercise 'words of wisdom', see pictures in their minds, prophecy and dream dreams that closer to paganism than biblical Christianity.

Sometimes even in churches that claim an allegiance to the Bible, the Bible is hardly opened. Instead of looking to God's Word for instruction, inspiration and guidance, people share 'pictures' they claim God has given them. Words of knowledge supplant the Word of God. As these esoteric forms of spiritual enlightenment increasingly outbalance Bible study the content of the communication will tend to deviate further and further from sound doctrine. Error will be inevitable.

Infiltration

Satan always attempts to foist his lies on the human race. Even in the church he continues his programme of illicit infiltration. Just because we claim to follow Jesus Christ, or claim allegiance to the Bible does not put us beyond the range of his attack. 'Our struggle is not against flesh and blood, but against the rulers, against the authorities, against the powers of this dark world and against the spiritual forces of evil in the heavenly realms.'[28]

Questions for discussion

Read 1 John 2:18-28 and 1 John 4:1-5.

1. There have always been many antichrists (2:18), how do you think we can recognize them in our generation? Does this passage give us any practical tests? Does chapter 4:1-5 add anything to these tests?

2. Chapter 2 verse 20 gives us two spiritual anchors. What are they? How are they developed in the passage? How can they help us in practice?

Introduction to Section 3

As we have tracked the re-emergence of paganism in its various forms over the previous chapters, we have given an ongoing critique from a biblical perspective. We now turn to focus on the case for Christianity in the light of the current developing neo-paganism. Here the arguments will be set out as to why biblical Christianity is true and paganism, in all its manifestations, is false.

In the following pages we will set out on the most exciting journey that is possible for a human being to make. We will explore how God has revealed himself to us; we will search out the foundations of Bible-believing Christianity. In doing this we will uncover why this is true and the 'new' spirituality of neo-paganism and the current mysticism is false. Because much of the Bible was originally set in a context where paganism was the main challenge, we will find there is plenty of material to gather as weaponry. We will be well armed.

Chapter 11
The God Who Made Heaven and Earth

'In the beginning God created the heavens and the earth.'
Genesis 1:1 puts it in these words: 'In the beginning God
created the heavens and the earth.'
Genesis 1:1

'The heavens declare the glory of God;
the skies proclaim the work of his hands.
Day after day they pour forth speech;
night after night they display knowledge.'
Psalm 19:1-2

'We are bringing you good news, telling you to turn from
these worthless things to living God, who made heaven
and earth and sea and everything in them. In the past, he
let all nations go there own way. Yet he has not left himself
without testimony: He has shown kindness by giving you
rain from heaven and crops in their seasons; he provides
you with plenty of food and fills your hearts with joy. Even
with these words, they had difficulty keeping the crowd
from sacrificing to them.'
Acts 14:15-18

'The God who made the world and everything in it is the
Lord of heaven and earth and does not live in temples built
by hands. And he is not served by human hands, as if he
needed anything, because he himself gives all men life and
breath and everything else. From one man he made every

nation of men, that they should inhabit the whole earth; and he determined the times set for them and the exact places where they should live. God did this so that men would seek him and perhaps reach out for him and find him, though he is not far from each of us.'
                                Acts 17:24-28

'The wrath of God is being revealed from heaven against all the godlessness and wickedness of men who suppress the truth by their wickedness, since what may be made known to them about God is plain to them, because God has made it plain to them. For since the creation of the world God's invisible qualities — his eternal power and divine nature — have been clearly seen, being understood from what has been made, so that men are without excuse.

For although they knew God, they neither glorified him as God nor gave thanks to him, but their thinking became futile and their foolish hearts were darkened. Although they claimed to be wise, they became fools and exchanged the glory of the immortal God for images made to look like mortal man and birds and animals and reptiles ... they exchanged the truth of God for a lie, and worshipped and served created things rather than the creator — who is forever praised. Amen.
                                Romans 1:18-25

One of the main arguments the Bible gives against paganism is from creation, which is deeply ironic when much of paganism actually worships creation. Human beings have always tended to worship what is made rather than the maker that stands behind it all.[1] For the Christian, creation is not part of 'the divine', but gives evidence, not of an impersonal life-force, nor of a host of spiritual beings, but of the Lord God Almighty, maker of heaven and earth.[2]

The Bible answers paganism by appealing to 'the God who made heaven and earth,'[3] who gives us life,[4] sustains our existence[5] and is sovereign over even the practical details of our lives.[6]

It is interesting and significant that at the time of the early spread of Christianity recorded in the New Testament, one of the main arguments used against paganism was the need and reality of an independent creator-God. This is recorded in Acts 14:15: 'We are bringing you good news, telling you to turn from these worthless things to living God, who made heaven and earth and sea and everything in them.' The man who said this, the apostle Paul, used the same approach when he was debating with the Greek philosophers in Athens in Acts 17:24-28: 'The God who made the world and everything in it is the Lord of heaven and earth and does not live in temples built by hands. And he is not served by human hands, as if he needed anything, because he himself gives all men life and breath and everything else. From one man he made every nation of men, that they should inhabit the whole earth; and he determined the times set for them and the exact places where they should live. God did this so that men would seek him and perhaps reach out for him and find him, though he is not far from each of us.'

The key question for us today is why does the Bible points us to creation as a key argument against paganism? What is so important about this approach that it is one of the most common biblical responses to a belief in the gods? Perhaps the answer is that pagan, neo-pagan, or New Age followers feel that the cosmos is caused by gods or forces, who although powerful, are not absolutely powerful — they are dependent beings, and as such still need an explanation themselves. A belief in spiritual forces and gods raises more questions than it answers. Such energies or beings simply do not explain the universe as we find it. They themselves would need an explanation.

The universe demands an ultimate explanation

For those who feel that 'God' is the force behind and within nature in all its manifestations, then a real problem arises. Those who take this perspective feel that there is no real distinction between nature and 'God', for the force not only infuses nature, but is one with nature.[7] The problem here is that if the 'god-force' is indistinct from nature, then 'it' or 'he' or 'she', depending on the particular perspective, is by definition dependent. This understanding has a dependent force within the cosmos — and such a force needs an independent cause. And for those pagans who emphasise spiritual beings and 'gods', then the problem is just as intense. The question naturally arises, who made those gods? They can't have made themselves. There has to be an ultimate being behind everything.

Whichever way we look at the pagan model or theory, it does not fit with a universe that is dependent. The biblical perspective is consistent with the data: a creator God who is independent and non-contingent explains the universe as we experience it: 'In the beginning God created the heavens and the earth.'[8]

What we see all around is what scientists call 'cause and effect'. Something acts on something else to produce a *result* or *effect*. Whatever we look at had something causing it, which in turn had something causing it, and that in turn had something causing it. And like a tumbling line of dominoes, the chain reaction can't be infinite.

Everything is *dependent* on something else; nothing acts by itself. Nothing is autonomous. Some scientists and philosophers use a special word for this — that word is *contingent*. In a former generation, if a young woman was asked out for a walk in the park, she might well have said something like, 'I would be pleased to go, *contingent* upon on the weather.' In today's speech, what she meant was, 'I will go, *dependent* upon the weather.' Contingent means dependent.

We live in a world where nothing happens by itself; things only occur because something else causes them to occur. Nothing is truly autonomous; everything in our universe is contingent; everything is dependent; everything is bound up in a relationship of cause and effect. The natural question that arises out of this is what caused the whole process? What started it all off? You can't have contingencies going back forever; you can't have an endless chain of causes. There has to be a First Cause. There has to be something (or perhaps someone) that started it all off.

The universe as we experience it is made of dependent stuff. This means that any hunk of it that we bump up against is unable to explain itself — we must appeal beyond it to something else to explain it. No single element of our world is self-explanatory. This is true of every part of our universe, but also, if you take the universe as a whole, the whole thing is contingent. Everything in our universe is contingent, or dependent — and therefore the whole universe must be contingent. If you have a whole load of contingencies and put them together, you don't suddenly get an explanation, you get a lot of contingency. A universe full of contingent stuff is a contingent universe. If all the parts are dependent, then the totality must be dependent. But what is it all dependent on?

Some people have suggested that an all-powerful absolute creator is not needed, all that is required is something more powerful that anything in our purely material cosmos. They say that such a force or being could have set the ball rolling, so to speak. But, of course this can't be true, for by definition what is needed is something independent or non-contingent — that is, Absolute. If the something that made our universe was immensely powerful, but still dependent, or contingent, then we would have to ask, well, what caused that? In other words, it would not solve the problem of a dependent universe. The only way a contingent universe could come into being is by something non-contingent, or Absolute. Anything just a bit more powerful, be it force or being, would not fit the bill. This theory is not consistent with the evidence.

Therefore, no one can simply point to some pagan god for an explanation, for they are seen as dependent beings themselves. They are dependent on some higher being yet still, or are a product of the life force, or *prana,* or impersonal energy that everything consists of. But as that is conceived of as part of our dependent reality, it still needs an independent cause.

Logically, the universe must be dependent on something non-dependent. By definition the cause must be non-contingent — something outside of our contingent and dependent universe must have caused it. This perspective is utterly consistent with what the Bible interestingly opens with, and then teaches throughout. Genesis 1:1 puts it in these words: 'In the beginning God created the heavens and the earth.' This necessity of an independent reality is consistent with the God described in the Bible.

Sometimes people respond to this by asking the question, 'Well then, if that is true, who made God?' And the answer is of course that nothing made God, because God by definition is independent or non-contingent. The whole argument for his existence here is based on the need for something Autonomous or Absolute — something that everything else is dependent upon — something of a different order of reality — something independent. If the whole argument is based on the need for something or someone unmade, then it requires a perverse misunderstanding of the argument to ask the question of who made the maker. The very point that indicates his existence is the need for something unmade, or non-contingent, or independent — or eternal.

What the Bible gives us is a model or theory as to how to view the universe: the universe is dependent on what it calls God, who is independent of it. All the evidence that we have been looking at is consistent with this perspective. That is not the same as saying that this evidence proves the existence of God — that would be stretching the data too far, making it prove more than it is able to bare. But it is quite fair to say that a belief in an ultimate Almighty God is consistent with this data.[9]

Design necessitates an ultimate designer

King David said of the Lord, 'I praise you because I am fearfully and wonderfully made; your works are wonderful, I know that full well.'[10] The beauty and complexity of his body made David cry out in adoration. The design in the life we see around us causes many to believe in a creator God and to worship him. It is no good appealing to some finite pagan god to explain this, for then their own complexity and design needs to be accounted for as well. We just cannot keep going back in an infinite regress to higher and higher, and increasingly complex, spiritual beings. And even worse, it is absurd to try to cut off the infinite regress by suddenly saying that it is all caused by some impersonal mindless cosmic energy or force.

The life-forms of planet earth certainly appear to be designed — after all, could raw, blind and random chance throw up something so intricate and beautiful? The language of DNA, when spoken by the nucleus of cells, makes molecules called amino acids.

These basic building blocks of life, when arranged specifically and precisely are built into bigger molecules called proteins. Proteins make life happen. Life is ultimately a molecular phenomenon. All organisms are made of molecules that act as the nuts and bolts, gears and pulleys of biological systems. The processes, interactions, control systems of this minuscule world is staggeringly complex, all the way from the tiniest bacterium through to the cells making up the reader and writer of this page. But how can we explain this Lilliputian world that allows, controls and causes all our movements and interactions? Michael Behe, Professor of Biochemistry at Lehigh University writes: 'Vision, motion, and other biological functions have proven to be no less sophisticated than television cameras and automobiles. Science has made enormous progress in understanding how the chemistry of life works, but the elegancy and complexity of biological systems at the molecular level have paralysed science's attempt to account for the origin of specific, complex biomolecular systems.'[11]

The way things are

Christianity can account for the way things are; it can give an adequate explanation for the world as we experience it. A pagan perception of the universe cannot deal with two key facts. First, everything we know of is dependent and therefore necessitates an ultimate non-contingent cause, which is beyond and separate from this existence. Neither an impersonal pantheistic life-force that is one with the universe, nor an ascending series of spiritual beings, can give an adequate explanation. Second, the complexity and design we see around us cannot come into being from either impersonal energy that pervades the cosmos, nor from a series of increasingly powerful and complex spiritual beings. Again, these do not provide an adequate explanation for what we see around us. These rationalizations are more to do with imagination than explanation: 'Men become superstitious not because they have too much imagination, but because they are not aware that they have any.'[12]

Questions for discussion

1. How does Genesis 1:1 teach us God is independent, or non-contingent?

Read Romans 1:18-32.

2. Follow the reasoning here from thinking to religion to morality to God's judgement. In the light of this, should good thinking strengthen or weaken true faith?

3. Where does good thinking come from in this passage?

4. In what ways do you think 'what may be known about God is plain?' (19) What do you think is meant by 'God's invisible qualities — his eternal power and divine nature?' (20)

5. If 'what may be known about God is plain', why is it that so many disbelieve?

6. Why are unbelievers 'without excuse?' (20)

7. Why do you think the very thing that reveals God ('from what has been made', 20) actually ends up obscuring God? ('They exchanged the truth of God for a lie, and worshipped and served created things rather than the creator' 25)

Read Psalm 19:1-6

8. Note the words, 'declare', 'proclaim', 'speech', 'knowledge', 'heard' and 'voice' in verses 1-4. What is communicated to humanity by the heavens? What is the content of this 'speech'?

9. Paganism often attaches divinity to various bodies in the heavens. What does this passage infer about such a belief? See also, Psalm 148:1-6; Deuteronomy 4:19; 17:3.

10. Can these bodies control or disclose our destiny in any way as astrology believes? See also, Isaiah 47:13; Jeremiah 10:2; Daniel 4:7.

11. In what way does the apostle Paul use verse 4 in Romans 10:8?

Chapter 12
God Has Spoken

To the Law and to the Testimony

'When men tell you to consult mediums and spiritists, who whisper and mutter, should not a people enquire of their God? Why consult the dead on behalf of the living? To the law and to the testimony! If they do not speak according to this word, they have no light of dawn. Distressed and hungry, they will roam through the land; when they are famished, they will become enraged and, looking upward, will curse their king and their God. Then they will look towards the earth and see only distress and darkness and fearful gloom, and they will be thrust into utter darkness.'
Isaiah 8:19-22

Why do I believe what I believe? The essential question with regard to religious belief and practice is the question of authority. What basis do I have for believing such and such? Why do I hold this view? Why do I insist on behaving in that manner? Why do I believe that is wrong and this is right? Where do my beliefs come from? What are they based on? With what authority do I hold that they are true? The authority for true Christians is the Bible; the Bible is the basis for all belief and conduct. Christians believe that God has spoken through the Bible.

But the question that naturally arises for any thinking person is why should I believe the Bible? Is this a reasonable thing to do, or is it the result of blind faith? Is dependence on the Bible really only the result of inner cravings that cry out certainty in an uncertain world? Is it merely the desire to have things in black and white when everything appears to be shades of confusing grey? Is the Bible true? Is it accurate? Has God really spoken through it? Is it trustworthy? After all, it is no good trusting the Bible if the Bible is not trustworthy.

Dangerous delusions

Of all the various forms of delusion in this world, religious delusion is the worst for its consequences go way beyond this life. The key question is how do we know what is a delusion and what is truth? How can we know that the Bible is the Scripture that is from God and all other religious Scriptures are delusions?

The world is stuffed full of religious Scriptures of various sorts, all claiming to offer spiritual wisdom. Hinduism has its Bhaga-vad-gita, Zoroastrianism, its Zend Avesta, Shintoism, its Kojiki and Nihongi, Buddhism, its Tripitaka, Taoism, its Tao Te Ching, Confucianism has its Analects, Islam, its Holy Qur'an, Sikhism, its Adi Granth and mystical Judaism, its Kabbalah. And then there are the more recent Book of Mormon and various pagan writings, like those of the Theosophists and Madam Blavatsky in particular. The list is almost endless. When looking out at this sea of religious Scriptures, why should we accept the Bible, and only the Bible? There can be no more important question.

And more than all this, the claim for supernatural religious rev-elation goes way beyond the claims for certain written Scriptures. Many pagan faiths depend on 'immediate' spiritual enlightenment that bypasses what they might think of as spiritually sterile scrip-tures. A direct encounter, an esoteric enlightenment, is what they claim for religious revelation and enlightenment. This is the way of the mystic and the shaman, common in most pagan faiths. The key question remains the same: Why should we turn to the Bible rather than hunt after these sorts of experiences?

Has God spoken? Has God spoken clearly? Can we know that God has spoken? Is the Bible God's message to humanity? It is vital to be able to determine whether the Bible is the Word of God and whether our trust, faith and obedience are justified.

Out of the ordinary

The first thing to consider when exploring this question is what we would expect if some document were God's revelation to humanity. Surely, it would be something out of the ordinary; there would be something very special about it; it would be unique. What follows here, initially, is not some proof that the Bible is the Word of God, but a demonstration that it is something that needs to be taken seriously. Historically, the Bible is an incredibly powerful and influential document. At the most basic level, this is the minimum we would expect for something purporting to be God's communication to the human race. Such a document should certainly be out of the ordinary, indeed, it should be unique.

A uniquely published book

The facts speak for themselves: 'The Bible has been read by more people and published in more languages than any other publication. More copies have been produced of the whole Bible and more extracts and selections than of any other book. There have been more copies produced of its entirety and more portions and selections than any other book in history. Some will argue that in a designated month or year more of a certain book was sold. However, over all there is absolutely no book that reaches or even begins to compare to the circulation of the Scriptures.'[1] The Bible, or portions of it, is currently available in over 2,500 languages and dialects.[2] This provides for well over 90% of the world's population. All this does not prove that the Bible is God's Word, but it is the sort of thing we would expect from such a document.

Cultural dynamite

The most basic facts about the Bible should make us think twice before rejecting it out of hand. For example, many of the phrases, which we use every day, can be traced directly to the old English, King James version of the Bible. For example, 'the skin of my teeth', 'to go from strength to strength' and 'pride comes before a fall' are all direct quotations. Other common phrases can be traced back to the Bible such as 'turn the other cheek' and 'blind leading the blind'. More than this, any of the Bible characters have become part of daily conversation, including 'The patience of Job', 'The wisdom of Solomon' and referring to someone as 'A Judas', meaning that they betray a friend.

Again, we are not here proving the Bible to be the Word of God; we are simply making two important points: first, a document this amazing should be given serious consideration; second, the Bible's has had an effect on society consistent with what we would expect from such a revelation.

Throughout history, it can be seen that this book has had an amazing effect on human life, culture and society. Alister McGrath, Professor of Historical Christianity at Oxford University says, 'The King James Bible was a landmark in the history of the English language, and an inspiration to poets, dramatists, artists and politicians. Without the King James Bible there would have been no *Paradise Lost*, no *Pilgrim's Progress*, no Handel's *Messiah*, no Negro spirituals, no Gettysburg Address. The culture of the English speaking world would have been immeasurably impoverished.'[3] It is impossible to understand English language, culture and society without some knowledge of the Bible.

Not only have those who believe it to be the actual Word of God been deeply moved by its pages, but many others have as well, who have held a variety of beliefs.[4] Napoleon stated, 'The Bible is no mere book, but it's a living creature with a power that conquers all who oppose it.' Charles Dickens wrote, 'The New Testament is the very best book that ever was or ever will be known in the world.' And the famous Victorian writer John Ruskin said, 'Whatever merit there is in anything I have written is simply due to the fact that when I was a child my mother daily read to me a part of the Bible and daily made me learn part of it by heart.' George Washington commented on the Bible: 'It is impossible to rightly govern the world without God and the Bible.' And Abraham Lincoln said, 'I believe the Bible is the best gift God has ever given to man.' On the other side of the Atlantic, W. E. Gladstone, one-time Prime Minister of Great Britain said, 'I have known 95 of the world's great men in my time and of these 87 were followers of the Bible.' The philosopher Immanuel Kant stated that, 'The existence of the Bible, as a book for the people, is the greatest benefit which the human race has ever experienced.' And the famous physicist, Sir Isaac Newton, believed 'There are more sure marks of authenticity in the Bible than in any profane history.' Even those who reject much of its content can't help themselves in recognising its value. Thomas Huxley, the argent evolutionist, stated, 'The Bible has been the Magna Charta of the poor and the oppressed. The human race is not in a position to dispense with it.' None of this forces us to accept the Bible to be the Word of God, but it simply makes it abundantly clear that this is a unique book that has had the most incredible influence on many of the 'movers and shakers' of history. Although all this does not prove the Bible to be God's revelation to us, it is certainly the type of thing we would expect from a book that is God's revelation to us. No one can ignore looking at the claims of the Bible seriously without undermining their intellectual integrity. Something that has influenced so many great leaders and thinkers surely demands our serious attention. This is the most amazing book of human history — it is truly amazing; it is unique — and that's exactly what we would expect from something that is the Word of God.

A unique effect on individuals

Again and again throughout the generations, readers have found that through reading the Bible's pages they have had the profound sense that something strangely supernatural was going on — the God behind the universe was communicating with them. This effect has been so amazing that some of these people have turned the world upside down. The Bible has an inherent power of its own, which people experience. When people read it, many testify to hearing God speak through its pages, having their lives revolutionized and discovering new meaning, peace and purpose to their existence.

The original disciples were utterly transformed by their belief in the resurrection of Jesus Christ. They were transformed from normal folk like mere artisans and tradesmen in an obscure corner of the Roman Empire into a body of people who totally revolutionized the world. These men, who claimed to have seen the risen

Christ, suffered for their beliefs — and some died for them. From the courage, devotion and energy of these people, a whole culture was overthrown and the world's largest religion was established. And this power of the risen Jesus to change lives was passed on — throughout the last 2,000 years, millions of people have had their lives revolutionized. They have fed the poor, cared for the sick, established schools, fought for justice and been the greatest force for good this world has ever seen.

This is very important, for if people feel that they 'hear' God speak to them then it is reasonable to test that claim by the difference it makes to their lives and those around them. With people claiming to hear God speak through the Bible, the claim is certainly given credence by the radical effect it has had on them and society in general.

A unique effect on society

This unique book has shaped much of our society's landscape for good. Those whose minds were inflamed by the Bible changed society — they fought against the slave trade, set up hospitals, founded schools, established orphanages and worked for religious liberty. Without the Bible, this world would be a poorer and more tragic place.

When the Bible was clearly preached in the eighteenth century in what has become known as 'the evangelical awakening' the effects on society were truly amazing. Those who turned to the teaching of the Bible campaigned successfully against the ravages of the salve trade, reformed conditions in the prisons, fought drunkenness that left thousands of families starving and inspired the founding of many hospitals and schools. More than this, they also campaigned until the cruel 'sports' of bull and bear bating were made illegal, sought for restrictions on pornographic literature and called for smallpox vaccinations for the people of London. It was people of biblical faith that were inspired to understand the dignity of work and the decency of a fair wage, as well as the right to express their views freely.[5]

It was due to the teaching of the Bible that many sought to set up schools. In the UK, twenty years before state education began in 1870, almost all schools were set up and run by chapels, churches and Christian charities. In 1780, Robert Raikes started a Sunday School, and by 1903 six million children across the country attended these places. For many it was the only education they received.

William and Catherine Booth, because of their biblical views, founded the Salvation Army, which became a major force for social welfare. As they shared the Christian message they provided clothing, food, shelter and employment training. Alongside this, many chapels and churches started soup kitchens and distributed to young mothers what became known as 'maternity parcels'.

Those who claimed some kind of allegiance to the Bible also initially provided the care of the sick and dying. For example, St Bartholomew's and Guys hospitals in London were both set up by Christians. It was values in inspired by the Bible that caused Christians to set up medical missions to provide free health care and medicine for the poor. Nearly three-quarters of all charity organizations in the late nineteenth century were run by Bible-believing Christians. The hospice movement began largely through the influence of Christians as was ACET (Aids Care Education and Training), an organization that cares for almost one in every ten of the people dying with AIDS.

In terms of justice, the Bible emphasizes the idea that everyone is subject to the law, even the national leaders, whether they by kings or Prime Ministers or Presidents. Enshrined here is the principle that no one is above the law. Lord Denning, the leading civil lawyer in England and Wales during the 1960s and 1970s, claimed that judges brought up in the Christian faith had moulded British common law. He concluded, 'If religion perishes in the land, truth and justice will also.'[6]

In the light of all this it is not surprising that during the British Coronation ceremony a Bible is presented to the monarch with the words: 'We present you with this book, the most valuable thing this world affords. Here is wisdom. This is the Royal Law. These are the lively oracles of God.'[7] In a message to the seventy-fifth anniversary celebration of the Bible Reading Fellowship, in January 1997, Her Majesty Queen Elizabeth the Queen Mother wrote, 'Many of the evils which beset us today would be avoided by strict adherence to the precepts of the Ten Commandments. In the New Testament can be found the words of Christ which contain the essential teaching for leading a spiritual life.'[8]

The Bible is not some ancient esoteric document that produces people who are 'so spiritually minded that they are of no earthly good'. The spirituality inspired by the Bible has had a unique beneficial effect on society. The record speaks for itself: the Bible is a power for good. This is exactly what we would expect if it is a message from the creator of the universe.

A uniquely persecuted book

It is remarkable in the extreme that history shows us that even though the Bible has produced such immense good for society, it is also the most persecuted book in history. People have always tried to ban and burn it. This is deeply ironic when the Bible actually produces exceptional citizens.

In A.D. 303 the Emperor Diocletian issued an edict to stop Christians from worshipping and to destroy their Scriptures. Twenty-five years later, Constantine, who succeeded Diocletian, ordered copies of the Scriptures to be prepared at the government's expense.

In 1526 copies of the Bible were smuggled into England and the cost of each copy on the black market was about equal to one week's wages for a farm worker. Around the year 1529, King Henry VIII had four secret agents hunting for a man he wanted to burn at the stake. The man's name was William Tyndale and his 'crime' was simply that he had translated the New Testament into an easy-to-read English. In the end he was caught and executed.

For despots and dictators of various hues, this book teaches people to think for themselves and lessens their control on the hearts and minds of the populations they enslave. Many Catholic, communist and fascist countries have banned and burned the Bible, Islamic states have worked against its distribution and others have seen fit to suppress it. It has been seen as one of the most dangerous pieces of literature this world has ever seen. This is why political leaders have used secret police, customs officers, soldiers, secret servicemen, legislation, threats, imprisonment and murder to suppress its distribution. On a more intellectual level, the Bible has received a sustained academic attack for well over two hundred years. Liberal scholarship has tried to criticize and mock the Bible into oblivion — but it has always failed. The writer Bernard Ramm has written, 'A thousand times over the death knell of the Bible has been sounded, the funeral procession formed, the inscription cut on the tombstone, and committal read. But somehow the corpse never stays put.'[9] The French philosopher Voltaire announced that in one hundred years from his time, Christianity would be swept from existence. Ironically, only fifty years after Voltaire's death, the Geneva Bible Society used his press and house to produce crate-fuls of Bibles.

The Bible is remarkable in its persecution and survival through time. Again, when this is considered in the light the claim of it being God's revelation to humanity, this sort of persecution and endurance is exactly what we would expect. From the original fall of mankind in the Garden of Eden, we read that Satan challenged God's Word[10] and that history would be one of warfare between this evil spiritual being and the rest of humanity.[11] Indeed, paganism always thrives when the Word of God is rejected.[12]

A unique historical validation

The Bible is utterly unique amongst the ancient documents of the world in that again and again it has been found to by archaeologically and historically accurate. In this it stands in stark contrast with various pagan writings. Indeed, much writing that is pagan in origin sets little importance upon historical veracity. Instead, it is often the case that the documents were inspired by some form of enlightenment or inspiration that is beyond verification; the revelation is by definition often mystical and mysterious. This hidden knowledge is only given to initiates, and its source is often actively hidden from 'outsiders'. Occult knowledge is for those 'who feel there is a group of initiates who have access to hidden truth' and who regard it 'as the means of attaining forms of knowledge not available in other ways'.[13] In direct contrast to this, biblical revelation can be checked to see whether it is historically and archaeologically accurate; if it is not true in these regards, it is not true in terms of what it reveals. The Bible invites us to check out the accuracy of its claims.[14] Everyone, not just special initiates, can look at the evidence for themselves and are free to read the revelation.

Although it has faced continual challenges, the Bible has always shown itself to totally correct. Nelson Glueck, a renowned Jewish Archaeologist, wrote, 'It may be stated categorically that no archaeological discovery has ever controverted a biblical reference.'[15] Sir William Mitchell Ramsay, D.C.L., Litt D., D.D., onetime Professor of Classical Art and Architecture at Oxford University, and later Regius Professor of Humanity at Aberdeen said regarding Luke, one of the writers of the New Testament: 'Luke is an historian of the first rank; not merely are his statements trustworthy ... this author should be placed along with the very greatest of historians ... Luke's history is unsurpassed in respect of its trustworthiness.'[16] And Sir Fredrick Kenyon, former director of the British Museum, and one of the greatest experts of ancient documents said, 'The last foundations for any doubt that the Scriptures come down to us substantially as they were written has now been removed. Both the authenticity and the general integrity of the books of the New Testament may be regarded as finally established.'[17]

With other ancient works we have very few manuscripts to work with. For example, we have 643 copies of Homer's *Iliad*, only nine or ten copies of Caesar's famous *Gallic War* (58-50 B.C.), twenty copies of Livy's *Roman History* (59 B.C.-A.D. 17), seven copies of the *Histories of Pliny the Younger* (c. A.D. 61-113) and merely two copies of Histories and Annals by Tacitus (c. A.D. 55-120). In contrast to this we have well over 5,000 manuscripts of the New Testament in its original Greek.

Equally significant is the point that with other ancient documents we only have manuscripts copied a long time after the originals were written For example, only one copy of Livy's *Roman History* was written closer than 400 to the original. And then for Caesar's Gallic Wars we have copies written no closer than 1,000 years after then evens it describes. In stark contrast to this the major manuscripts of the Bible were copied only 300 years after the original events, and some fragments are far closer than that. The famous John Ryland's Fragment is thought to date from A.D. 117-

138 and three fragments of papyrus in Magdalene College, Oxford, are dated to within living memory from the original events. No other document of history has such strong validation.

F. F. Bruce, onetime Professor at Manchester University wrote, 'There is no body of ancient literature in the world which enjoys such a wealth of good textual attestation as the New Testament.'[18] If we reject the Bible on historical grounds, then to be consistent we must reject much history that we learn at school and never doubt. To put it bluntly the Bible is the most attested and substantiated ancient document. Or, to put it another way, in the history of the world, it is unique, which is just what we would expect if God was speaking through it.

A unique ability to see into the future

One of the most remarkable credentials of the Bible is that can be shown again and again to have accurately predicted the future. Only God knows what will happen in the future and if this is predicted accurately and precisely then it generally shows that the message comes from him.

This accurate prediction is actually a test the Bible itself gives for discovering whether God is speaking, or a fraudster. The Old Testament puts it in this way: 'You may say to yourselves, "How can we know when a message has not been spoken by the Lord?" If what a prophet proclaims in the name of the Lord does not take place or come true, that is a message the Lord has not spoken.'[19]

Paganism is full of prophecies and predictions all the way from the diviners of ancient civilizations, through people like Nostradamus,[20] to the current fascination with astrology. The Bible is unique, however, in its precise predictions and exact fulfilments. These are not hidden away in some occult fashion, but are there for all to examine. Due to the limitations of space, only one prophecy and fulfilment can be considered here.

One of the most remarkable prophecies in the Bible is that concerning the ancient city of Tyre. Between 592 and 570 B.C. the prophet Ezekiel wrote in chapter 26 of his prophecy:

A prophecy against Tyre

[1] In the eleventh year, on the first day of the month, the word of the LORD came to me: [2] Son of man, because Tyre has said of Jerusalem, 'Aha! The gate to the nations is broken, and its doors have swung open to me; now that she lies in ruins I will prosper', [3] therefore this is what the Sovereign LORD says: I am against you, O Tyre, and I will bring many nations against you, like the sea casting up its waves. [4] They will destroy the walls of Tyre and pull down her towers; I will scrape away her rubble and make her a bare rock. [5] Out in the sea she will become a place to spread fishnets, for I have spoken, declares the Sovereign LORD. She will become plunder for the nations, [6] and her settlements on the mainland will be ravaged by the sword. Then they will know that I am the LORD.

[7] For this is what the Sovereign LORD says: From the north I am going to bring against Tyre Nebuchadnezzar king of Babylon, king of kings, with horses and chariots, with horsemen and a great army. [8] He will ravage your settlements on the mainland with the sword; he will set up siege works against you, build a ramp up to your walls and raise his shields against you. [9] He will direct the blows of his battering rams against your walls and demolish your towers with his weapons. [10] His horses will be so many that they will cover you with dust. Your walls will tremble at the noise of the war horses, wagons and chariots when he enters your gates as men enter a city whose walls have been broken through. [11] The hoofs of his horses will trample all your streets; he will kill your people with the sword, and your strong pillars will fall to the ground. [12] They will plunder your wealth and loot your merchandise; they will break down your walls and demolish your fine houses and throw your stones, timber and rubble into the sea. [13] I will put an end to your noisy songs, and the music of your harps will be heard no more. [14] I will make you a bare rock, and you will become a place to spread fishnets. You will never be rebuilt, for I the LORD have spoken, declares the Sovereign LORD.

[15] This is what the Sovereign LORD says to Tyre: Will not the coastlands tremble at the sound of your fall, when

the wounded groan and the slaughter takes place in you?
[16] Then all the princes of the coast will step down from their thrones and lay aside their robes and take off their embroidered garments. Clothed with terror, they will sit on the ground, trembling every moment, appalled at you. [17] Then they will take up a lament concerning you and say to you: 'How you are destroyed, O city of renown, people by men of the sea! You were a power on the seas, you and your citizens; you put your terror on all who lived there. [18] Now the coastlands tremble on the day of your fall; the islands in the sea are terrified at your collapse.

[19] This is what the Sovereign LORD says: When I make you a desolate city, like cities no longer inhabited, and when I bring the ocean depths over you and its vast waters cover you, [20] then I will bring you down with those who go down to the pit, to the people of long ago. I will make you dwell in the earth below, as in ancient ruins, with those who go down to the pit, and you will not return or take your place in the land of the living. [21] I will bring you to a horrible end and you will be no more. You will be sought, but you will never again be found, declares the Sovereign LORD.

The basic elements of the prophecy here are, Nebuchadnezzar will destroy the mainland city of Tyre (v.8), many nations will come against her (v.3), she will be made into a bare rock (v.4) and fishermen will spread there nets over the site (v.5). Furthermore, the debris of the old city will be thrown into the sea (v.12), never to be built again (v.21).

The fulfilment is staggering in its precision. In 585-573 B.C. the 'city of Tyre withstood a prolonged siege by the Babylonian king Nebuchadnezzar II'[21] and then made terms of peace and acknowledges Babylonian suzerainty. When he broke the gates down he found the city almost deserted as the majority of the people had fled to an island about half a mile off the coast and fortified a city there. The mainland city was destroyed (first prediction).

From 538 it was ruled by Persia until attacked by the Greeks led by Alexander the Great in 332, who took it after a seven-month siege. It is then that the third part of this amazing prophecy was fulfilled. As the Encyclopaedia Britannica puts it: 'He completely destroyed the mainland portion of the town and used the rubble to build an immense causeway (some 2,600 feet [800 metres] long and 600-900 feet [180-270 metres] wide) to gain access to the island section. After the town's capture, 10,000 inhabitants were put to death, and 30,000 were sold into slavery. Alexander's causeway, which was never removed, converted the island into a peninsular.'[22] Here is the fulfilment the fifth prophecy. A secular historian notes that the bare rock where the former city stood, is now 'a place where fishermen at still frequent the spot spread their nets to dry,'[23] showing the coming to pass of the forth prediction. The second prediction, that many nations will come against her, is seen by the fact that through the years she was attacked by not only the Babylonians and the Greeks, but also by the Moslems and the Crusaders. The sixth prophecy is shown to be fulfilled by the fact that 'in 1984, UNESCO designated the historic town a World Heritage site. In the late 20th Century the ruins were damaged by bombardment, most notably in 1982 and 1996 during Israeli offensives in southern Lebanon. The site is threatened by urban growth, looting, and the decay of stone because of airborne pollution. In 1998 UNESCO created a special fund for the preservation and archaeological excavation of the ancient treasures of Tyre.'[24] In our generation Tyre is a small port where, 'fishing vessels lay at anchor ...and is 'a haven ...for fishing boats and a place for spreading nets.'[25] Tyre, once the commercial centre of the Mediterranean world and the mistress of the seas, has never recovered her glory; the original location is an archaeological site full of ruins. Nearby, nearby the place that now bares that name, is a mere fishing village. In every detail the prophecy of Ezekiel has come true.

This prophecy concerning Tyre has another dimension that is of great significance in our discussion on paganism. It is worth noting that Tyre often symbolized much to do with pagan belief and Satan's kingdom: 'The ninth century saw Jezebel, a daughter of Ethbaal (Itobal) the Tyrian king-priest, married to Ahab of Israel.'[26] Jezebel was the witch-queen of Israel and epitomized the pagan infiltration of that land. Her father was a priest-king, an evil opposite of Melchizedek, the priest-king of Salem, that is Jerusalem.[27] While Melchizedek was king of God's city, Jerusalem, Ethbaal was seen as king of Satan's city. The king of Tyre in Ezekiel 28 symbolized Satan himself. Even more interesting is that Ezekiel 28 is often taken to describe in symbolic language the fall of Satan. The beautiful archangel Lucifer became evil in his pride and rebellion, was cast out of heaven and became the Devil, and the angels that fell with him became the demons. This deceiver then continued to attack humanity, turn them from the Word of God and to his own devilish religion, which has been worked out in the numerous ways described in this book. Whereas the priest king of Tyre symbolizes Satan, Melchizedek of Salem symbolizes and prefigures Jesus Christ.[28] Taken together the prophecy against Tyre has momentous significance: it reveals the fall of Satan and his religious delusions.

However, from the perspective of our main point here in demonstrating the authority of the Bible as the Word of God, the prophecy's main significance is that the prediction against the physical city of Tyre came exactly true. This is only one example of the vast numbers of biblical prophecies; many others could be given, but that would be a book in its own right.[29] From cases like this, the veracity of the Bible as the Word of God can be demonstrated again and again. This is in stark contrast to the generalisation of much pagan prediction. It should be noted at this point that some of the most amazing prophecies and their fulfilment in the Bible have to do with Jesus Christ, but these will be dealt with specifically in chapter 13.

A unique account of miracles

Again and again the Bible has been shown to be an accurate historical record. Even after over two centuries of sustained attack by liberal academics, who have tried to show it to be little more than a myth, the Bible has continually managed to reassert itself. Whether we look at the archaeological evidence, the scientific data, the number of early manuscripts, or the criteria for analysing the accuracy and reliability of our present documents, the Bible continually shows itself to be correct. Whichever way we look at the evidence, the Bible is believable.

In every instance where we can test the Bible we find that it is factually accurate, even down to find details. This being so, it is not a step of blind faith to trust the writers where we cannot test them. Therefore it is quite reasonable to accept its testimony with regard to miracles.

What is more, the authors of the various parts of Scripture demonstrate the most profound sense of personal morality and honesty — they wrote what they believed to be the case. Once these points are put together we can see that it is utterly amazing what the Bible actually communicates in terms of the supernatural. The Bible does not shrink back from recording miracles.

Some people dismiss the Bible out of hand because it contains miracles, without realising that such a prejudiced opinion is based upon a supposition of blind faith that miracles are impossible. David Hume, the avowed anti-Christian philosopher was so dogmatic about this that he refused even to consider possible evidence of such occurrences. This can hardly be the attitude of a seeker after truth. To deny evidence simply because it points to something we have not experienced is to be biased in the extreme.

The basic issue at stake is whether we will accept the supernatural at all. If there really is a God, then logically he may suspend any law of nature if he chooses to do so. And if Jesus was truly God, this power must have been extended to him as well. The belief that miracles cannot happen supposes that we live in a universe that is a closed system of rules of cause and effect that cannot be broken. But as we saw earlier, the very existence of a chain of cause and effect reactions actually show that there is something beyond the universe — we live in an open system: there is a non-contingent cause behind our cosmos. If there is a non-contingent cause that caused the whole thing, then it is quite consistent to believe that that ultimate cause can occasionally change or supersede those chains of cause and effect we see around us. We live in an open system — miracles are therefore possible.

This is not to say that we would see the laws of nature broken all the time — that would lead to chaos. The point of the laws of nature is that generally and normally they are laws, and so are rarely broken. But theoretically the possibility exists. This is exactly what we see in the Bible. We don't see miracles all over the place, but we do see them. And generally, when we see them they are grouped around special events. They are there for a specific purpose: to validate those events.

As we peruse the length and breadth of the Bible, we see that, in particular, miracles are grouped around the giving of the Law of God and the establishment of a very special people, who were going to show how a relationship with God works out in practice. And then we see another cluster at a crisis point in Israel's history when they were being called back from rebellion and sin to serve the Lord again in accordance with that divine revelation given earlier. But the greatest cluster of miracles surrounds and are performed by the Lord Jesus Christ.

Another aspect of miracles, particularly in connection with paganism is the fact that miracles are always greater than magic. Pagans do certainly occasionally manage to do conjure supernatural events at times, but they are always significantly less powerful than a miraculous act of God. A case in point would be when Pharaoh summoned his wise men, sorcerers and magicians to change their staffs into snakes, but Aaron's staff swallowed them up.[30] Usually, however, the pagan magicians are utterly powerless as in the conflict on Mount Carmel.[31] Particularly in the life of Jesus, the power of demons is demolished.[32] The Apostles also had power over occult powers.[33] The enormous significance of this is that it shows who rules the universe. God is the almighty One; Jesus is Lord.

Supernatural claims

The Bible claims to be a supernatural revelation to us. Again and again throughout its pages it claims to the written Word of God. In the Old Testament the phrase 'Thus says the Lord' appears hundreds of times.[34] Furthermore, God is often said to speak 'through' the prophets.[35] The Old Testament prophets knew that the Spirit of God governed what they said. For example, one of them put it like this: 'I am filled with power, with the Spirit of the Lord.'[36] And another states, 'The Spirit of the Lord spoke through me; his word was on my tongue.'[37]

The New Testament writers also claimed to speak and write with the authority of God. One puts it in this way: 'We speak, not in words taught by human reason but in words taught by the Spirit,

expressing spiritual truths in spiritual words.'[38] Another passage expresses the Bible's radical claim in these words: 'All Scripture is
inspired by God and is profitable for teaching, rebuking, correcting
and training in righteousness.'[39] The Bible claims nothing less for
itself than to be the written Word of God.

A unique validation from Jesus Christ

One of the most important validations of these claims of Scripture
is the testimony of Jesus Christ. At first sight this seems to be a
circular argument: using the testimony of Jesus Christ within the
Bible to defend the whole of the Bible. However, with a little more
thought, it can be seen that this is certainly not the case; the argument is not circular. The basic argument is as follows. Scripture can
be shown to be historically accurate and from this historically accurate record we can learn about Jesus Christ. At this point we have
not got to show that the Bible is the supernatural Word of God, we
just have to accept that it is a reasonably accurate historical record.
From the historical testimony about Jesus it can be seen that he
is God the Son, God revealing himself in human form. (This will
be worked out in detail in the next chapter.) Jesus, who can be
seen to be God incarnate from history, gives his validation of the
Scriptures as the Word of God. Therefore, we can now accept the
Bible, not merely as accurate history, but as divine revelation. The
argument is not circular, but spirals up from historical record to
divine revelation.

    Jesus clearly regarded the Scriptures as the Word of God, an
authoritative revelation from God himself.[40] He recognized the authority of the Old Testament, constantly quoting from it and without
question accepting its accuracy and authority. Jesus saw the Old
Testament as God speaking.[41] He also gave authority to the New
Testament. Jesus promised the Apostles that God would specially
gift them so that they would be able to remember all that he had
said,[42] and that they would be taught all spiritual truth.[43] Just before
Jesus was taken up into heaven he gave these men a command
to take his teaching to all nations, and he promised to help them
and subsequent believers in this task until he returned to earth. It is

one of these Apostles, Peter, who regarded Paul's writings as Scripture as well.[44] So Jesus validates the Bible that we have today, not merely as accurate history, but as the Word of God.

God has spoken

When all this is put together we have an amazing result — the only conclusion is that God has supernaturally spoken through the Bible. Whatever way we look at it, the evidence is remarkable. This is a uniquely published book; it is cultural dynamite, having effected in an extraordinary way a great number of thinkers and influential leaders; it has had a unique effect on individual people who have then had a unique and beneficial effect on society; ironically, and in spite of this, it is also a uniquely persecuted book. On top of this, the Bible is unique in its historical accuracy, unique in its ability to predict the future and its account of miracles. All this supports its own claim to be the Word of God, a claim that is given supreme validation by Jesus Christ. Here is God's message to humanity; here is God speaking.

In the light of this, it can clearly be said to those who are pagans, or who are tempted by paganism: 'When men tell you to consult mediums and spiritists, who whisper and mutter, should not a people enquire of their God? Why consult the dead on behalf of the living? To the law and to the testimony! If they do not speak according to this word, they have no light of dawn. Distressed and hungry, they will roam through the land; when they are famished, they will become enraged and, looking upward, will curse their king and their God. Then they will look towards the earth and see only distress and darkness and fearful gloom, and they will be thrust into utter darkness.'[45]

Questions for discussion

1. Read Psalm 19:1-6 and Romans 1:18-20 and v.25. Paganism is essentially nature religion. Pagans love to 'connect' with and 'listen' to nature, looking at these passages, is that totally wrong, or is it a subtle perversion of a truth? How do these passages help us to

find an initial contact point in conversation with pagans? (See also Acts 17:24-31.) Although creation does reveal something of God's glory, what are the limitations of this revelation?

2. Read Psalm 19:7-11 and 2 Timothy 3:14-17. What benefits does the written revelation from God have that God's handiwork in nature does not have?

3. Read Psalm 19:12-14. What should our response be to God's revelation in nature and his Word?

4. Read Genesis 3:1-5. What are the basic deceptions that Satan used in this passage and still uses today?

5. Read Romans 1:18-32. What does this passage show happens when people turn away from the limited but important truths that God's handiwork in creation does reveal?

6. Read Isaiah 8:19-22. What does this passage reveal happens when people turn away from God's Word? What is the antidote to this condition?

Further Reading

John Blanchard, *Why Believe the Bible*, Evangelical Press, 2004.

Brian H. Edwards, *Nothing But the Truth*, Evangelical Press, 1993.

Paul Barnett, *Is the New Testament History?* Hodder and Stoughton, 1986.

Graene Goldworthy, *According to Plan: The Unfolding Revelation of God in the Bible*, Intervarsity Press, 2002.

Josh McDowell, *Evidence that Demands a Verdict*, Paternoster, 1998.

John W. Wenham, *Christ and the Bible*, Baker Book House, 1994.

Chapter 13
The Supremacy of Jesus Christ

*'God exalted him to the highest place and gave him a name
that is above every name, that at the name of Jesus every
knee should bow, in heaven and on earth and under the
earth, and every tongue confess that Jesus Christ is Lord, to
the glory of God the father.'*
Philippians 2:9-11

'Jesus said, 'Anyone who has seen me has seen the Father.'
John 14:9

One of the obvious things of the many varieties of paganism, neo-paganism and the New Age Movement is the belief in many spiritual beings, or gods. From a biblical perspective, there are spiritual beings, but these are called demons, or evil spirits, and they are in the service of their master, the devil. These beings are in constant conflict with God and his people.[1] Although the Bible teaches that there are these evil spiritual beings, as well as angels, who are righteous and do God's bidding,[2] there is only one ultimate Lord.[3] Jesus is God's clearest revelation of himself to humanity. Jesus said, 'Anyone who has seen me has seen the Father.'[4] He also said, 'I am the way and the truth and the life. No one comes to the Father except through me.'[5]

Even for those who believe in the existence of some ultimate 'God' or 'Spirit' from the evidence of creation[6] it must be said that that knowledge is incomplete. And it is not only incomplete; it is also perverted and polluted.[7] Furthermore, no way is given as to how we might approach him and be acceptable to him, let alone come into a relationship with him. God's character and expectations of us are revealed in the Bible, the Word of God, and within that the fullest revelation of who God is[8] and how we can approach him[9] is given in Jesus Christ. This is a deathblow to a mysticism filled with obscure and often contradictory perceptions of spirituality. In Jesus, God the Father is clearly seen; in Jesus the way to approach him is clearly marked out.

In one passage of the Bible Jesus Christ is called the Word of God.[10] Jesus is God's clearest and most supreme communication to us; he is God's message to us. Imagine if God wanted to clearly disclose himself to us, how would he do it? Surely, it would be quite coherent to suggest that in some way he would come into our world. After all, writing to someone is one thing, going and meeting them is another. By entering into our world and taking on our humanity he would be able to reveal himself to us in a way far more clearly than through prophets, or miracles. This is exactly what the Bible claims. One of Jesus' original followers put it like this: 'The Word became flesh and lived for a while among us. We have seen his glory, the glory of the one and only Son, who came from the Father, full of grace and truth.'[11]

This is mind boggling in the extreme — that the creator should step into his creation; that the eternal and timeless one should wrap himself in temporal flesh. The concepts here are quite staggering: the infinite maker of everything contracts himself to a finite body. Our minds quite naturally reel and are confounded, if not confused. This is possibly the most profound thought and truth in the universe, and so it is not surprising that our finite minds struggle and intellectually wheeze and pant. The Bible puts it this way regarding Jesus Christ:

> Who being in very nature God,
>   did not consider equality with God
>   something to be grasped,
> but made himself nothing,
>   taking the very nature of a servant,
>   being made in human likeness.[12]

Now, if this Jesus is indeed God, we would expect him to be unique. And this is exactly what we find in the Bible.

Whatever way we look at Jesus we can see that he is utterly unique — which is exactly what we would expect if he is God's anointed Messiah, or Christ — his messenger to humanity. You may notice an overlap between some of the arguments for the Bible and those for Jesus Christ. This is no accident, the arguments for the written Word of God, the Bible, and the living Word of God, Jesus Christ, are both based around their uniqueness. Like several strands in a rope make it stronger, so the overlapping strands of their uniqueness combine to make a cord that is an unbreakable argument.

A unique footprint in history

Before we look at uniqueness of Jesus in detail there is a vital issue that needs to be dealt with. And this is a vital question: did Jesus really exist at all? If Jesus did not exist, then Christianity is not true.

Many people today, including those who have absorbed some quasi-pagan perspective, often feel that Jesus is a merely mythical figure. Indeed, sometimes people say things like, 'Everyone knows that Jesus never existed!' In response to this it needs to be said that there is a certain truism in 'what everyone knows, no one knows'. When people use phrases like 'it is obvious' or 'in point of fact', it is generally not obvious and rarely a fact. A lack of evidence is obscured by a misleading use of overconfident language.

Where does truth end and legend begin? Think of King Arthur, Father Christmas, Robin Hood and Jesus Christ. Are they all legend? Are they part fact and part fable? Are they fable based on fact? And can we know anyway? In the end it is only by looking at hard historical evidence that we can tease out the fact from the fiction. Is there sufficient data to show that what we know about Jesus is true, or is the whole thing a trick? Is Jesus Christ man or myth, history of hoax?

The testimony of those who have serious looked into this is important here. F. F. Bruce, the late Rylands Professor of biblical criticism at the University of Manchester stated, 'Some writers toy with the fancy of a "Christ-myth," but they do not do so on the ground of historical evidence. The historicity of Christ is as axiomatic for an unbiased historian as the historicity of Julius Caesar. It is not historians who propagate the "Christ-myth" theories.'[13]

Could this Jesus be made up? Theodore parker wrote, 'It takes a Newton to forge a Newton. What man could have fabricated a Jesus? None but a Jesus.'[14] And Will Durant aptly noted, 'That a few simple men should in one generation have invented so powerful and appealing a personality, so lofty an ethic, and so inspiring a vision of human brotherhood, would be a miracle far more incredible than any recorded in the Gospels.'[15]

Whatever you may think about it, you can't ignore a body of some 1,500,000,000 people spread all over the world who claim that they trace their faith back to a historical figure, Jesus of Nazareth. And then there are a significant number of non-Christian writers who all testify to the existence of Jesus. To name but a few, Pliny (A.D. 61-114), Suetonius (A.D. 69-140), Tacitus (A.D. 55-118) all refer to the historical person of Jesus of Nazareth. Probably writing shortly after A.D. 115, Tacitus includes a brief mention of Nero's persecution of the Christians in A.D. 64: 'Nero ... treated with the most extreme punishments some people, popularly known as Christians, whose disgraceful activities were notorious. The originator of that name, Christus, had been executed by order of the procurator Pontius Pilatus.'[16] And then Josephus, the Jewish historian, wrote in the early second century: And there arose about this time [referring to the time of the Roman governor Pontius Pilate, A.D. 26-36] Jesus, a wise man, if indeed we should call him a man; for he was a doer of marvellous deeds, a teacher of men who received the truth with pleasure. He won over many Jews and also many Greeks ... And when Pilate condemned him to the cross at the instigation of our own leaders, those who loved him from the first did not cease. For he appeared to them on the third day alive again, as the Holy prophets had predicted and said many other wonderful things about him. And even now the race of Christians, so named after him, has not yet died out.'[17] On top of this, the Bible, an accurate historical record, clearly demonstrates Jesus historical reality.[18]

Taking all this into account, it is not surprising that Otto Betz concluded that 'no serious scholar has ventured to postulate the non-historicity of Jesus.'[19]

A unique character

Jesus had a unique character, or personality. We could spend a long time looking at his poise, his majesty, his love, his humility, his thoughtfulness, his devotion. Wherever he went he cared for the lonely, the sick, the social outcasts, and all in need. No one can fail to admire the beauty of his character; but there is one feature, which makes him unique, and that is his moral perfection. There was honesty and integrity about Jesus' life which meant that neither his closest friends who were with him 24 hours a day, nor his enemies, could find any fault with him. Peter said that he was 'without blemish or defect'[20] and 'committed no sin',[21] and John said that Jesus is 'the righteous one'[22] 'and in him is no sin'.[23]

A unique teacher

Thomas Jefferson, although not a Bible-believing Christian, admitted, 'I hold the precepts of Jesus as delivered by himself, to be the most pure, benevolent and sublime which has ever been preached to man.'[24] The moment Jesus opened his mouth he showed incredible power as a teacher. Soldiers who were sent to arrest him fell back in amazement and returned empty-handed, saying, 'Nobody taught like this man'.

Jesus taught with his own authority, rather than quoting the philosophers and teachers who preceded him. This thirty-year old carpenter was so devastatingly good as a teacher that he threatened the religious academic professionals of the day, and the jealousy aroused contributed to his ultimate arrest and execution.

No revolution throughout history can be compared to that which has been produced by the words of Jesus. Without money and arms he has conquered more millions than any emperor of history. He spoke such words as have never been spoken before of since and without writing a single line, 'he set more pens in motion and furnished themes for more sermons, orations, discussions, learned volumes, works of art and songs of praise than the whole army of great men of ancient and modern times'.

Jesus spoke with such originality and had such profound insight that, even in the estimation of those who have no belief in his claims, he is respected as being in the first rank of those of genius and probably the greatest moral reformer and martyr who has ever lived.

A unique effect on individual lives

The original disciples were utterly transformed by their belief in the resurrection of Jesus Christ. They were transformed from normal folk like mere artisans and tradesmen in an obscure corner of the Roman Empire into a body of people who totally revolutionised the world. These men, who claimed to have seen the risen Christ, suffered for their beliefs — and some died for them. From the courage, devotion and energy of these men, a whole culture was overthrown and the world's largest religion was established.

And this power of the risen Jesus to change lives was passed on — throughout the last 2,000 years, millions of people have had their lives revolutionised. They have fed the poor, cared for the sick, established schools, fought for justice and been the greatest force for good this world has ever seen.

A unique effect on history

Jesus' effect on history indicates that his claims are true. Someone once wrote: "He never wrote a book. He never held an office. He never had a family or owned a house. He didn't go to college. He never visited a big city. He never travelled more than 200 miles from the place where he was born. He did none of the things one usually associates with greatness. He had no credentials but himself . . . [Twenty] centuries have come and gone and today he is the central figure of the human race. All the armies that ever marched, all the navies that ever sailed, all the parliaments that ever sat, all the kings that ever reigned, put together, have not affected the life of man on earth as much as that one solitary life!'[25]

Even the atheist author and historian H. G. Wells has made this admission, as if, in spite of himself, he must recognise something about Christ: 'I am a historian, I am not a believer. But this penniless preacher from Galilee is irresistibly the centre of history.'[26] And Kenneth Scott Latourette stated, 'As the centuries pass the evidence is accumulating that, measured by his effect on history, Jesus is the most influential life ever lived on the planet.'[27]

Unique fulfilment of prophecies

One example of the Bible's many prophecies is where it predicts, hundreds of years before the event that the Messiah would be born in Bethlehem.[28] The prophecy says, 'But you, Bethlehem Ephrathah, though you are small among the clans of Judah, out of you will come for me one who will be ruler over Israel, whose origins are of old, from ancient times.' And then, years later we read in the New Testament the history of where Jesus was born in Bethlehem.[29]

Others predictions include that the coming Messiah will be a son of David,[30] that he will work in the area known as Galilee,[31] be killed by being pierced,[32] die a criminal's death[33] and yet will come back to life again.[34] With regard to Jesus' betrayal, the Old Testament amazingly prophecies startling details, including his actual betrayal by a close friend,[35] for 30 pieces of silver,[36] that this money would be thrown into God's house[37] and the money used to buy a potter's field.[38] These are just a few, by way of illustration — there are too many to consider them fully.

Some have objected to this by saying that Jesus intentionally made his life fit the prophecies. But although this allegation might seem to be possible for a few of the prophecies, many concern events Jesus could never have arranged, including his ancestry, how he was betrayed for a specific amount of money, how he was put to death, the fact that his bones remained unbroken and that soldiers cast lots for his clothing.

Another objection is that it is possible that several people in history have fitted these predictions, and that Jesus happened to have a better spin-doctor, so he is the one everyone remembers. However, the probability of this occurring is so unlikely that for all practical purposes it is impossible. For example, to take but a few of the prophecies into account, that person would have to be a Jew, from the tribe of Judah, from the family line of Jesse, and from the royal line of King David, who was born in Bethlehem. That eliminates most people in the world. Then he would have to be betrayed by a friend, sold for 30 pieces of silver, have his hands and feet pierced, be executed with thieves and buried in a rich man's tomb. How many people in history fit all these criteria — and there are many more precise prophecies than this.

Some people have tried to explain these prophecies away by saying that they were written at, or after, the times they purported to describe. In other words, they were a political, or religious, comment at that time rather than prediction. This is easily answered, as most scholars would estimate that the original documents were written at least 400 years prior to the events predicted, and even if that is not believed, we have a Greek translation of the Old Testament that was translated about 200 B.C.

Unique miracles

Jesus' miracles cannot be ignored — they are described in almost every strand of the Gospels and even in Jewish writings as well. He made the lame walk, the dumb speak, the blind see, and even brought some dead people back to life. Nor was his power confined to the realm of healing; he also demonstrated his control over nature. He ordered water to become wine and fed a crowd of five thousand from five little loaves of bread and two small fish. The storm subsided and the tempestuous waves were stilled at his command. By having such command over the powers of nature, Jesus showed that he was the all-powerful creator. pagans worship nature; Christians worship the one who created nature and who controls it. They look at the beauty of a window; we look through it at the glorious wonders beyond.

The apostle John stated at the end of his Gospel, where he had recorded many miracles: 'Jesus did may other things as well. If every one of them of them were written down, I suppose that even the whole world would not have enough room for the books that would be written.'[39] He also stated earlier what the main purpose of these miracles was: 'Jesus did many other miraculous signs in the presence of his disciples, which are not recorded in this book. But these are written that you may believe (or may continue to believe) that Jesus is the Christ, the Son of God, and that by believing you may have life in his name.'[40] The miracles are there to cause us to believe Jesus is God's anointed messenger and that through him we can have eternal life.

A unique resurrection

Millions upon millions of Christians throughout the last two thousand years have believed that Jesus came back to life after being executed by the Roman authorities. More than that, they believe he is still alive today. And this is not the mere fairy-tale fantasy of deluded simpletons — many learned researchers, scholars and lawyers have had a hard look at the evidence and have concluded that these claims are true.

For example, Sir Edward Clarke, K.C. wrote, 'As a lawyer I have made a prolonged study of the evidences for the events of the first Easter Day. To me the evidence is conclusive, and over and over again in the High Court I have secured a verdict on evidence not nearly so compelling.'[41]

And then there is J. N. D. Anderson, former lawyer and professor of oriental law at the University of London, who wrote: 'The most drastic way of dismissing the evidence would be to say that these stories were mere fabrications, that they were pure lies. But as far as I know, not a single critic today would take such an attitude. In fact, it really would be an impossible position. Think of the number of witnesses, over 500. Think of the character of the witnesses, men and woman who gave the world the highest ethical teaching it has ever known, and who even on the testimony of their enemies lived it out in their lives. Think of the psychological absurdity of picturing a little band of defeated cowards cowering in an upper room one day and a few days later transformed into a company that no persecution could silence — and then attempting to attribute this dramatic change to nothing more convincing than a miserable fabrication they were trying to foist upon the world. That simply wouldn't make sense.'[42]

Stupendous claims

Whatever way we look at Jesus, he is unique. And this uniqueness validates the stupendous claims he made for himself. Among other things he claimed to be the Messiah or Christ, God's special messenger, to forgive sins, to own the titles the 'Son of Man'[43] and the 'Son of God'[44] and to be the one who would conduct the final judgment. Taken together, these are a claim to be God!

Jesus' contemporaries were not in any doubt as to the strength of his claim: 'The Jews tried all the harder to kill him; not only was he breaking the Sabbath, but he was even calling God his own Father, making himself equal with God.'[45] When Jesus was being tried by the ruling Jewish authorities, the following exchange took place:

> At daybreak the council of the elders of the people, both the chief priests and the teachers of the law, met together, and Jesus was led before them.
>
> 'If you are the Christ,' they said, 'tell us.'
>
> Jesus answered, 'If I tell you, you will not believe me, and if I asked you, you would not answer. But from now on, the Son of Man will be seated at the right hand of the mighty God.'
>
> They all asked, 'Are you then the Son of God?' He said, 'You are right in saying I am.'
>
> Then they said, 'Why do we need any more testimony? We have heard it from his own lips.'[46]

This Jesus is God revealing himself to us in the clearest possible way. Jesus Christ embodies God's message to humanity – he is the living Word of God.[47] Through Jesus we can come to know the Father. This is no mere historical or intellectual exercise, this Jesus is alive today and by the Holy Spirit makes God the Father known to us. We can know this Jesus today; he can put his Spirit in our hearts.

Safe and Secure

It is because Jesus is Lord, believers need not fear paganism or the occult. As we shall see in more detail later, believers in the Lord Jesus Christ have been forgiven and now have access to the Father. Jesus took their guilt on the cross and now they are clean and have been given eternal life.[48] Furthermore, God has put his Holy Spirit within them to empower them in this new life and to secure them for all eternity.[49] True believers are safe: 'If God is for us, who can be against us? He who did not spare his own Son, but gave him up for us all — how will he not also along with him, graciously give us all things? Who will bring any charge against those God has chosen? It is God who justifies. Who is he that condemns? Christ Jesus, who died — more than that, who was raised to life — is at the right hand of God and is also interceding for us. Who shall separate us from the love of Christ? Shall trouble or hardship of persecution or famine or nakedness or danger or sword? ... For I am convinced that neither death nor life, neither angels nor demons, neither the present nor the future, nor any powers, neither height nor depth, nor anything else in all creation, will be able to separate us from the love of God that is in Christ Jesus our Lord.'[50] Because Jesus is Lord, we are eternally safe and secure if we trust and follow him

The power of prayer

The power of Jesus Christ does not just mean that we are eternally safe and secure; it also means that we have God's power now. The spiritual beings behind paganism and the occult shudder at the power of Christian prayer. When someone trusts and follows Jesus Christ they are given new life by the power of the Holy Spirit who equips them now[51] and secures them for eternity.[52] One of the things the Holy Spirit does now is to help us in prayer.[53] Prayer is a new power for the believer in Jesus.

Jesus gives us a wonderful example of the life of prayer, and more than that, he taught us how to pray according to the framework given in the prayer he gave to his disciples.[54] In this, we are taught that we can approach God as our heavenly Father. Jesus not only reveals the Father to us, and gives us access to Him by forgiving us, he also introduces us into a relationship with the Father. pagans grave 'spirituality' and to connect into Nature and the 'elemental spirits' of the universe; Christians have access to the Lord God Almighty, who is their heavenly Father. Because of Jesus we can pray. And through prayer we can know the Lord better: 'I keep asking that the God and Father of our Lord Jesus Christ, the glorious Father, may give you the Spirit of wisdom and revelation, so that you may know him better.'[55] The occult revels in hidden mysterious knowledge; Christians glory in the mystery that God has made known, which is Christ in us, the hope of glory.[56]

Questions for discussion

Read John 14:1-13.
Troubled Thomas' interaction with Jesus.

1. Why were the disciples troubled? (v.1 — also refer to previous verses)

2. What is Jesus answer to their concerns? Why? What relevance does this have to our concerns today?

3. Why is Thomas confused? (v.5)

4. What is Jesus' answer to Thomas' confusion? In what ways is this relevant to us today?

5. What do verses 6-11 teach us about Jesus?

6. What can we do today that will be greater than what Jesus did? (v12 – clue: some things depend on Jesus having died, risen and sent his Spirit)

7. Do verses 13 and 14 teach us that we can get what we want in prayer, what God wants, or something else?

8. What basis does Jesus give Thomas for believing in him? (v.11)

Read John 20:24-31.
Doubting Thomas' encounter with Jesus.

9. Why do you think Thomas' doubted when he had seen Jesus do so many miracles? (14:11; 20:30-31)

10. What was special about this new miracle?

11. Jesus miracles in general, and the resurrection in particular should lead us to exclaim with Thomas, 'My Lord and my God!' (28) Why do you think the resurrection of Jesus led him to this conclusion? Was this any greater than the rising of Lazarus?

12. We are all in the position of those mentioned in verse 29. What reasons do we have for faith in Jesus? (30-31)

Chapter 14
The Law of the Universe

Jesus replied, "Love the Lord your God with all your heart and with all your soul and with all your mind" This is the first and greatest commandment. And the second is like it: "Love your neighbour as yourself." All the Law and the prophets hang on these two commandments.'
Matthew 22:37-40

One of the most startling things about contemporary paganism is the almost total lack of morality. This is not to say that there is no moral or ethical teaching, but there is so little that it is almost impossible to find. It is simply not a central part of the way they see the universe. One current dictionary on the occult, for instance, has no entry whatsoever on 'ethics' or 'morality'.[1] Nor does perhaps the most academic work on the subject, which is based on the author's lecturing courses run at the University of London, Sussex University and King Alfred's College, Winchester.[2] Another book, this time on Eastern Philosophy, has absolutely nothing in the index under, righteousness, good, evil, ethics or morality.[3] The book is written by someone from the West, and although it may not be a totally accurate representation, it does give a westerners impression. Therefore these are the facets most likely to be assimilated into the current western blending of the various forms of paganism we see developing at the moment. A perusal of the contemporary literature of the rising neo-paganism reveals very scant regard for ethical issues. If they are there, they are buried deep; they're not on the surface; they're not obvious, they're not central; they don't have priority.

Magical morality

Wiccans do claim they have a very positive ethic: 'If you harm none, do what you will.' However, it is admitted that 'on the face of it, it looks like a licence to do anything'. Nevertheless, it is stated that it means that 'so long as you cause no harm to any person, animal or thing, you may follow your True Will. True Will is not a personal choice or want, but the purpose of your existence on Earth; the reason you are alive is to discover this and work towards it. If you cause harm to anyone, that harm will be reflected back on you, if not in this life then in another incarnation, there is no escape. However, if you do good, then that too is reflected back to you.'[4] Some Wiccans believe, 'bad luck comes in threes, and if you cast a spell and send out bad intent, it will always come back to you in three ways on three levels.'[5] The difficulty here is the superficiality of the ethics presented; they are so general that anyone can almost make of them what they want. What exactly is harm? What really is my True Will? And how do I find out what it is for me, without simply trying to get what I want? Basically, it seems to be a licence to absolute freedom.

Apart from these simplistic ideas, much pagan literature is almost a blank sheet with regard to ethics and morality. This is particularly seen to be the case as soon as we ask specific questions like, what is good? What is evil? How do I know what is wrong and will harm my neighbour? Is there such a thing as justice, and if so, what is just and what is unjust? From the literature it would be impossible to work out any detailed morality for our personal lives or society at large.

One of the reasons for this lack of teaching on right and wrong in much of paganism is the underlying belief that there is no good God, or evil devil. Indeed, at an ultimate level, there is no good and evil. The crucial reality is ethically neutral. One writer puts it like this: 'Magicians do not believe the stories in the Bible about God having an adversary called Satan. That is part of orthodox religion and not part of paganism. Pagans believe that there are two forces: one is called 'cosmos' and strives towards order and wholeness; the other is called 'chaos' and trends towards dissolution and re-formation. Both are positive forces; one constructing, the other breaking down through change. If the second force did not exist, nothing that died would ever decay, and no transformations could occur from fallen leaves into compost and into strong new growth. These forces need to balance and be in harmony. Evil is what people consciously or unconsciously do in the world, there is no being or energy which is of itself evil.'[6] From this two points can be understood: first, pagans do not give any emphasis on saying what precisely is evil and what precisely is good. Secondly, this undefined insipid view of morality is only something that occurs in what individual people do, there is no absolute good or evil in the universe. Good and evil are merely relative and personal; they are not absolute and eternal. The result of this is that people are given no guidance as to how they should live.

Apart from this simplistic view of human morality that is proffered by contemporary paganism, it is worth noting that many older forms of western paganism were not only amoral, but immoral. We only have remember the behaviour of, say, the ancient Greek gods to get a glimpse of this.

Common conscience

Having highlighted the paucity of moral instruction in paganism, it must be recognized, however, that when the various ancient pagan systems of thought have been the dominant religious and social force in a society, they have had a restraining role on individual wickedness. This is recognized by the apostle Paul in his letter to the Romans, where he says, 'Everyone must submit himself to the governing authorities, for there is no authority except that which has been established by God.' He then goes on to they that the one in authority is 'God's servant to do you good.'[7] We must remember that the governing authorities Paul was writing about were not secular, like so many today, but were religious, and religiously pagan at that. The Roman Empire was absolutely pagan, and even the emperor was worshipped as a god. Paul is teaching here that God has instituted what we often call the state, or governing authorities, for our good. This must be true, even if they are pagan like in most ancient civilisations, atheistic like the former and present communist states, or run by modern day dictators and despots like the Roman emperors certainly were. Even when the 'system of morality' is far from a biblical one, it is still better than anarchy. Anthropological studies have shown the controlling and restraining influence of even societies dominated by witch doctors and shamans.[8] God in his grace, through human conscience, causes social structures to develop that restrain the evil behaviour of the individual.[9] God is gracious. Of course, in such societies that are far removed from biblical influence there would be things that Christians feel are deeply wrong; nevertheless they are still used to restrain evil.

It needs to be understood though, that restraining excessive individual wickedness is very different from promoting positive righteousness. For this there needs to be the Law of God that gives detailed moral requirements. Only when there are righteous standards, based on the Law of God revealed in the Scriptures, is it possible to lead a nation not only to restrain sin, but also to develop godly standards and expectations. Even this, although it may suppress outward iniquity and develop external righteous expectations, will not produce a godliness that God desires. For that the gospel is needed.

Another vital point is that, although even pagan social structures are used to restrain evil, there is always a risk, due to the absence of the Law of God, that the wickedness will sometimes increase terribly and get out of control. This was seen in the cities of Sodom and Gomorrah and also the Canaanite cities that God sent Israel to destroy. In such cases God's judgement is near.

So, while admitting that God even uses pagan social structures to restrain some evil, it is certainly also the case that the belief systems behind these structures are often very weak in moral content. And in the various manifestations of the current rebirth of paganism and its reinvention in neo-paganism, it is clear that ethical considerations are almost all but absent. Values of right and wrong are barely there at all, and when they are they are pushed into the corners of the worldview, rather than being a central pillar, upon which everything depends.

Scriptural superiority

This is all in stark contrast to this the biblical perception of reality has righteousness at its heart. At the centre of all reality is a throne, and on that throne is a lamb looking as if it has been slain.[10] Here, at the heart of heaven, is shown the severity of righteousness and the cost of mercy. The moral Law meant that the lamb should be slain, but God's mercy caused the lamb to be slain so that we might be forgiven. Here is righteousness and mercy. Whereas pagans have no good or evil beyond the ill-defined actions of individuals, biblical Christianity puts righteousness and mercy at the heart of everything; they spring from God's nature.

The Bible puts righteousness and mercy at the heart of everything. From the very beginning of the Bible right up to its last pages the Bible unpacks a morality that is based on God's character. The concepts of right and wrong, good and evil, and morality and immorality are central and essential to the biblical worldview. Righteousness and unrighteousness are not something subsidiary or secondary, they are primary and central. The creator of the universe is a moral being; he is righteous.

From the very beginning the righteousness of God is demonstrated. God described creation as good;[11] his first words to man was a moral command: 'you must not eat from the tree of the knowledge of good and evil, for when you eat of it you will surely die.'[12] After Adam and Eve fell there were terrible consequences to their moral rebellion, including pain in childbirth, harm to relationships, loss of intimacy, shame, toil in work, damage to creation and death. God shows his righteousness by casting Adam and Eve out of the Garden, but shows his mercy in promising a future deliverer and covering their shame.

In the chapters that follow righteousness and unrighteousness are central to the unfolding revelation with the accounts of the murder of Abel, the flood at the time of Noah and the promise of righteousness to Abraham. As soon as God prepares his people to enter the Promised Land he gives them the Law. On Mount Sinai he gave his righteous commands, that if obeyed would produce a blessed community. Alongside this, God gave the sacrificial system, the priesthood and the Tabernacle. All these were given so that if people break the Law and fail their God they might find forgiveness. In the Law God revealed his righteousness; in the sacrificial system he revealed his grace and mercy. All this points to the coming deliverer who will fulfil all the righteousness commands on his people's behalf and take the consequence of their sin in his place. Jesus Christ is central to the unfolding narrative of the Bible and his role central to the human problem of unrighteousness and its consequences.

Much of the rest of the Old Testament after the giving of the Law is really a series of case studies, where we see again and again in practice what happens to individuals, communities and nations if they reject God's righteous Law. Through the wanderings in the desert, the capture of the Land, the rule of the judges, the reign of the kings, the call of the prophets and the exile and the return, God's righteous commands are worked out. The consequences of obedience and disobedience are seen in scenario after scenario. The whole Old Testament is a revelation and a working out in practice of the Law of God. If this ethical understanding was extracted from the Old Testament, the whole thing would make no sense at all. It would all collapse in a meaningless heap.

The New Testament, likewise, has as a central concept God's righteous Law. Through Jesus' life he showed us what human existence can be like when this amazing Law is obeyed. Through Jesus' teaching, particularly the Sermon on the Mount, he shows that this Law, rightly understood, judges not only our actions, but also our motives, our thoughts and desires. More and more clearly we realise that we continually fail these standards — we sin. We break God's Law - we are transgressors. Our thinking and actions twist God's requirements continually — we commit iniquity. Morality and ethics, sin and guilt are central to Jesus' life and teaching. The Bible looks forward to a day of judgement where all our shortcomings, all our transgressions and all our iniquities in attitude, motive and action will be judged. But more than this, for those who cast themselves on God's mercy in Christ, Jesus' totally righteous life becomes the righteousness to cover our sin, and his death on the cross becomes the way our sins are justly punished. Jesus Christ takes our guilt and punishment in our place and we can at peace with the holy and righteous God of the universe.[13]

The rest of the New Testament works all this out in detail with its implications for believers. It teaches that God gives his Holy Spirit, among other reasons, to help us to gradually become more like the Lord Jesus Christ. The Law of God, particularly as it is taught and exemplified in the life of Jesus, becomes the standard we strive for, not now to gain acceptance before God, but out of gratitude because we are accepted through Christ. Gratitude is a primary motive, and the power of the Holy Spirit is the enabling strength.[14] The aim of the Pagan is often merely mystical enlightenment and power to reach his or her perceived full potential. It is to become knowledgable and powerful; it is to become like God; it is Satan's original lie.[15] Among other things, the Holy Spirit also keeps us secure in Christ until we die and finally stand before our Lord, accepted and received into glory.[16] The New Testament looks forwards to a new heaven and new earth, where there will only be righteousness.[17]

The central thrust of all this is that it is to do with righteousness. The biblical revelation is about a righteous God who allows humanity to rebel against him and become unrighteous, but who provides a way to restore them through the life and death of the righteous Messiah, Jesus. At the end of time the unrighteous face eternal punishment, but those who turn to Jesus find mercy for their unrighteousness become righteous and enter a new earth where only righteousness exists. Everything is to do with morality, with ethics, with righteousness. This is nothing subsidiary, or an appendage; it is at the heart of the very essence of biblical Christianity.

And here is the real travesty with paganism in its various contemporary manifestations: the concept of righteousness is either totally absent, or at best some frail and dilute ethics are weakly attached to the periphery of the belief system. God help us if such a perspective ever becomes predominant.

The point of prayer

Pagan prayer is to do with power to survive in this world and power to get what the practitioner wants. It has little or nothing to do with righteousness. In essence it is a selfish exercise. By contrast, Christian prayer has morality at its core. When the Lord

Jesus taught his disciples to pray, they were to submit their wills to his divine will,[18] they were to ask to be forgiven for their sin,[19] they were to forgive others who had sinned against them,[20] they were to ask that they were not led into temptation to do wrong[21] and they were to ask to be delivered from the evil one.[22] It is primarily to do with the issues of righteousness and unrighteousness, good and evil, sin and purity, right and wrong. The Christian life is a battle against evil, whether from our own fallen natures,[23] or compounded and inflamed by spiritual forces of evil.[24] Prayer is central to this fight. The tragic irony is that the spiritual forces of darkness that we fight are the very same forces that the pagan worships and seeks help from.[25] It is therefore hardly surprising that paganism leads to increasing unrighteousness.[26]

Salt in society

The righteousness that Christians see as so important is not merely something that concerns them and other believers. They are commanded to make a difference in the world God has put them. Fundamentally, this means sharing the gospel with those around them.[27] However, this does not merely mean sharing the good news of forgiveness in Jesus Christ, but also influencing society for good and showing their righteousness in action.[28] They are to make their faith in Christ and their submission to his Word affect every part of their thinking and actions.[29] This means that believers should make society a better place by working for righteousness and fighting wickedness wherever they find it. In essence then, Christians are to make the world around them more righteous, by calling people to accept the gospel, by being an example of godliness and by applying God's righteous Law into every area of society that they have influence.

Unlike paganism, biblical Christians believe in the reality of good and evil, and they also believe that they are to make a difference for good in this world, by both word and deed. The reader can judge for themselves as to the value of a religion that has morality at its core and works for righteousness, or one that merely straps on a few moral comments, but fundamentally works for personal self-advancement.

Questions for discussion

1. Read Exodus 20 and Matthew 5-7. What do these two statements of morality have in common and in what ways are they different?

2. Read Matthew 22:34-40. What is the essence of the Law of God recorded here?

3. Read Romans 7:7-25. What is the primary function of the Law?

4. Read Romans 8:1-17. What is the relation between the Spirit and the Law in the life of a believer?

5. Read Galatians 5:16-6:10. What relationship is there between this passage and God's Law? What function does the Law have for the believer? How does the Spirit help us in regard to the Law?

Chapter 15
God Has Provided a Way Back to Himself

'For there is one God and one mediator between God and men, the man Christ Jesus, who gave himself as a ransom for all men.'
1 Timothy 2:5-6

The heart of the failure of paganism is not only that is does not recognise the One Lord God Almighty, maker of heaven and earth, it is also that even where glimpses of his existence are recognised, no way is offered for us to know him. If he is believed in at all, he is the distant sky God, or hidden within nature, or behind a myriad of spiritual beings or so-called gods. He is obscured from sight.

The greatest secret in the universe

The occult offers illicit hidden mystical knowledge, but is does not know 'the mystery that has been kept hidden for ages and generations, but is now disclosed to the saints.'[1] It is to true Christians, often called saints[2] in the Bible, that 'God has chosen to make known ... the glorious riches of this mystery, which is Christ in you, the hope of glory.'[3] The ironic truth is that even though the occult and paganism make so much of mystical knowledge to connect with the 'spiritual', they know nothing of 'the mystery of God, namely Christ, in whom are hidden all the treasures of wisdom and knowledge.'[4]

Ever since the fall of humanity, when Adam ate the forbidden fruit from the tree of the knowledge of good and evil,[5] we have been alienated from God and destined to die.[6] The results of this cataclysmic event have meant that in life we are subjected to toil

and frustration,[7] pain in procreating new life,[8] tensions in our relationships[9] and a lack of real intimacy with each other,[10] spiritual
conflict[11] and the continual prospect of death.[12] Worse of all, we
have been separated from God, the source of all life: we hide from
him[13] and he has banished us from his presence.[14] After death we
will be separated from him for all eternity.[15] Throughout human
history the reality of this situation has demonstrated itself again
and again. And yet, God had a secret rescue plan that was hinted
at even back then.[16] Clues of that mystery were gradually revealed
bit by bit through the whole Old Testament.[17] And then in the New
Testament we see the mystery finally fully revealed. God's rescue
plan is centred on Jesus Christ. The mystery is now disclosed for
all to know.[18]

A thorough diagnosis

One of the fundamental areas that paganism fails is that it does not
properly diagnose the full extent of the human problem. It claims,
in essence, that if we gain mystical knowledge, connect into spiritual power of some kind and achieve a higher state of consciousness, we will rise to a greater level of existence. Essentially, what it
diagnoses as our problem is a lack of esoteric knowledge, a degree
of impotence for coping with the problems of life and an inability
to see the universe from a 'higher' perspective. At its simplest level,
many neo-pagans claim that our problem is that we do not realise
that we are all gods; we are all divine. We should think of ourselves
as far greater than we generally do.[19]

From a biblical standpoint this diagnosis is utterly false. Generally, our problem is generally not that we are better than we think,
but that we are far worse. Pride is wrong. What paganism leaves
out of the equation is the whole area of ethics and morality; it
does not deal with the problem of sin. This is because it does not
understand who God is. The Bible shows that God is holy and
that he demands that we should be holy. Our fundamental problem is that we have broken his laws in thought and deed.[20] Once
we understand this, it becomes clear that God's rescue plan must
deal with the problem of moral failure. It was a moral failure that
got us in a mess in the beginning, and it is our continual moral

failure that reinforces and confirms our fallen state. All paganism offers us is more illicit mystic knowledge and it was illicit knowledge that caused the problem originally.[21] If someone is poisoned, there is no hope in taking more of toxin. An antidote is required. The knowledge and experience of evil has to be removed. Sin has to be forgiven.

People have a problem with being called a sinner; we don't like it. But unless we accept the diagnosis we will never take the cure that is offered. No one would want to go through the agony of chemotherapy unless they knew they had cancer. Who would want to undergo serious surgery unless they thought it was absolutely necessary. We have to accept the diagnosis if we are going to submit ourselves to the cure.

In the Ten Commandments[22] God sets out the essentials of righteousness. But in the Sermon on the Mount Jesus shows us that it is not merely the actions that are prohibited, it is also the thought life behind the actions and word that flow from those thoughts that condemn us.[23] For example, in regard to the command not to murder, Jesus said: 'You have heard that it was said to the people long ago, "Do not murder, and anyone who murders will be subject to judgment." But I tell you that anyone who is angry with his brother will be subject to judgment.'[24] And then, in connection with adultery, Jesus said, 'You have heard that it was said, "Do not commit adultery." But I tell you that anyone who looks at a woman lustfully has already committed adultery with her in his heart.'[25] And it is no good just obeying part of the law and thinking that is sufficient. James says, 'whoever keeps the whole law and yet stumbles at just one point is guilty of breaking all of it. For he who said, "Do not commit adultery," also said, "Do not murder." If you do not commit adultery but do commit murder, you become a lawbreaker.'[26] More than this, on one occasion Jesus summarised the whole Old Testament law by saying, '"Love the Lord your God with all your heart and with all your soul and with all your mind." This is the first and greatest commandment. And the second is like it: "Love your neighbour as yourself." All the law and the Prophets hang on thee two commandments."'[27] It is not therefore surprising that the apostle Paul writes in his letter to the Romans, 'All have sinned and fall short of the glory of God.'[28]

Whether we like it or not, no one can escape the diagnosis: we have all fallen short of God's required standards; we have all broken his law. This means that everyone is separated from God,[29] his wrath is being revealed against us,[30] and we 'are storing up wrath against ourselves for the day of God's wrath, when his righteous judgment will be revealed. God "will give to each person according to what he has done".[31]

Looking for a cure

When you know you are sick you start looking for a cure. This can be a disorientating business, for where are we to look? Old-fashioned maps were different from ours: instead of having north at the top, they were positioned so that the top of the map faced east. The reason for this was that they then faced Jerusalem and the holy land. It is this practice that led to the term orientation: our maps were turned towards the orient and so we became orientated. In a similar way, it is as we turn towards Jerusalem and the land of Israel that we can find our spiritual bearings. In that land, and in that city about two thousand years ago, Jesus did something that provided a cure for our sin and removed God's righteous wrath from us.

Paganism utterly fails at this point: not only does it not diagnose the true human problem, neither can it provide a solution. Neo-paganism is impotent in removing our guilt; it can't bring us peace with a holy God. Mysticism offers false medicine; instead of a panacea, it offers poison.

Understanding the cure

The death of Jesus

Through Jesus Christ dying on a cross, God offers us healing for our condition of alienation from our maker and judge.[32] This one incident is perhaps the most significant event of global history: it has radically changed the course of the world's unfolding drama and still shapes our global politics to this day. The politics and power struggles of our world cannot be understood without reference to the death of Christ. By ignoring, proclaiming, misconstruing and contradicting the affair of the crucifixion, communities often take their sides in our contemporary world.

But it is not just at the level of politics and ideology that this event is so relevant to the current situation: in a far more personal, emotional and experiential way, a vastly growing number throughout the planet testify that this one happening helps them make sense of their lives.

God is holy and just, and is bound by his very nature to punish our sin, but he is also loving and merciful. How can the two be reconciled? How can God be just and loving? How can he be holy and merciful? How can he condemn our sin and yet forgive us? How can God's perfect justice and perfect love meet? The answer is in the death of Jesus on the cross.

On the cross Jesus took our punishment in our place. He was bearing what we should have borne. In Jesus, on the cross, God absorbed the offence and punishment for our wrongdoing himself. His justice is vindicated, and yet his mercy is shown.

So, in essence, what is Good News of the death of the Christ all about? Let me explain. This key question is this: if God is totally pure and righteous, and I am aware of my moral failings in thought, attitude, motive, word and deed, then how can I ever be acceptable to him. If, as the Scriptures teach, God demands total perfection, then I am utterly lost. If heaven can only be entered by those who are perfect, then surely no one can enter it.

It is at precisely this point that the Christian conception is so different from all others. All the others teach in one way or another that we simply must try to be good enough, so that in the end our good deeds outweigh our bad. The Bible teaches that this is an impossibility, and for a couple of good reasons. First, no one has totally good deeds, all of our motives are mixed and are therefore not totally pure. Second, even if it was hypothetically possible for someone's good deeds to outweigh their bad, this would not solve the essential problem. If God is totally pure, the bad deeds, even if less than the good, are still sufficient to condemn us. God demands perfection — the good cannot undo the bad.

So, we have an immense and practical problem, how can we get rid of all the bad within us and so be acceptable to God? The

Bible teaches that God is just and must punish all wrong, whether in thinking, attitudes or actions, and yet it also tells us that he is loving and wants to let us off, so to speak. How can God's justice and love be reconciled? How can the bad within us be justly dealt with? And this is where the death of Jesus comes in.

Now comes the amazing concept of the cross, the idea that has revolutionised peoples' thinking and experience throughout the ages. The essential idea is this: when Jesus died on the cross, he was taking the punishment for our evil instead of us. Jesus became our substitute, sacrificing himself to pay the penalty for wickedness. Because he is Son of God, he is powerful enough to do this; because he is human he can legitimately represent us.

The astonishing upshot of all this is that forgiveness is possible for those who seek it; the past can be cleansed. And that is not just a religious thing; it has immense psychological significance. If God can forgive me, then I can forgive myself. Peace of mind is possible. And if this is true, then I can forgive others — and there is the possibility that they can forgive me. Here is the only basis for restitution and reconciliation at every level, from breakdown in marriages, all the way to tackling the legacy of the anguishing bloodbath that occurred in places like Rwanda and the Balkans.

In a world where feelings of guilt, breakdown in relationships, conflict between communities and all-out war are all around us, the possibility of personal forgiveness, as well as the basis to forgive others, is utterly vital.

The life of Jesus

Jesus did not merely take our badness, he also declared us good. It is not just that he has paid off our moral overdraft, but also that he filled our account with his righteousness. Someone once asked whether Jesus could have paid the price of our sins if he had died as an infant, like when Herod massacred the children of Bethlehem. The question is interesting because hidden within it is another question: why did Jesus have to live to adulthood in order to be able to give us forgiveness? Of course, if Jesus had died as a child we would not have his teaching or example, but more is at stake than this. Our problem before God is not merely that our sin has to be removed, but that we need to have righteousness credited to our account. It is not just that we need the penalty for breaking God's law taken from us, but also that we need to have obedience to the law given to us. We don't only need unrighteousness removed, but also positive righteousness needs to be credited to us. In the court of heaven we need to be declared forgiven *and* righteous. But righteousness is not merely not doing wrong, it is also positively doing good; it is not merely committing no sin, it is also actively achieving a perfectly righteous life. Righteousness is not only the absence of sin, it is also the presence of active obedience.

Jesus lived to adulthood so that he could grow up under the law and obey it in *every* single respect. Jesus was the perfect law keeper.[33] It is this law keeping, or positive righteousness that is given to those who turn to Jesus. When a believer approaches God they are clothed or covered in the righteousness of Jesus Christ and so are fully acceptable.[34] Both the taking away of our sin by Christ's death and the covering of our shame by the righteousness of Christ's life are God's free gift and cannot be earned or deserved.[35]

Applying the cure

About two thousand years ago, just after these things originally happened, Peter, one of Jesus disciples, spoke this message to the people of Jerusalem. His words had an amazing effect on them. 'When the people heard this, they were cut to the heart and said to Peter and the other apostles, "Brothers, what shall we do?"'[36]

Peter replied, 'Repent and be baptized, everyone of you, in the name of the Lord Jesus so that your sins may be forgiven. And you will be given the gift of the Holy Spirit. The promise is for you and your children and all who are far off — for all whom the Lord will call.'[37]

In many ways, we are the people who are 'far off.' Two thousand years later, in a different part of the world and in a very different culture, the message is still the same for us.

Jesus himself said, 'For God so loved the world that he gave his one and only Son, that whoever believes in him shall not perish but have eternal life. For God did not send his Son into the world to condemn the world, but to save the world through him. Whoever believes in him is not condemned, but whoever does not believe stands condemned already because he has not believed in the name of God's one and only Son. This is the verdict: Light has come into the world, but men loved darkness instead of light because their deeds were evil. Everyone who does evil hates the light, and will not come into the light for fear that his deeds will be exposed. But whoever lives by the truth comes into the light, so that it may be seen plainly that what he has done has been done through God.'[38]

Elsewhere, Jesus said, 'Ask and it will be given to you; seek and you will find; knock and the door will be opened to you. For everyone who asks receives; he who seeks finds; and to him who knocks, the door will be opened.'[39] Later, he went on, saying, 'Enter through the narrow gate. For wide is the gate and broad is the road that leads to destruction, and many enter through it. But small is the gate and narrow the road that leads to life, and only a few find it.'[40]

In start contrast to paganism, with its obscured view of any ultimate God, its plethora of higher beings, like gods, and its emphasis on self-achieved spiritual evolution, the Bible plainly declares: 'there is one God and one mediator between God and men, the man Christ Jesus, who gave himself as a ransom for all men.'[41] For the Christian, heaven is a free gift, it is not earned or deserved.[42]

In Conclusion...

Some might be overly concerned with the current rise of the mystical way of thinking, feeling that this will be a more difficult context for the church than the recent years of dead liberal Christianity, agnosticism, atheism and secularism. But surely this is not the case. Of course paganism offers Christianity a considerable challenge, but we must also remember that the church initially grew in a fundamentally pagan context.

The main thrust of the Scriptures is against paganism, not secularism. Paganism may be an old enemy, but it is one we have already defeated. On the other hand, dead liberal Christianity has often inoculated unbelievers against the real thing. Also, agnosticism and atheism, with their outworking in the secularisation of our society, have distanced people from asking spiritual questions and sensing something of their immense significance. Ironically, and in contrast to this, the 'new spirituality' offers believers an opportunity unknown for generations in the West. Mr Average and Mrs Normality are now increasingly aware of a spiritual dimension, are often fascinated by it and yet utterly confused and lost. Many today, superficially at least, are seekers. This may be a God-given opportunity.

Here is the challenge: under God's grace and through his power we can intelligently proclaim the true spirituality to a generation that is spiritually open. We can offer a relationship with the Lord of the Universe through the one mediator, Jesus Christ. For us, ultimate reality is not confusing or frightening. At the heart of the cosmos is a throne: God our Father is in charge. In the middle of the throne is a lamb, looking as if it has been slain: God is merciful and loves us in a way that is beyond full comprehension. We can be forgiven.

Contemporary paganism merely offers a mindful of shadows — but we offer the light. The current mysticism invites us to immerse ourselves in a world of uncertainty and final terror. We hold out Jesus Christ, the way, the truth and the life — the only way to the Father in heaven.

Notes

Introduction

1. Anodea Judith, *The Truth about Neo-Paganism*, Llewellyn Publications, 1994.
2. 1 Chronicles 12:32
3. Romans 16:19
4. 1 Kings 14:24
5. 2 Kings 23:10
6. Acts 17:23
7. Acts 17:28. There are two quotations here. The first, 'In him we live and move and have our being', is from the Cretan poet Epimenides (c. 600 B.C.) in his *Cretica*. The second, 'We are his offspring', comes from the Cilician poet Aratus (c. 315-240 B.C.) in his *Phaenomena*, as well as Cleanthes (331-233 B.C.) in his Hymn to the pagan god Zeus. Paul quotes pagan Greek poets elsewhere (Titus 1:12 and 1 Corinthians 15:33).
8. 1 Peter 3:16
9. John 14:6

Chapter 1

1. *The Book People*, October 2002, Advertising sheet for mail order book company.
2. Kalfors, Mariano, *White Witching: The Good Magic-Maker's Guide to Spellweaving*, Anness Publishing Ltd, 2002, back page.
3. Kalfors, Mariano, *White Witching*, p.7.
4. Green, Marion, *Practical Magic: A Book of Transformations, Spells and Mind Magic*, London, Anness Publishing Ltd, 2001.

5. Algie, Nessa, *First Steps to Numerology*, Axiom Publishing, 2001.

6. *Dreams: Your Innermost Thoughts Revealed*, Strathearn Books, Ltd., 1987.

7. *Bath Spa University College Postgraduate Prospectus* 2003/2004, pp.54-55.

8. Take Dr Clark for example, at California State University who advocates a variety of Eastern and occult methods for the educational curriculum. For other examples see the article, *New Age Education* in the *Encyclopaedia of New Age Beliefs*, by John Ankerberg and John Weldon, Harvest House, Eugene, Oregon, 1996.

9. Anodea Judith, *The Truth about Neo-Paganism*, Llewellyn Publications Ltd., 1994.

10. Anodea, *The Truth about Neo-Paganism*.

11. *Know Your Destiny: Mystic Meg's Magazine*, Summer 2001, News Group Newspapers, Ltd.

12. *Know Your Destiny*, Summer 2001, p.3.

13. Ecclesiastes 3:11

14. This can easily be verified by looking at the reading material on the web sites of various US bookstores, as well as more international companies, like Amazon.

15. Geddes and Grosset, *Dictionary of the Occult*, p.3.

16. First John and Colossians are particular examples.

17. Geddes and Grosset, *Dictionary of the Occult*, p.3.

18. www.pagan.co.uk. Pagan Solicitors – Cupar, St Andrews, Fife.

19. Mariella Frostrup in *The Independent*, quoted on the back of *Kindred Spirit*, Issue 61, Winter 2002/2003.

20. The city of Bath, for example, has three pagan bookshops, but no Christian bookshop.

21. Quoted in *Pagan Invasion*, Volume 4, *The East Seduces the West*. 1991, Jeremiah Films Inc. Also quoted on http://www.johankerberg.org/Articles/new-age/NA0802W2.htm; http://www.johankerberg.org/Articles/PDFArchives/new-age/NA2W0802.pdf. This is an article by Dave Hunt (*Occult Invasion*, Harvest House, 1998). The quote is also cited on http://www.dci.dk/?artikel=311&emne=Hinduisme which has the following: 'In January 1979 Indian newspapers reported that the second

"World Congress on Hinduism" took place in Allahabad. Between 40,000 and 50,000 delegates from allover the world attended. The congress which lasted for two or three weeks was headed by four chairmen, the four shankaracharyas who lead the large order of swamis, and its honorary president was Dalai Lama. One newspaper reported that a speaker at the congress had said something to the effect of: "Our mission in the West bas been crowned with a fantastic success. Hinduism is new becoming the decisive World religion and the end of Christianity has come near. Within another generation there will be only two religions in the world, Islam and Hinduism."'

22. Quoted in *Pagan Invasion*, Volume 4, *The East Seduces the West*. 1991, Jeremiah Films Inc. www.jeremiah films.com

23. This appears on the official website of the Vishva Hindu Parishad, on a page headed 'Aims and Objectives'. http://www. vhp.org/englishsiteb-objectives/aim_object.htm, downloaded Sept. 2004. The full quote is: 'To establish an order of Dharmapracharaks, both lay and initiate, for the purpose of propagating dynamic Hinduism representing the fundamental values of life comprehended by various faiths and denominations originated in Bharatvarsha, such as, Bouddha, Jain, Arya Samaj, Sikh, Veershaiva, Shakta, Shaiva, Vaishnav, etc. and to open, manage and assist Centres for training such Dharmapracharaks.' In context, the above is listed under 'Education' as activity that is or may be undertaken to further the objects of the Association

24. Sultphen, Dick, New Age activist, writing in the 1980s. Quoted in, Strohmer, Charles, *Building Bridges to the New Age World*, CPAS, Warwick, 1996.

25. Acts 19:19

26. 2 Kings 17:7-20

27. 1 Timothy 2:5

Chapter 2

1. As recognized in the media in articles like, 'Attacks on horses linked to Satanic rituals' where the author writes, 'Members of Britian's growing community of pagans...' *The [London] Observer*, Sunday Novemeber 10, 2002. Also claimed by pagan

writer, Anodea Judith to be 'the fastest growing religion in America today. *The Truth about Neo-Paganism*, Llewellyn Publications, 1994. Furthermore, the topics under 'top.searches' on various search engines in the Internet often have pagan themes. For example, 'Nostradamus' was one of the top.searches on Yahoo in early 2005, just after the tragic Asian Tsunami.

2. Quoted in Greenwood, Susan, *The Encyclopedia of Magic and Witchcraft: An Illustrated Historical Reference to Spiritual Worlds*, Hermes House, 2004.

3. www.panda.org/endangeredspecies writes, 'Nobody knows how many species are being lost each year, nor even the total number of species that exist. Biologists estimate that there are between 5 and 15 million species existing on the Earth today, of which only about 1.5 million have been described and named...Yet almost all species (plant and animal) are under threat to some degree from the activities of men... It is said by some, if not most, experts that habitat loss is the greatest threat to the variety of life on the planet today. Already around half of the world's original forests have disappeared, and they are still being removed at a rate 10 times higher than any possible level of regrowth. As tropical forests contain at least half of the Earth's species, the clearance of some 17 million hectares each year is causing dramatic loss of biodiversity. Moreover, habitat loss is identified as a main threat to 85% of all species describes in the IUCN's Red Lists (those species officially classified as 'threatened' and 'endangered'). http:www.Audubon.org/campaign/esa/ark.html says, 'Scientists estimate that in 200 years preceding the passage of the ESA, more than 500 species became extinct in the United states.' When specific details are given, the true picture become easier to grasp. For example, in his research on the US National Parks Service in his book, *A Walk in the Woods*, Bill Bryson discovered that in the Smokies alone, twelve muscle species have become extinct in recent years. In the last century 42 species of mammal have disappeared from America's National Parks. In just the year 1957, the Parks Service managed to make a mistake that wiped out 31 species of fish — and one, which scientists had never seen before (Black Swan, 1997, pp.126-127.)

4. Lovelock, James, *Gaia: A New Look at Life on Earth*. Oxford University Press, 1982.

5. The name Gaia, after the Greek Earth Goddess, was also known as *Ge*, from which root the sciences of geography and geology derive their names.

6. Lovelock, *Gaia*, p.ix.

7. Lovelock, *Gaia*, p.viii.

8. Lovelock, *Gaia*, p.8.

9. Lovelock, *Gaia*, p.9.

10. Lovelock, *Gaia*, p.ix.

11. As set out initially in, Dawkins, Richard, *The Selfish Gene*, Granada Publishing Ltd, 1978.

12. Lovelock writes, 'Gaia was condemned as teleological by my peers and the journals *Nature* and *Science*, would not publish papers on the subject (Lovelock, *Gaia*, p.vii).

13. As expressed most clearly by Dawkins in *The Selfish Gene*, *The Blind Watchmaker*, *River Out of Eden* and so forth.

14. This reasoning behind this movement is perhaps most clearly expressed by Michael Behe in his book, *Darwin's Black Box*, Touchstone, 1996.

15. Genesis 1 and 2

16. Lovelock, *Gaia*, p.10.

17. Acts 14: 14-15; Colossians 1:15-16

18. Colossians 1:17; Acts 17:24-28

19. Acts 14:17

20. Judith, Anodea, *The Truth about Neo-Paganism*, Llewellyn, 1994. I have recorded the author's capitalization for Sun and Moon accurately as it expresses her veneration for these bodies.

21. Take for example one edition of *Resurgence*, Jan/Feb 2002, No. 216. There several articles of ecology and agriculture: 'When They Once Meet: Reflections On Humanity's Uneasy Coexistence with the Natural World', p.34; 'Wild World: We Should Value and Preserve Wilderness on Its Own Terms', p.36; 'Eating Oil: Food Supply in a Changing Climate', p.39.

22. Theroux, Paul, *National Geographic*, December 2002, p.17.

23. Genesis 1:1

24. Romans 1:25

25. Romans 1:20
26. Ephesians 2:2; Ephesians 6:12; 1 John 4:1-6; Colossians 1:15-17; 2:6-23
27. Simpson, Liz, *The Healing Energies of Earth*, Gaia Books Ltd, London 1999, p.15.
28. Simpson, *The Healing Energies of Earth,* p.15.
29. Schumacher College is an independent international centre for ecological studies, based in Totnes, Devon.
30. Goodwin, Brian, *Patterns of Wholeness: Introducing Holistic Science, Resurgence,* No. 216, January/February, 2003, p14.
31. *Resurgence*, No. 216, January/February 2003, p.83.
32. Shamanism is a pagan path claiming contact with supernatural entities for a variety of purposes. In traditional shamanism the shaman functions as a healer, spiritual leader and mediator between the spirits and people. Sometimes shamans are termed witchdoctors by westerners. The Native American religious tradition is representative of shamanism.
33. *Resurgence*, No. 216, January/February 2003, p.83.
34. Russell, Bertrand, *History of Western Philosophy*, pp.26-27, Routledge Edition, 2000. Original edition first published in 1946.
35. Simpson, *The Healing Energies of Earth*, back cover.
36. Simpson, *The Healing Energies of Earth*, p.15.
37. Romans 1:20; Psalm 19:1
38. John 14:6
39. Genesis 1:25
40. Genesis 2:15
41. Genesis 3:11
42. Genesis 9:9-10
43. Leviticus. 25:1-7
44. Of course, the Holy Spirit was also present (Genesis 1:2). Indeed, therefore, Father Son and Spirit were intimately involved in creation. This plurality is also demonstrated in Genesis 1:26.
45. John 1:1
46. Matthew 4:35-41
47. Colossians 1:15-17
48. Revelation 21:21
49. 2 Peter 3:7; 10

50. Genesis 3:17-19
51. Romans 8:22-23
52. Romans 8:19-21

Chapter 3

1. *Enhancing Your Mind, Body Spirit*, De Agostini UK Ltd, Summer 2003.
2. Sometimes other classifications labels used to covering the same ground such as mysticism or spirituality. The point is the same: under these titles a plethora of publications exist, including those covering New Age medicine and alternative therapies.
3. *The Health Magazine*, Meseloak Marketting Limited, Summer 2002, p.19.
4. *Body and Soul, The [London] Times*, Saturday May 22, 2004, p.17. Buy surfing the web it can be seen that other national newspapers in a range of countries have similar publications.
5. George, Sue, *Stress Relief Made Simple*, p.45, Haldane Mason, UK, Revised edition 2001.
6. George, Sue, *Stress Relief Made Simple*, Haldane Mason, UK, Revised edition 2001, p.49.
7. Alexander, Jane, *Five Minute Healer: A Busy Person's Guide to Vitality and Energy, All Day, Every Day,* Gaia Books, 2000, p.150.
8. Deuteronomy 18:10-11
9. Deuteronomy 13:1-5
10. Exodus 7:11; 22; 8:7
11. 2 Thessalonians 2:9
12. 2 Thessalonians 2:9-12
13. Genesis 2:19-20. Adam naming the animals involves some kind of classification and ordering. Once a name has been given, some kind of authority, power and knowledge is gained. This is true in every are of human exploration: knowledge is power, and to get knowledge words must be employed.
14. Genesis 1:28
15. Genesis 2:15-17
16. Exodus 7:11,22; 8:7,18; Acts 16:16-18; 19:15-16

17. 2 Thessalonians 2:9-12
18. For example, Willow bark used to be chewed in Druid England as a pain killer. Willow bark contains acetylsalicylic acid, a chemical similar to aspirin. The purple foxglove contains an active ingredient from which the heart drug digitalis can be extracted. Many, if not most, drugs have natural origins.
19. This publication was sold in the main supermarkets in 2003-2004.
20. *The New Guide to Therapies*, p.203.
21. *The New Guide to Therapies*, p.209.
22. *The New Guide to Therapies*, p.209.
23. *Hands of Light: A Guide to Healing Through the Human Energy Field*, New York, Bantam Books, 1988.
24. See, for example, Kurt E. Koch, *Demonology: Past and Present*, Kregel, 2000; *Occult Bondage and Deliverance*, Kregel, 2006; Frederick S. Leahy, *Satan Cast Out: A Study in Biblical Demonology*, Banner of Truth, 1990; *The Victory of the Lamb: Christ's Triumph Over Sin, Death and Satan*, Banner of Truth, 2001.

Chapter 4

1. Matthew 5:40.
2. Brecher, Paul, *The Way of the Spiritual Warrior: Soft Style Martial Arts for Body, Mind and Spirit*. Goodfield Press Ltd., 2000, p.17.
3. As in according to ancient Daoist theory.
4. Brecher, Paul, *The Way of the Spiritual Warrior*, p.19.
5. Brecher, Paul *The Way of the Spiritual Warrior,* p.19.
6. Keegan, Paul, 'Into the Void', *Boston Business*, February March, 1990, p.71. Quoted in, *Encyclopedia of New Age Beliefs*, John Ankerburg and John Weldon, Harvest House Publishers, Oregon, USA, 1996. p.261.
7. Smith, Adam, 'Powers of Mind — Part II: The est Experience,' (interview with Werner Erhard), *New York*, September 29, 1975. Quoted in, *Encyclopedia of New Age Beliefs*, John Ankerburg and John Weldon, Harvest House Publishers, Oregon, USA, 1996. p.262.

8. *The Financial Times*, Weekend January 25/January 26, 2003.

9. *The New Guide to Therapies*, Paragon, London, 2002, p.162.

10. *The New Guide to Therapies*, p.162.

11. Baker, Marina, *Spells for Teenage Witches*, 2000, pp.7,9,15; Kalfors, Mariano, *White Witching: The Good Magic-Maker's Guide to Spell Weaving*, 2002, p.33.

12. Kalfors, Mariano, *White Witching*, p.33.

13. Leviticus 19:26

14. Leviticus 20:27

15. Acts 19:19

16. *The New Guide to Therapies*, p.132.

17. *The New Guide to Therapies*, p.132.

18. Alexander, Jane, *The Five Minute Healer: A Busy Person's Guide to Vitality and Energy All Day, Every Day.* Gaia Books Ltd, 1999, p.23.

19. George, Sue, *Stress Relief Made Simple*, Haldane Mason Ltd, 2000, p.13.

20. *The New Guide to Therapies*, p.132.

21. *The New Guide to Therapies*, p.70.

22. See, for example http://www.johnankerberg.org/Articles/new-age/NA0802W2.htm http://www.johnankerberg.org/Articles/_PDFArchives/new-age/NA2W0802.pdf. Also see, http://www.dci.dk/?artikel=311&emne=Hinduismewhich has the following: 'In January 1979 Indian newspapers reported that the second 'World Congress on Hinduism' took place in Allahabad. Between 40,000 and 50,000 delegates from allover the world attended. The congress which lasted for two or three weeks was headed by four chairmen, the four shankaracharyas who lead the large order of swamis, and its honorary president was Dalai Lama. One newspaper reported that a speaker at the congress had said something to the effect of: "Our mission in the West bas been crowned with a fantastic success. Hinduism is new becoming the decisive World religion and the end of Christianity has come near. Within another generation there will be only two religions in the world, Islam and Hinduism."' This appears on the official website of the Vishva Hindu Parishad, on a page headed 'Aims and Objectives', http://www.vhp.org/englishsite/b-objectives/aim_object.htm, downloaded Sept. 2004. The full

quote is: 'To establish an order of Dharmapracharaks, both lay and initiate, for the purpose of propagating dynamic Hinduism representing the fundamental values of life comprehended by various faiths and denominations originated in Bharatvarsha, such as, Bouddha, Jain, Arya Samaj, Sikh, Veershaiva, Shakta, Shaiva, Vaishnav, etc. and to open, manage and assist Centres for training such Dharmapracharaks.' In context, the above is listed under 'Education' as activity that is or may be undertaken to further the objects of the Association.

23. *The New Guide to Therapies*, p.70.
24. This sounds so like the Satanic lie of Genesis 3:5: 'and you will be like God'. Divinity is seen as permeating us, if only we have the consciousness and enlightenment to realize it – God is in me. This is a reoccurring theme in paganism and the New Age.
25. *The New Guide to Therapies*, p.78.
26. Isaiah 8:20
27. 2 Kings 16
28. Isaiah 8:19-20
29. Isaiah 8:21-22

Chapter 5

1. Restall Orr, Emma, *Honouring the Ancient Dead, British Archaeology*, Issue 77, July 2004.
2. Judith, Anodea, *The Truth about Neo-Paganism*, Llewellyn Publications, 1994. p3.
3. Restall Orr, *Honouring the Ancient Dead*.
4. Judith, *The Truth about Neo-Paganism*, p.2.
5. Judith, *The Truth about Neo-Paganism*, p.35.
6. Judith, *The Truth about Neo-Paganism*, pp.35-46.
7. Judith, *The Truth about Neo-Paganism*, p.46.
8. Greenwood, Susan, *The Encyclopedia of Magic and Witchcraft: An Illustrated Historical Reference to Spiritual Worlds*, Hermes House, 2004, p.247.
9. Greenwood, *The Encyclopedia of Magic and Witchcraft*, p.161.
10. Some philosophy over the last half a century had undermined the assumptions upon which traditional science is based. Postmodernists like Jacques Derrida, for example, argue that the

meaning of language is fluid, its understanding depending on a variety of factors. As science is thought about and communicated in language, this removes its basis of truly 'knowing'. On one hand, Scienceism, takes science as the almost sole master and authority of knowledge. On the other, postmodernism implies it can't be certain about anything. A biblical view of science recognises that God created both us, and our world — and gave us the command to explore it and be stewards over it. Science then, in studying God's 'book' of creation has real, but limited authority. The book of nature has to be read with the other book of revelation, the Bible. Science based on a biblical conception of reality allows us to explore it with our senses and think, communicate and predict with our language, because God made the world, our brains and our language in order that they work together and are compatible with each other. Nevertheless, the falleness of the human condition must be realistically accepted: scientists are inevitably biased, finite and fallen creatures like the rest of humanity. The shift away from scienecism is an opportunity for Christians as well as for pagans.

11. This was reported in much of the media at the time, for example, *The Western Daily Press*, October 28, 2004, p.10.
12. This will be looked at in detail in a later chapter.
13. Celtic and other peoples with their religious beliefs migrated around much of Europe.
14. Seville, Christine, *Practical Wicca: Spells and Rituals to Heal and Harmonise Your Life*. Silverdale Books, 2003, p.6.
15. Seville, *Practical Wicca*, p.7.
16. Seville, *Practical Wicca*, pp.8-9.
17. Kalfors, Mariano, *White Witching: The Good Magic-Maker's Guide to Spellweaving*, Hermes House, 2002, p.10.
18. Kalfors, *White Witching*, p.10.
19. Green, Miranda, *Exploring the World of the Druids*, Thames and Hudson, 1997, p.160.
20. Seville, *Practical Wicca*, p.31.
21. Judith, Anodea, *The Truth about Neo-Paganism*, p.25.
22. Green, Marion, *Practical Magic*, p.30.
23. Green, Marion, *Practical Magic*, p.30.
24. Judith, *The Truth about Neo-Paganism*, p.25.

25. Colossians 1:26-27; Romans 16:25-27; Matthew 13:10-17
26. Psalm 19:1-4; Acts 14:15-17; Romans 1:18-20
27. Romans 2:14-16
28. See Exodus and the giving of the Law as well as the instructions for the Tabernacle and sacrificial system.
29. See Exodus chapters 1-20; Hebrews 12:18
30. See the four Gospels and all the miracles and signs that permeate the life of Jesus; Hebrews 2:1-4
31. Seville, *Practical Wicca*, front flyleaf.
32. Judith, *The Truth about Neo-Paganism*, p.43.
33. Judith, *The Truth about Neo-Paganism*, p.45.

Pulling The Threads Together

1. Mainly through alternative health supplements, articles, programs and features.

Chapter 6
1. Russell, Bertrand, *History of Western Philosophy*, 1946, Routledge edition, 2000, p.78.
2. Remember this web concept is at the heart of the current advancing perspective on science called holistic science. Also remember, this web is what is called in Anglo-Saxon the Wydd, or weird. Furthermore, when a Wiccan, or witch, casts a spell they see themselves as connecting into this larger web and then casting their own web, focussing the visible and invisible forces of the web for their purposes.
3. Seville, Christine, *Practical Wicca*, Silverdale Books, 2003, p.8.
4. Geddes and Grosset, *Dictionary of the Occult*, David Dale House, 1999, p.69.
5. Genesis 10:8-9
6. Genesis 11:1-9
7. This idea of the Spirit or Force of the universe having two sides or aspects is found in many older and newer forms of pagan belief. For example, yin and yang in far eastern belief, and the dark and light sides of the Force in Star Wars.
8. Riane Eisler, *The Chalice and the Blade*, Harper and Row, 1987, pp.17-18.

9. Numerous books have been published about Atlantis, all with varying degrees of credibility.

10. Angebert, Jean-Michel, *The Occult and the Third Reich*. Introduction by Lewis A. M. Sumberg, former Chairman of the History Department of the University of Tennessee, MacMillan Publishing, 1974.

11. Luke 17:26

12. Judith Anodea, *The Truth about Neo-Paganism*, Llewellyn, 1994, p.11.

13. Lord Byron (George Gordon Noel Byron) *Don Juan* (Canto 1, st.83).

14. Grayling, A. C. *The Meaning of Things: Applying Philosophy to Life*. Phoenix, 2001, p.100.

15. Kennedy, Ludovic, *All In The Mind: A Farewell to God,* Hodder and Stoughton, 1999, p.133.

16. Judith, *The Truth about Neo-Paganism*, p.12.

17. Seville, *Practical Wicca*, p.19. Whatever the arguments over inserting the specific English word 'witch', what true witches are involved in is clearly banned in Scripture.

18. Kennedy, *All In The Mind,* p.134.

19. Sampson, Philip, J. *Six Modern Myths Challenge Christian Faith*, IVP, 2000, p.133.

20. Sampson, *Six Modern Myths*, p.135.

21. Sampson, *Six Modern Myths*, p.139.

22. Sampson, *Six Modern Myths*, p.141.

23. Sampson, *Six Modern Myths*, p.138.

24. Anthropologist Marvin Harris cited in, Sampson, *Six Modern Myths*, p.138. Harris Marvin, *Cannibals and Kings: The Origins of Cultures*, New York: Vintage, 1978, p.165.

25. Green, J. Miranda, *Exploring the World of the Druids*, Thames and Hudson, London, 2002, pp.40, 71-72. See also, Seville, *Practical Wicca,* p.11.

26. Sampson, *Six Modern Myths*, p.138.

27. Acts 16:16-18

28. Jensen, P. F., 'Calvin and Witchcraft', *Reformed Theological Review*, 34:76-86.

29. Matthew 13:24-30

30. James 2:19

Chapter 7

1. This would be modified today in the light of the new physics of Einstein, where matter and energy are interchangeable according to $E=mc^2$. In essence it is the same thing; all that exists is matter/energy.

2. Darwin, C. *Letter to W. Graham* in F. Darwin, ed., *The Life and Letters of Charles Darwin*. New York, D. Appleton & Co., 1905.

3. Rendall, Ruth, *Murder Being Once Done*, Harper Collins Audio Books, London, Original publication, 1972, Audio Book publication, 1996. Side 1.

4. Although these different perspectives, including nihilism, developed sequentially, after they came into being they persisted in various forms. Nihilism, for example was still expressing itself generations later in the Punk movement around 1980. It is still present in moderated forms today.

5. The other strand of existentialism was theistic existentialism, which was born in the middle of the 19th century as a response to dead Christian orthodoxy.

6. Too often, vital biblical faith had been replaced by either liberalism or traditionalism. These weakened or dead varieties of Christianity acted like an inoculation, producing an immune reaction against the real thing. Western culture and society had built up an allergic reaction against true Christianity.

7. The word 'God' here is the ultimate reality from the eastern perspective, not the God of the Bible. This reality is infinite and impersonal, rather like the 'The Force' in Star Wars. As this idea is absorbed by the West,this ulimate reality is sometimes thought of as personal, but it is still not the God of the Bible.

8. It is fascinating to note how an evolutionary perspective saturates the New Age Movement. Whereas Darwinism looks back to explain our origins with out reference to God, the New Age looks forward to anticipate our climax and fulfilment with out reference to him either.

9. Greenwood, Susan, *The Encyclopedia of Magic and Witchcraft: An Illustrated Historical Reference to Spiritual Worlds*, p.226.

10. Greenwood, *The Encyclopedia of Magic and Witchcraft*, p.170.

11. Although the word 'God' is used here, this is not the biblical conception of God that is in mind.
12. See for example, Constance, Clumbey, *The Hidden Dangers of the Rainbow*, Huntington House, 1983; *The Occult and the Third Reich*, Angebert, Jean-Michel, McMillan, 1974; *The Spear of Destiny*, Ravenscroft, Trevor, 1973.
13. A term referring to spiritual beings.
14. Quoted in, Constance, *The Hidden Dangers of the Rainbow*, p.44.
15. The kabala, or Kabbalah, is the Jewish mystical tradition, especially the system of esoteric mystical speculation and practice developed in the twelfth and thirteenth centuries. This general approach was present on Old Testament times and also had 'Christian' versions after the time of Christ. It is a form of occultism and mysticism that takes on the outward appearance of either Judaism or Christianity.
16. Quoted in, Constance, *The Hidden Dangers of the Rainbow*, p.45.
17. Greenwood, *The Encyclopedia of Magic and Witchcraft*, p229.
18. *Dictionary of the Occult*, p.160.

Chapter 8

1. Grayling, A. C. *The Meaning of Things: Applying Philosophy to Life*, Phoenix Paperbacks, Orion Books, 2001, p.60.
2. Quoted in Grayling, *The Meaning of Things*, p.60.
3. See, for example, the research results of a project conducted by a partnership of *The London Institute of Christianity* and the Diocese of Coventry. *Beyond the Fringe: Researching a Spiritual Age*. The report of Revd Yvonne Richmond's exploration in the Diocese of Coventry into the spirituality of people outside the church. Consultant and analysist, Nick Spencer, The London Institute of Christianity, Cliff College Publishing, 2005.
4. Quoted in, Burns, K., *Eastern Philosophy: The Greatest Thinkers and Sages from Ancient to Modern Times*, Capella, Arcturus Publishing Ltd, 2004, p.24.
5. Albert Einstein said, 'Buddhism has the characteristics of what

would be expected in a cosmic religion for the future: it transcends a personal God, avoids dogmas and theology; it covers both the natural and the spiritual, and it is based on a religious sense aspiring from the experience of all things, natural and spiritual, as a meaningful unity.' Helen Dukas and Banesh Hoffman, Eds., 'Albert Einstein: The Human Side', Princeton Univefrsity Press, (1954). Quoted on http://religioustolerance.org/buddishm.htm.

6. See for example, Davies, P., *God and the New Physics*, Touchstone, 1984.

7. Capra, F., *The Tao of Physics: An Exploration of the Parallels Between Modern Physics and Eastern Mysticism*, Flamingo, Londion, 1976; Talbot, M., *The Holographic Universe*, Harper Collins, London, 1991.

8. See, for example, in the New Age journal, *Nexus*, the article, *An Introduction to Parallel Universes*, *Nexus*, April-May, 2005, vol. 12, no. 3.

9 This is similar to ancient gnosticism, which holds that 'salvation' comes from special knowledge. This is deeply ironic when the fall was caused by Satan offering Adam and Eve a special kind of knew knowledge, a new 'more full' perception of reality (Genesis 3:5).

10. 'You will be like God.' Genesis 1:5

11. Genesis 1:1

12. Genesis 3:8, 24; Romans 1:18-2:5

13. 1 Timothy 2:5

14. This is illustrated in the personal testimony of Mark Philips, a one-time New-Ager who became a Christian: Philips, M. *Truth Seeker*, IVP, Leicester, England, 1998.

15. See, for example, in the New Age journal, *Nexus*, the article, *A brief account of the true nature of the 'UFO entities.'* *Nexus*, April-May, 2005, vol. 12, no. 3.

16. Ephesians 6:12

17. 1 Corinthians 8:4-6

18. 1 Corinthians 10:20

19. Matthew 4:1-11; 8:28-34; 10:8; 12:22-29; 17:14-23; Mark 5:1-20; 9:14-32

20. 2 Corinthians 11:14

21. Acts 16:16-18

22. Acts 19:13-16-20
23. Exodus 7:11-12; 22; 8:7
24. 2 Thessalonians 2:7-12
25. 2 Peter 2:10-12
26. For instance: 'White witches believe that we are part of the 'Wyrd' or 'web of life', intimately connected to all things and to one another via invisible forces and energies.' Our word 'weird' comes from the Anglo-Saxon 'Wyrd' — 'which people thought of as an all-powerful sense of destiny that shapes the world. It can be imagined as a magical web in which all of life is interconnected', Kalfors Mariano, *White Witching*, Hermes House, London, 2002, p.10.
27. Colossians 1:15-20
28. Hebrews 9:27
29. *Dictionary of the Occult*, pp.3-4.
30. *Dictionary of the Occult*, pp.208-209.
31. Greenwood, *The Encyclopedia of Magic and Witchcraft*.
32. Genesis 2:16-17; 3:1-5,7,13
33. Isaiah 8:19-22
34. See, for example, the research results of a project conducted by a partnership of *The London Institute of Christianity* and the Diocese of Coventry. *Beyond the Fringe: Researching a Spiritual age*. Cliff College Publishing, 2005. Section 3.3, pp.57-61, Section 4.2, pp.69-72. Section 5.2, pp.85-103.
35. 1 Corinthians 10:14 24; Galatians 5:20.
36. Kabbalah is the Jewish mystical tradition, especially the system of esoteric mystical speculation and practice that developed in the twelfth and thirteenth centuries.
37. *Dictionary of the Occult*, pp.216-217.
38. *Dictionary of the Occult*, pp.5-6.
39. One New Age journal, *Resurgence*, illustrates this in an article called, *One Truth, Many paths*. Referring to the founder of the Interfaith Seminary in London (founded 1996) the author writes, '"Interfaith", she says, has "until very recently meant people from established religions coming together to talk about how not to kill one another. We are taking the concept further. Our vision is not just tolerance, but acceptance. We believe there is One

God or Truth and many paths to it."' *Resurgence*, March/April 2005. No. 229.
40. See, for example, the British government's attempt in 2005 to bring in a law against inciting what was termed' religious hatred'. The issues are discussed in the booklet, *Serious Organised Crime and Police Bill: Clause 119. Why a religious hatred law would harm religious liberty and freedom of speech*, The Christian Institute, Newcastle upon Tyne, UK, January 2005.

Chapter 9

1. Quoted in, Helen Dukas and Banesh Hoffman, Eds., *Albert Einstein: The Human Side*, Princeton University Press, 1954.
2. See, for example, Targ, R., *Limitless Mind: A Guide to Remote Viewing and Transformation of Consciousness*, New World Library, California, 2004. Russell Targ Ph.D. is a physicist and founder of the Stanford Research Institute Program, California.
3. *Bath Spa University College Postgraduate Prospectus* 2003/2004, pp.54-55.
4. See, for example, Baker, M., *Spells for Teenage Witches*, Kyle Cathie, Ltd, London, 2000, Mander, G., *The Essential Book of Empowerment*, Michael O'Mara Books, London, 2000; Green, M. *Practical Magic: A Book of Transformations, Spells and Mind Magic*, Hermes House, London, 2001; Kalfors, M., *White Witching: The Good Magic-Maker's Guide to Spellweaving*, Hermes House, London, 2002.
5. Greenwood, S., *The Encylopedia of Magic and Witchcraft*, Hermes House, London, 2004, p.227.
6. Two international institutions proffering this perspective include, The Center for Ecoliteracy, Berkeley, California, USA, and The Schumacher College, Dartington, Devon UK, which offers an MSc in Holistic Science.
7. It is not that individual scientists like Lovelock believe in magic or are pagans, but rather that some of their ideas are used, if not hijacked.
8. Erwin Schrodinger, *Science and Humanism*, quoted in, Targ, R., *Limitless Mind: A Guide to Remote Viewing and Transformation*

of Consciousness, New World Library, California, 2004, p.xi.

9. See, for example, Anodea Judith, *The Truth about Neo-Paganism*, Llewellyn Publications, St Paul, USA, 1194, pp.17-18.

10. Davies, Paul, *God and the New Physics*, Touchstone, 1984, p.225.

11. Davies, *God and the New Physics*, p.225.

12. Davies, *God and the New Physics*, p.225.

13. *Britannica Concise Enclyclopeadia*, 2004, http:/www.Britannica.com/ebc/article?eu=385634. The article continues: 'Applications include the study of turbulent flow in fluids, irregularities in biological systems, population dynamics, chemical reactions, plasma physics, meteorology, the motions of groups and clusters of stars, transportation dynamics, and many other fields.'

14. Bryson, Bill, *A Short History of Nearly Everything*, Doubleday, 2003, p.153.

15. Bryson, *A Short History of Nearly Everything*, p.129.

16. Or indeed, how the casting of a spell here can effect something miles and miles away. They feel the causal relationship is unknown, but it is nevertheless there. See the section on visualization.

17. Bryson, *A Short History of Nearly Everything*, p.130.

18. Davies, *God and the New Physics*, p.226.

19. This is a whole new field of brain science called neurotheology.

20. Holmes, B. *New Scientist*, Issue 2287, 21 April 2001.

21. Holmes, B. *New Scientist*, Issue 2287, 21 April 2001.

22. Holmes, B. *New Scientist*, Issue 2287, 21 April 2001.

23. www.bbc.co.uk/science/horizen/2003/godonbrain.shtml

24. BBC — Science and Nature — Horizon — *God on the Brain*, BBC2, Thursday 17 April 2005; Holmes, B. *New Scientist*, Issue 2287, 21 April 2001.

25. Holmes, B. *New Scientist*, Issue 2287, 21 April 2001.

26. Holmes, B. *New Scientist*, Issue 2287, 21 April 2001.

27. Greyson, B. *Dissociation in people who have near-death experiences: out of their bodies or out of their minds? The Lancet* – Vol. 355, Issue 9202, 5 February 2000, pp.460-463.

28. Pirn van Lommel, Ruud van Wees, Vincent Meyers and Elfferich, *Near-death experiences in survivors of cardiac arrest: a pro-*

spective study in the Netherlands, The Lancet, 2001, 358:2039-2045.

29. Parnia, S. d'Arcy, K., *Research body will shed more light on near death experiences*, News Release from University of Southampton, England, 16 February, 2001, http://www.soton.ac.uk/pubaffrs/0128.htm. Ref: 01/28.

30. Petre, Jonathan, *Patients near death see visions of hell, The Telegraph*, 25 May, 1997, see also, Petre, Jonathan, *Soul-searching doctors find life after death, The Telegraph*, 22 October, 2000.

31. Pirn van Lommel, Ruud van Wees, Vincent Meyers and Elfferich, *Near-death experiences in survivors of cardiac arrest: a prospective study in the Netherlands, The Lancet*, 2001, 358:2039-2045.

Chapter 10

1. Brown, D. *The Da Vinci Code*, Corgi, 2003, pp.313-315.

2. Exodus 32:5. Although the calf was an idol and a pagan god, probably similar to the Egyptian bull-god *Apis*, Aaron claimed they would hold a 'festival to the Lord.' 1 Kings 12:25-33. Jeroboam attempted to combine the pagan calf symbol with the worship of the Lord, though he attempted no physical representation of the Lord — no 'god' stood on the backs of his bulls.

3. See Judges 2:6-23

4. *The Da Vinci Code* mixes history, myth and fantasy, producing a powerful delusion to contemporary readers. Certainly there are aspects of Christianity that were foreshadowed in pagan religions, but that is hardly surprising. Through guesswork and the biblical revelation, it would not have been difficult for demons to develop subtle lies that darkly pre-empt certain aspects of the revelation of Christ. In the passage quoted there is the important true point that the Church, because of the political expediency of the rulers, the Church became a political animal, and political animals always compromise. It is clear that Christianity absorbed far more of paganism that we often suppose. Regarding the role of Constantine in particular, Eusebius of Caesarea (c.260-c.341) was very positive concerning the Christianising of the empire:

'Men had now lost all fear of their former oppressors; day after day they kept dazzling festival; light was everywhere, and men who once dared not look up greeted each other with smiling faces and shining eyes. They danced and sang in the city and country alike, giving honour first of all to God our sovereign Lord, as they had been instructed ... Old troubles were forgotten and all religion passed into oblivion; good things present were enjoyed, those yet to come eagerly awaited (*History of the Church*, Bk. 10, para. 9) However, *The Da Vinci Code*, along with many other publications, is probably right in stating that Constantine was more of a political genius than a spiritual reformer. We must remember, it was after he claimed to be converted to Christ (when, before his battle for Rome he said he saw the sign of the cross in the sky, and above it the words *In hoc signo vinces* (in this sign conquer)) that he showed less than Christian conduct. He murdered both his son Crispus and his wife Fausta.

5. Green, M., *Practical Magic: A Book of Transformations, Spells and Mind Magic*, Hermes House, London, 2001, p.73.

6. Seville, C., *Practical Wicca*, Silverdale Books, Leicester, 2003, p.73.

7. Green, *Practical Magic*, p.73.

8. See http://rapidnet.com/-jbeard.bdm/Psychology/posit.htm. Positive Confession/PMA — Prosperity Gospel and the New Age, Biblical Discernment Ministries, 25 May 2005.

9. Yonggi Cho, Paul, *The Fourth Dimension* (Logos, 1979), foreword.

10. See for example, Greenwood, S. *The Encyclopedia of Magic and Witchcraft: An Illustrated Historical Reference to Spiritual Worlds*, Hermes House, London, 2004, pp.41,67; Kalfors, M. *White Witching: The Good Magic-Makers Guide to Spellweaving*, Hermes House, London, 2002, p.29.

11. Ankerberg, J. and Weldon, J., *Encyclopedia of New Age Beliefs*, Harvest House, Eugene, Oregon, 1996, pp.39-40.

12. Kelsey, M. *The Other Side of Silence: A Guide to Christian Meditation*, SPCK, 1977, p.136.

13. *Journal of the Royal Society of Medicine*, Vol. 85, no. 7, July 1992, p.383.

14. Morrison, A., *The Serpent and the Cross*, Kand M Books, Plas Gwyn, Trelawnyd, Wales, 1994, p.293.

15. Hurding, R. F., *Roots and Shoots: A Guide to Counselling and Psychotherapy*, Hodder and Stoughton, London, 1985, p.59.

16. Freud, Sigmund, *An Autobiographical Study*, in Standard Edition, Vol. 20 (1925) p.1, quoted in Hurding, *Roots and Shoots*, p.59.

17. Quoted in, Morrison, *The Serpent and the Cross*, p.306. Original reference: Paul Roezen, *Freud and His Followers* (Penguin, 1979), p.113.

18. Again note the pantheistic conception inherited from Mesmer and ancient paganism.

19. See Wilhelm Reich, *The Murder of Christ* (Farrar. Straus and Giroux, 1953), cited in, Morrison, *The Serpent and the Cross*, p.300.

20. This is similar to many pagan religions, including some mentioned in the Bible.

21. See for example professing Christian leaders who have advocated Jungian style therapies: Paul Yonggi Cho, Richard Foster, John Wimber and the Arbuthnotts, to name but a few. Typing in 'Healing of the memories' into a search engine on the internet produces a strange mix of Christian and pagan protagonists.

22. Brome, V., *Jung: Man and Myth*, Paladin, 1980, p.113.

23. Hurding, *Roots and Shoots*, p.79.

24. Hurding, *Roots and Shoots*, p.80.

25. For example, the laws of physics, the applications of engineering or the knowledge of modern medicine.

26. *Dictionary of the Occult*, Geddes and Grosset, Scotland, 1999, p.3.

27. Genesis 3:4-5

28. Ephesians 6:12

Chapter 11

1. Romans 1:25

2. See for example, Jeremiah 10:16. Here the fact of God as 'Maker of all things' is used to combat pagan idolatry.

3. For instance, Acts 14:15; Acts 17:24-28
4. Acts 17:25.
5. Acts 14:17.
6. Acts 17:26.
7. Pagan thought generally makes the divine inseparable from the normal, and therefore an explanation for everything must come from that one integrated divine-normal reality. It must be self-explanatory. It is vital to the argument of contingency and design sketched out in this chapter. William A. Dembski is fascinating and apposite on this point: 'We need to understand that it is impossible to be neutral about God's relations to the world. Is God the source and sustenance of the world, or does the world exist in and for itself? ... This is not a scientific question but a metaphysical, yes, even a religious question. To see this it is instructive to examine the earliest Hindu scriptures, the *Rig Veda* ... a fundamental characteristic of Vedic literature was "a sense of a cosmic order or law pervading the universe ... This cosmic law is the ground of being, the first principle, the ultimate reference point. It is embedded in nature and undergirds nature. This cosmic law supplants divine creation. There can be no transcendent God within such a framework. The gods of the Vedas are not prior to nature but intrinsic to it. These are gods who control nature are as much as they are controlled by it. Indeed, they are inseparable from nature. Hindu pantheism is perhaps the most developed expression of religious naturalism ... naturalism leads irresistibly to idolatry ... Although in ancient times graven images were the most obvious sign of idolatry, idolatry is not so much a matter of investing any particular object with any extraordinary significance. Rather it is a matter of investing the world with a significance it does not deserve. We need to ask ourselves why anyone would want to worship a material object in the first place. The ancients certainly new as well and we that a carved figure by itself holds no special significance. What is significant about a craven image is not the image itself but what it signifies. Some images in the East, for instance, are hollow on the inside and have a hole so that the reality signified by the image may enter the image and thus become the proper object of worship for the worshipper ... The problem is that all our images can signify only

other things in creation and not the One who gave creation its being in the first place. A graven image signifies something else in the world, some power, some influence, some favour that the worshipper wants to tap into. The tacit assumption here is that what needs to be tapped into is part of the world, not the God who created the world in the first place. Idolatry is always a denial of the Creator and thereby transforms creation into nature' (Dembski A. Willaim, *Intelligent Design: The Bridge between Science and Theology*, IVP, 1999, pp.99-102.)

8. Genesis 1:1
9. I have presented this argument more fully in my book, The *Edge of Known Reality and Beyond*, Evangelical Press, 2005.
10. Psalm 139:14
11. Behe, Michael J., *Darwin's Black Box*, Touchstone, 1998, p.x.
12. Santayana, quoted in, Grayling, A. C., *The Meaning of Things: Applying Philosophy to Life*, Phoenix, an imprint of Orion Books, 2002, p.133.

Chapter 12

1. McDowell, *Evidence that Demands a Verdict*, Volume 1, Alpha, 1998, p.18; See also, *Cambridge History of the Bible*, Cambridge University Press.
2. Source: International Bible Societies: http//www.ibs.org/aboutibs/index.php; http//www.ibs.org/bibles/about/19.php.
3. McGrath, Alister, *In the Beginning: The Story of the King James Bible*, Hodder and Stoughton, 2002, prologue.
4. The following quotes and others can be found in *The New Encyclopaedia of Christian Quotations*, Compiled by Mark Water, John Hunt Publishing, Alresford, Hampshire, UK and also at http://www.retakingamerica.com/great_quotes_bible_001.html: or also the Christian Resource Center at http://www.biblelife.co.uk/article.php?id=445.
5. All six Tolpuddle Martyrs were convinced Christians and two were lay preachers. In 1834 they were sentenced to seven years transportation to Australia for organizing the Tolpuddle Friendly Society of Agricultural Workers to improve their wages from seven shillings a week. In 1934 the Trades Union Congress placed

the following inscription on the grave of one of the six: 'James Hammett, Tolpuddle Martyr, Pioneer of Trades Unionism, Champion of freedom.'

6. Quoted in, Edwards, B. H. and Shaw, J. I, *AD*, Day One Publications, 1999, p.5.
7. Quoted in the introductory help notes by Gideon International to the NIV Bible, Hodder and Stoughton.
8. Quoted in, Edwards and Shaw, *AD*, p.12.
9. Quoted in McDowell, J. *Evidence that Demands a Verdict*, Volume I, Alpha, 1998, p.21.
10. Genesis 3:1
11. Genesis 3:15
12. Isaiah 8:19-22
13. *Dictionary of the Occult*, Geddes and Grosset, 1999, p.166.
14. 1 Corinthians 15:3-7
15. Glueck, Nelson, *Rivers in the Desert; History of Negev*. Philedelphia: Jewish Publications Society of America, 1969, p.31.
16. Ramsay, W. M. *The Bearing of Recent Discovery on the Trustworthiness of the New Testament*, Grand Rapids: Baker Book House, 1953. Quoted in McDowell, J. *Evidence that Demands a Verdict*, Volume I, p.71.
17. Kenyon, G. F. *The Bible and Archaeology*, Harper and Row, p.288.
18. Bruce, F. F. *The Books and the Parchments*, Rev. ed. Westwood: Fleming H. Revell Co., 1963, p.178.
19. Deuteronomy 18:21-22. However, it also needs to be understood that this is a negative criterion. So, although it is true that if something does not come true the message is not from God, it is not necessarily true that that because a prophecy is fulfilled it is from God. When a false prophet makes a fulfilled prediction, this may be a test of God's people. Deuteronomy 13 deals with prophecy theologically: if the prophet uses gods other than the true God, he is not of Yahweh. Through Moses, the theme was sealed on all future prophecy by setting the norm of the theology, which all future prophets must accept. If a prophet presented fulfilled predictive prophecy, yet claimed a theology out of keeping with the norm set down through Moses, the people had a false prophet. Jeremiah 23 expands on Deuteronomy 13 by painting

the false prophet as immoral (v. 10-14) and condoning others' immorality (v. 17); he preaches of peace, not a God-like peace, but an artificial, manufactured peace. The true prophet preaches a message of conviction and repentance (v. 29) and calls the people to righteousness and obedience (v. 22).

20. The predictions of the sixteenth-century French physician, Nostradamus, have fascinated the world for more than four centuries, so much so that during this time they have never been out of print.
21. *Encyclopaedia Britannica*, Deluxe Edition, 2004, CD, article on Tyre.
22. *Encyclopaedia Britannica*, Deluxe Edition, 2004, CD, article on Tyre. See also, *The Wycliffe Dictionary of Biblical Archaelogy*, Ed. Charles F,.Pfeiffer, article on Tyre.
23. Myers, Philip Van Ness. *General History for Colleges and High Schools*, Boston, Ginn and Company, 1889, p55, quoted in, McDowell, J. *Evidence that Demands a Verdict*, Volume I, p.276.
24. *Encyclopaedia Britannica*, Deluxe Edition, 2004, CD, article on Tyre.
25. Jidejian, Nina, *Tyre through the Ages*, Beirut: Dar El-Mashreq Publishers, 1969, quoted in, McDowell, J. *Evidence that Demands a Verdict*, Vol. I, p.277.
26. *The Wycliffe Dictionary of Biblical Archaeology*, article on Tyre.
27. Genesis 14:18
28. Hebrews 7
29. An excellent summary of the prophecies and their fulfilment is given in, McDowell, J. *Evidence that Demands a Verdict*, Volume I, chapter 11.
30. Exodus 7:8-13
31. 1 Kings 18:16-46
32. For instance, see, Luke 4:31-37
33. See Acts 8:1-25; Acts 16:16-20; Acts 19:11-20.
34. Numbers 22:38; Deuteronomy 18:18-20; Jeremiah 1:0; 14:14; 23:16-22; 29:31-32; Ezekiel 2:7; 13:1-16
35. 1 Kings 14:18; 16:12; 34; 2 Kings 9:36; 14:25; Jer. 37:2; Zech. 7:7; 12
36. Micah 3:8

37. 2 Samuel 23:2
38. 1 Corinthians 2:13
39. 2 Timothy 3:16
40. An excellent book on this subject is Wenham, J.W., *Christ and the Bible*, Baker Book House, Grand Rapids, Michigan, 1984.
41. He quoted it authoritatively (Matthew 4:4; Mark 14:27); he referred to it as the Word of God (Mark 7:11-13; John 10:34f); he believed the whole Old Testament to be authoritative (Luke 24;25-27) and he fulfilled it (Luke 24:25, 27).
42. John 14:26
43. John 16:13
44. 2 Peter 3:15-16
45. Isaiah 8:19-22

Chapter 13

1. Ephesians 6:12; Luke 4:33
2. See for example, Luke 1:1120; 26-38; 2:8-14
3. Philippians 2:9-11
4. John 14:9
5. John 14:6
6. Psalm 19:1-1-6; Romans 1:18-20; Acts 17:22-28
7. Romans 1:18-23
8. John 14:9
9. John 14:6
10. John 1:1-18
11. John 1:14
12. Philippians 2:6-7
13. Bruce, F. F. *The New Testament Documents: Are They Reliable?* IVP, 1972, p.119.
14. Quoted in, *The New Encyclopaedia of Christian Quotations*, John Hunt, 2000, p.177.
15. Quoted in, *The New Encyclopaedia of Christian Quotations*, John Hunt, p.177.
16. *Annals* XV.44. Quoted in France, R. T., *The Evidence for Jesus*, Hodder and Stoughton, 1986, p.21-22.
17. Josephus, *Antiquities* xviii.33, quoted in, Barnett, P. *Is the New Testament History*, Hodder and Stoughton, 1986, p.28.

18. The case for the historical accuracy of the Bible is made in chapter 12.
19. Betz, Otto. *What Do We Know About Jesus?* SCM Press, 1968, p.9.
20. 1 Peter 1:19
21. 1 Peter 2:22
22. 1 John 2:1
23. 1 John 3:5
24. Quoted in, *The New Encyclopaedia of Christian Quotations*, p.171.
25. Anonymous
26. Wells, H. G. *Outline of History*, Penguin, 1931.
27. Quoted in, *The New Encyclopaedia of Christian Quotations*, p.171.
28. Micah 5:2
29. Matthew 2:1; Luke 2:4-7
30. Jeremiah 23:5
31. Isaiah 9:1
32. Psalm 22:16
33. Isaiah 53:12
34. Isaiah 53:11; Psalm 16:10
35. Psalm 41:9
36. Zechariah 11:12
37. Zechariah 11:13b
38. Zechariah 11:13b
39. John 21:25
40. John 20:30-31
41. Quoted in Stott, J.R.W. *Basic Christianity*, Downer's Grove: IVP, 1971, p.47.
42. Anderson, J. N. D. *The Resurrection of Christ*, (copyright) *Christianity Today*, 29 March 1968, quoted in Josh McDowell, *Evidence that Demands a Verdict*, Volume 1, Paternoster Publishing, 1998 revised edition.
43. Mark 2:28; 9:9; 9:31
44. Luke 22:70; Mark 3:11; Matthew 4:3, 6.
45. John 5:16-18
46. Luke 22:66-71.
47. John 1:1

48. Ephesians 2:1-10
49. Ephesians 1:13
50. Romans 8:31-39
51. Galatians 5:16-26; Romans 12:1-8
52. Ephesians 1:13-14
53. Romans 8:26-27
54. Matthew 6:5-15
55. Ephesians 1:17
56. Colossians 1:27

Chapter 14

1. *Dictionary of the occult*, Geddes and Grosset, David House, Scotland, 1999.
2. Greenwood, S. *The Encyclopaedia of Magic and Witchcraft: An Illustrated Historical Reference to Spiritual Worlds*, Hermes House, 2004.
3. Burn, K. *Eastern Philosophy: The Greatest Thinkers and Sages from Ancient to Modern Times*, Arcturus Publishing, 2004.
4. Green, G. *Practical Magic: A Book of Transformations, Spells and Mind Magic*, Hermes House, London, 2002, p.30.
5. Seville, C. *Practical Wicca: Spells and Rituals to Heal and Harmonise Your Life*, Silverdale Books, Leicester, 2003, p.42.
6 Green, *Practical Magic*, p.30.
7 Romans 13:1-4
8 Greenwood, *The Encyclopaedia of Magic and Witchcraft*, pp.78-91.
9 Romans 2:14-15
10. Revelation 5:6
11. Genesis 1:10; Genesis 1:31
12. Genesis 2:17
13. This will be dealt with in far more detail in the next chapter.
14. Galatians 5:16-26
15. Genesis 3:5
16. Ephesians 1:13-14
17. Revelation 21:1-5
18. Matthew 6:9-10
19. Matthew 6:12a

20. Matthew 6:12b; 14-15
21. Matthew 6:13
22. Matthew 6:13b
23. Romans 7:14-25;12-14
24. Ephesians 6:10-20
25. 1 Corinthians 10:20
26. Romans 1:23-32
27. Colossians 4:7-9; 1 Peter 3;15-17
28. Mathew 5:13-16; Ephesians 2:10; James 1:27
29. Romans 12:1-2; 2 Corinthians 10:5

Chapter 15

1. Colossians 1:26
2. Saints are God's people, those he has chosen, called and declared holy by trusting in and following his Son Jesus.
3. Colossians 1:27
4. Colossians 2:2
5. Genesis 2:9; 17;3:5-7
6. Genesis 3:22-24
7. Genesis 3:17-19
8. Genesis 3:16a
9. Genesis 3:16b;12
10. Genesis 3;7.
11. Genesis 3:15.
12. Genesis 2:17;3:3;19.
13. Genesis 3:8-10.
14. Genesis 3:23-24.
15. Revelation 20:11-15.
16. Genesis 3:15 – 'he will crush your head.'
17. The Old Testament is like a scroll that is gradually unrolled to reveal more and more of this mystery. Theologians often call this gradual increase in revelation 'progressive revelation'. As the pages are turned, pictures are given of the coming Christ: prophet, priest and king, suffering servant. God's justice that is pure and demands retribution, and his mercy that can forgive and save are unveiled in a whole host of ways, including the

Law, the Tabernacle, the sacrificial system and the case studies of the history of Israel.

18. Colossians 4:3
19. Genesis 3:4 shows us that the temptation to view ourselves as gods goes back to the very first temptation offered to humanity.
20. Genesis 3:11; Romans 3:23
21. Genesis 3:4-5
22. Exodus 20:1-21
23. See, for example, Matthew 5:17-30
24. Matthew 5:21-22
25. Matthew 5:27-28
26. James 2:10-11
27. Matthew 22:37-40
28. Romans 3:23
29. Isaiah 59:2
30. Romans 1:18
31. Romans 2:5-6
32. Malachi 4:2; Acts 28:27-28
33. Matthew 3:15; 5:17; Galatians 4:4-7; Romans 10:4; 2 Corinthians 5:21.
34. Just as God sacrificed an animal in the Garden of Eden to use its skin to cover Adam and Eve's shame and nakedness, so Christ's death allows his righteousness to covers our sin.
35. Ephesians 2:8
36. Acts 2:37
37. Acts 2:37-39
38. John 3:16-21
39. Matthew 7:7
40. Mathew 7:13-14
41. 1 Timothy 2:5-6
42. Ephesians 2:8-9